13 Sharks

13 Sharks

The Careers of a Series of Small Royal Navy Ships, from the Glorious Revolution to D-Day

John D Grainger

Pen & Sword
MARITIME

First published in Great Britain in 2016 by
Pen & Sword Maritime
an imprint of
Pen & Sword Books Ltd
47 Church Street
Barnsley
South Yorkshire
S70 2AS

ISBN 978 1 47387 724 5

A CIP catalogue record for this book is available from the British Library

Typeset in Ehrhardt by
Mac Style Ltd, Bridlington, East Yorkshire
Printed and bound in the UK by CPI Group (UK) Ltd,
Croydon, CR0 4YY

Pen & Sword Books Ltd incorporates the imprints of Pen & Sword
Archaeology, Atlas, Aviation, Battleground, Discovery, Family History,
History, Maritime, Military, Naval, Politics, Railways, Select, Transport,
True Crime, and Fiction, Frontline Books, Leo Cooper, Praetorian Press,
Seaforth Publishing and Wharncliffe.

For a complete list of Pen & Sword titles please contact
PEN & SWORD BOOKS LIMITED
47 Church Street, Barnsley, South Yorkshire, S70 2AS, England
E-mail: enquiries@pen-and-sword.co.uk

Contents

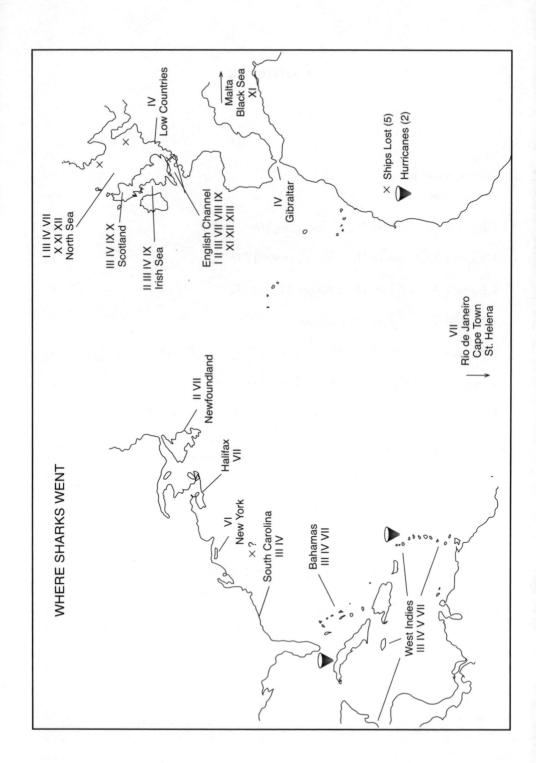

WHERE SHARKS WENT

I III IV VII
X XI XII
North Sea

III IV IX X
Scotland

II III IV IX
Irish Sea

IV
Low Countries

English Channel
I III VII VIII IX
XI XII XIII

IV
Gibraltar

Malta
Black Sea
XI

× Ships Lost (5)
◣ Hurricanes (2)

VII
Rio de Janeiro
Cape Town
St. Helena

II VII
Newfoundland

Halifax
VII

VI
New York
× ?

South Carolina
III IV

Bahamas
III IV VII

West Indies
III IV V VII

Abbreviations

ADM – Admiralty documents in the National Archives, Kew, and the National Maritime Museum, Greenwich.

Clowes, *Royal Navy* – William Laird Clowes, *The Royal Navy, a History from the Earliest Times to 1900*, 7 vols. (London 1898–1903).

Colledge-Warlow – JJ Colledge and Ben Warlow, *Ships of the Royal Navy*, 2nd ed. (Newbury 2010).

CSP Dom., Col. – Calendar of State Papers, Domestic Series, Colonial Series.

DNB – *Dictionary of National Biography*

NRS – Navy Records Society.

SP – State Papers in the National Archives, Kew.

Syrett-DiNardo – David Syrett and RL DiNardo, *The Commissioned Sea Officers of the Royal Navy, 1660–1815*, 2nd ed. (NRS, 1994).

TNA – The National Archives, Kew.

Introduction

Pity the poor shark. It is one of the larger and supposedly one of the fiercest predators in the oceans, but when its name was taken for a series of ships serving in the Royal Navy, these were all small, and until the last four, it has to be said that they were largely inoffensive vessels – while of those last four, three were speedily destroyed when they went into action.

The origin of the term 'shark' is scarcely understood. It first appears in English in the report by Sir John Hawkins of his voyage to the West Indies in 1568.[1] It is said to have been adapted from an Austrian-German term, *schirke*, for the sturgeon, but this, it must be said, seems fairly unlikely.[2] How did Hawkins, in the West Indies, catch such an obscure name for a fish he had never met before, and transfer it from one species to another? For, after all, sharks are not uncommon in British waters, though those of the Caribbean are perhaps fiercer, at least in reputation, than the British variety. It could therefore be a term known to fishermen, but which only got into print in Hawkins' report. (It is noticeable that the languages of the nations whose sailors went to the Caribbean in Hawkins' time all have different words for sharks – in French *requin*, in Spanish *tiburon* or sometimes *caiman*, in German *haifisch* or simply *hai*, in Italian *squalo*. These all show an independent origin, and none collected the name from another European tongue, which argues against Hawkins' supposed Austrian-German derivation.)

Alternatively, and this is one explanation I myself particularly like, it may be a term adopted in the Caribbean from a local language, specifically from the Aztec Nahuatl language, learned there by Hawkins and his men between bouts of threatening, fighting, and trading with the Spaniards. This would be the only term ever acquired in English from Nahuatl, but it would be appropriate given the equivalent fierceness of the Aztec people and the fish. Unprovable, alas, but pleasantly romantic.

The Royal Navy *Sharks*, of which there have been thirteen to date, lasted for a variety of periods of time, and suffered a variety of fates. One simply sank at its mooring, having been there for too long; another foundered in a storm; one was captured, and another was seized by its mutinous crew and surrendered to the enemy; two were renamed, but this did not save them, for one was the only ship of the Allies to be sunk off the Normandy coast on D-Day. Most of the rest were worked until the Admiralty could not maintain them any more, and were then sold or scrapped. This was the normal fate – mutinies perhaps excepted – for most of the small ships of the Royal Navy, which were used in all sorts of roles, of which fighting came a long way down the preferred list; they were all too frequently sent into danger on behalf of their larger brethren; at least two *Sharks* survived in part because they were faster than most other ships of the time.

But these ships were an essential part of any navy, and their work was always necessary. When the line-of-battleships were in harbour or going about in fleets and squadrons, ships like the *Sharks* could speed off on their own, carrying messages, reconnoitring, escorting convoys, carrying passengers – tasks which may well have been more interesting and entertaining than merely maintaining station in a fleet, or keeping the ship clean. One *Shark* was used by two of the greater admirals of the late seventeenth century as their command post; another provided a constantly available transport service between England and Ireland for people who were distinguished enough to be able to command a free ride. They patrolled the coasts of England, Scotland and Ireland to intercept law-breakers and invaders. They were scouts and spies, carried messages and showed the flag, and two of them operated actively against Jacobite rebels.

They fought when necessary, of course, but such small vessels had to pick their enemies with care. So they tackled pirates and smugglers and privateers, and were happy enough to see them escape without having to fight; poorly armed merchant ships of the enemy were especially prized as targets, though it has to be said *Sharks* did not capture many of them. They scouted enemy positions from close to. When all ships grew bigger, in the twentieth century, the *Sharks* suffered for their size and their armament, and three were sunk. Another, however, fired its guns in anger against Russian revolutionaries, just as a predecessor had fought French revolutionaries and another had fought American rebels, and others fought against Jacobite armies. Their crews ran the full gamut of naval behaviour from mutiny and frequent desertion to a posthumous Victoria Cross. Several of their captains died in the service, a fate which happened also to far too many men of the crews, though much more frequently from accident or disease than from enemy fire.

So this is a study of an aspect of Royal Naval history which largely eschews the great battles – though not entirely – because the ships being studied generally avoided being involved in such fights. Yet their work was just as essential as that of the greatest battleships in maintaining the presence and power of the navy in all waters. It is, however, quite typical of the accounts of the events in which *Sharks* were involved that the ships themselves are scarcely ever mentioned, even in lists of ships in fleets of which they were a part, where they are too often consigned to such notices as 'various smaller ships and vessels'. One of the purposes of this account is to indicate the injustice of this for the ships, their captains, and their crews, and to point out that accounts which ignore the smaller ships of the navy are necessarily incomplete. They were as essential to British naval power and assertion as *Victory* or *Hood* or any aircraft carrier.

A Note on Sources and Footnotes

Small ships like the *Sharks* do not, as pointed out above, feature in either battle reports or modern narratives. It is therefore necessary to base an account of their careers on the logs produced by captains and masters and lieutenants. There are difficulties in using such sources, for they are rarely very informative, except that they do provide the bare essentials of ports called at, courses followed, and sometimes the positions of the ships; just occasionally there are longer entries, though it takes a major event to force a ship's captain to a larger statement with details – a hurricane or a battle might just do it; one captain had published a book before becoming a *Shark* captain; he was satisfyingly loquacious. But the most important aspect of using logs as the basic source for this study is that they provide a virtually continuous record of the ships' actions – and where a log is missing, that can be almost as informative. This does involve recording a lot of detail, but that is largely the point in demonstrating the work these ships did. Yet such sources must also be supplemented by outside sources, letters, where they exist, and the general naval and political context.

The basic sources used in this account are therefore the logs of the ships and the captains' journals, most of which survive, and which supply the informational spine along which other narrative limbs are attached as necessary. These are supplemented by any other items, such as references in such Admiralty letters and records which can be found; often, however, it is necessary to explain the context from other sources. In each case, I have noted the log's reference in the National Archives at Kew on its first use, but not then in detail afterwards; any direct quotation not annotated is thus from the log; other sources are annotated in the usual way.

Finally I refer throughout – except in a direct quotation – to a ship as 'it', in accordance with present Royal Navy (official) practice, and not by the old term 'her'.

Chapter 1

Shark I: a Brigantine, 1691–1698

I

The first naval *Shark* was built at Deptford, in the old naval dockyard founded in King Henry VIII's reign, and was launched on 20 April 1691. The need for ships of all sizes, and perhaps particularly for small ships, was great. The Revolution Settlement of 1688–1689 was no more than a year or two old, and the cause of the self-exiled King James VII and II had been taken up by Louis XIV of France, who had been building up his own navy for the past decade. Little was yet certain about the political condition or future of the British Islands: in Scotland there was plenty of sentiment still for a Stuart king; mainly Catholic Ireland had fallen almost entirely to Catholic James II. Small ships were going to be useful in the next years in the intricate and difficult waters off Ireland and in the English Channel and the North Sea. *Shark*, with just four guns, was classed as a brigantine, a vague term which covered a wide variety of vessels – essentially it meant a small ship with two masts. It was the first of a new type, of which seven more, all larger than *Shark*, were built; the type was not thought to be a success, though *Shark* itself was certainly well used in its short life.[1]

The first crew began installing the rigging, gathering stores, and so on, on 28 October 1691. The first captain was Lieutenant Jedediah Barker.[2] He began with a crew of just eight men – the mate John Higginbotham, the boatswain-and-gunner Charles Moore and five seamen. No log of the ship's progress has survived for the nine months of Barker's captaincy, but some idea of where the ship went can be gleaned from its muster book.[3]

The complement of the ship was supposed to be thirty men, but in the nine months from October 1691 to July 1692 seventy-four men were listed as joining the ship. Twenty-seven of them were marked as 'discharged', that is, they were transferred to another ship or station; the new ship was clearly being used as a catch and source for seamen for the fleet as a whole. Two of the men died; eighteen are marked as 'run' – deserted – including two of Barker's first five crewmen. The dates of these events are noted in the muster, allowing us to make a rough estimation of the ship's activities. By July 1692 the remaining crew numbered twenty-seven, a little under complement. (There is a discrepancy in the numbers; about ten men cannot be accounted for.)

It took until the end of 1691 to complete fitting out, and then from January to March the ship was in the Downs, the great waiting place for the navy, at the eastern choke point of the Channel between Kent and the Pas de Calais, where a guard was always kept in peace and war, to supervise traffic in peace, and in wartime to intercept any threatening fleet aiming to invade England, either from northern France, or from the Low Countries – Belgium was the Spanish Netherlands, and Holland had been a regular English enemy in the past fifty years – or from the French Channel ports. This last was the clear and present danger at the time *Shark* was fitted out. The ship made occasional visits to Dover for water and fresh supplies, and it was back in the Thames estuary, at Sheerness, for a time in April, no doubt for technical adjustments. In May it sailed to Gosport and Portsmouth.

A brigantine was a small ship, in *Shark's* case 58ft long and with a beam of 15ft. It was rigged in an unusual, experimental, way, with a square sail and a topsail on the foremast, and a larger triangular fore and aft sail, called a lugg, on the mainmast. This was not a rig easy to control, and at least one of its captains disliked it sufficiently to ask for the lugg sail to be replaced by a square. It was not a design which in the end was much favoured by the Royal Navy, but it has persisted to this day as a civilian craft rig.

In its first months the ship's career was unexceptional, but two incidents are obliquely recorded in the muster which indicate that it was soon involved in some of the great events in the Channel in 1692. On 24 May 1692 able seaman John Land was killed in an 'engagement'. The ship had been at Portsmouth until at least 11 May, when one sailor is noted to have deserted. It thus had left the Downs, gone to Portsmouth, and then went to sea between 11 and 24 May. But 24 May is the date of several incidents in the Battle of La Hougue, or Barfleur. This was when the two fleets of France and the Anglo–Dutch allies met in a great fight off the coast of Normandy. This was their second fight, the first, off Beachy Head, having been a victory for the French, but one they had failed to follow up by an intended invasion of England.[4]

Now in the second battle, in late May 1692, the French were beaten, and *Shark*, with its four guns, had been part of the battle.[5] On 23 May the boats and fireships of the fleet went into the Bay of La Hougue on the eastern side of the Cotentin Peninsula to burn several of the stranded French line-of-battle ships;

next day – 24 May, the day AB Land died – they went in again. On each visitation half a dozen of the great French ships were burned, and numbers of transports and storeships as well. It may thus be assumed that this was the 'engagement' referred to in the ship's muster book; Land was no doubt shot by a Frenchman as his ship drove into the French coast to assist in the burning and destruction of the French ships.

The second incident came two weeks later, at Portsmouth. On 6 June Captain Barker was transferred to 'discharged into' – the *St Vincent* fireship. This was a former French ship captured not long after the Battle of La Hougue.[6] Since Barker was given the command it is probable that the capture was accomplished by *Shark*, and that his new command was Barker's reward; he took fourteen of the men from *Shark* with him on his transfer; this would form the nucleus of his new crew.

Next day, 7 June, a new captain for *Shark* arrived, Thomas Stepney. He came from the 100-gun flagship of the fleet, *Britannia*, and his appointment was no doubt at the instigation and favour of Admiral Edward Russell, the commander-in-chief of the fleet and the victor of the recent battle. Stepney was thus now given his own ship, and it is at this point that the first of the surviving captains' logs begins, and so provides more detailed information about the activities of *Shark*.[7] (No doubt Barker took his *Shark* journal with him.)

The first task, no doubt stimulated by the experience of the great battle, was to double the number of guns on the little ship. By Admiral Russell's order, *Shark* was sent to acquire four more guns while at Spithead. This took a week, then it went to sea once more. By 19 June, *Shark* was off the 'Island of Basto', as Stepney put it, which is presumably the Ile de Batz, just off the north coast of Brittany, near Roscoff. 'I spyed a sail close into shore', he explained, but when he chased it, it got away, as did another, which was spotted amid some rocks; Stepney was sensible enough not to attack an enemy vessel amid a rock-strewn enemy coast.

Shark was evidently part of a squadron under Captain George Mees, which had been detached from the fleet to examine the coast of Brittany from Cape Frehel westwards.[8] They failed to find any possible landing place – for the intention after the naval victory had been to land a force somewhere on the French coast, though no one could decide where. The summer of 1692 was a particularly stormy one and *Shark* lost its topmast on 21 June; the ship was back with the fleet by then, and received a replacement from *Britannia*. *Shark* was exactly the sort of vessel which the admiral wanted for close reconnaissance of the enemy's coast and ports, able to get close to the enemy coast and yet it would be no great loss if it was wrecked on the rocks or captured by the French. Keeping the ship and others like it fit was clearly one of Admiral Russell's priorities. The fleet crossed and recrossed the Channel, and by 21 July it, and *Shark*, was back at Spithead.

Shark was sent, presumably with some message, as far as Plymouth in the next days, returned in stages to Torbay on the 20th, and was then ordered back to Portsmouth. It was a lone voyage, perhaps to locate any separated ships, or perhaps to try to contact a squadron under Sir John Ashby which had been told to keep in touch through the port of Dartmouth. Captain Stepney was ordered to complete his stores to a month's supply on 23 July, and the next day the fleet sailed again on another fruitless Channel cruise. It was back in Portsmouth by 4 August.

Admiral Sir Cloudesley Shovell was now detached to pursue an idea of King William for an attack on Dunkirk, a well-fortified city which was a notorious privateer base. Shovell took with him to the Downs a convoy of transports carrying some of the troops originally intended for the now-abandoned descent on France, and *Shark* was part of the convoy escort. The port of disembarkation was to be Ostend, and *Shark* was sent on ahead to deliver a letter from the army commander, the Duke of Leinster, to the governor of the town. Captain Stepney took the opportunity to make a fairly detailed sketch map of the place in his log, indicating gun emplacements, city walls, and the anchorages. The squadron and its convoy arrived on 23 August. Three of the ships went aground in the shallow waters, and it was decided to actually put the troops ashore at Nieuport instead. This was a smaller port but closer to Dunkirk, which was the target of the expedition. But Nieuport was an even shallower and smaller port than Ostend, and only ships with less than 8ft draught could go in, so all the small ships and the boats of the squadron were employed to carry the troops to the shore.

This task did not, it seems, include *Shark*, for it was sent back at once to Ostend to redirect the artillery, which had been sent by the king by boat along the canals and the Maas River, and was apparently landed at Ostend, to be moved on to Dunkirk by road. After this the ship remained at Ostend for several days. This was clearly intended and not just a matter of adverse weather. Captain Stepney used part of the time to clean and tallow his ship, a task which usually took some time, leaving the ship temporarily immobilized. Shovell required *Shark's* services again on 5 October, and for the next month the ship visited a series of French and Flemish and English ports, sometimes delivering letters, sometimes reconnoitring, sometimes collecting provisions. These were not always easy tasks, for the season was getting late. On 1 October Stepney sailed from Nieuport to Ostend with a letter for the Dutch Admiral Evertsen, but it took the ship five days to get into the harbour to deliver it.

Then on 9 October the ship carried Shovell to the Maas estuary to supervise the return of the guns which had been lent to the expedition by King William. After all the preparations, Dunkirk had been adjudged to be too strong, behind its Vauban-designed fortifications, to be attacked; the expedition captured Dixmude instead, which was hardly a proper compensation, but perhaps better than nothing. On 15 October *Shark* was ordered back to Ostend where the whole expedition had been gathered to return to England. Three days later the ship was off Dover and was sent on to Sheerness and then to Deptford. On 14 November it was laid up for the winter.

(This episode provides a perfect example of the neglect of the work of these small ships where larger vessels or high ranked officers are involved. In a recent biography of Shovell, *Shark* is mentioned once (but not in the index), and the context ignores its clearly essential passages back and forth, providing the necessary communication links between the several commanders.)[9]

For a ship which was essentially less than a year old it had been an exciting introduction to its navy career. Involved in a battle, drawing the favourable attention of two admirals, having had two captains, budding off a crew to another ship, deeply involved in a major expedition – these were all events which few ships could list in their history over a period of lifetime, let alone a mere single campaigning season. And yet in most accounts of these events the ship is never mentioned.

II

After a winter being laid up, the whole process of fitting out, collecting stores, and recruiting a new crew had to be done again. The new captain was Edward Durley, another sailor whose first independent command this was. (He arrived as a lieutenant; he was promoted to captain by 25 May 1695.)[10] He took command of *Shark* on 13 April 1693, with just three other men for his crew, and when he sailed for Spithead on 7 May he was still short of a few men.

For some reason Durley had great difficulty in holding on to his physician (a problem which also arose for other *Shark* captains). The first man he recruited,

Samuel Lopes, one of his first crew members, deserted before the end of May; the second was recruited the day after Lopes went, but was discharged within a fortnight; the third died in October; it was only his fourth, Edward Mosorvoo, who stayed the course. Two of these were clearly foreigners, be it noted. During the year thirteen other men deserted, some of them in late May or early June, the others in September and November – the dates reflecting the times the ship was in harbour, of course, when desertion was possible.[11] There was thus the usual constant seepage of sailors away from the ship, by desertion, and by discharge, though only one man died.

By way of the Downs *Shark*, in company with two line-of-battle ships and several small vessels, sailed to Spithead, arriving on 27 May 1693. The ship was at once assigned to a fleet commanded by Admiral Sir John Ashby, which sailed on the last day of May. (Six men, including Lopes the physician, managed to desert while the ship was at Spithead.) This fleet was covering for a huge convoy of 400 British and Dutch ships which were heading for a variety of Mediterranean destinations. They sailed together as far as Ushant, and there Ashby's fleet left the convoy, it being supposed that its presence was preventing the French from coming out from Brest – but the French were already out, though no one had noticed, and no check was made. The convoy, which was the famous 'Smyrna convoy', was ambushed off Cape St Vincent, losing ninety-three ships, a near quarter of the total. It would have been worse but for a gallant fight by some of the Dutch warships in defending the merchantmen.[12]

After the separation off Ushant indecision reigned in Ashby's fleet, probably because Ashby was already ill; he died at sea on 13 June, and the fleet returned to moor off Berry Head in Devon until a new commander, Admiral Lord Berkeley, arrived. And then, when he did take command, all Berkeley did was to bring the fleet back to Torbay. *Shark* had meanwhile sprung a leak and had been sent in ahead to make repairs. At 'Bricksome' (Brixham) pier on 14 July no obvious leak was found, but the ship was caulked. The fleet sailed again on the 21st, slowly moving as far west as Scilly, then returning to Torbay. Berkeley left the fleet on 22 August, using *Shark* to take him to Starcross on the Exe estuary, from where he went on to Exeter – another admiral using *Shark* as his personal transport.

That was the sum total of the fleet's activities in the fighting season of 1693. *Shark's* actions in that year were, of course, much more typical of a naval vessel's work, even in wartime, than the excitements of the year before. By 3 September *Shark* was back at Spithead. That day, an official from the

Admiralty, Mr Dumer, reported on the state of the fleet, and included *Shark* with a group of three other brigantines and some fireships which were to be 'immediately prepared'.[13]

This preparation was to be for an attack on the Breton port of St Malo, to be mounted later in September. The main weapon was not to be a landing and then a venture into the harbour, suggestions which had been repeatedly rejected as too difficult or too dangerous by more than one council of senior officers the year before. This time it was proposed to bombard the port from out at sea. The organizer was Captain John Benbow, one of the coming men of the navy.

The reasons for suggesting that *Shark* was involved are two: although the captain's log for the autumn and winter of 1693–1694 is missing, the muster book records the ship's presence at Guernsey on 26 November, after the bombardment, when a pilot, John Amy, was discharged. This island was the source of all the pilots used for the expedition, and this therefore presumes that Amy was one of them. These were men who will have known the approaches to St Malo, which was notoriously difficult, a twisting and rock-strewn channel.

The second reason is that later, when he was organizing a similar bombardment elsewhere, Benbow used the *Shark* as his personal reconnaissance vessel. It would seem to have gathered a useful reputation as a ship in which admirals – Russell, Shovell, Berkeley, Benbow – had an interest, no doubt because it was both new and handy and could penetrate to shallow waters where bigger vessels could not go. I suggest that this attack on St Malo was another of these instances, and that Benbow used *Shark* for his personal close reconnaissance of the attack.[14]

The expedition was composed of a group of smaller ships, none larger than a fourth-rate – small line-of-battle ships of perhaps fifty guns – and including the four brigantines Mr Dumer from the Admiralty had specified, of which *Shark* was one. A highlight of the attack was the detonation of a 'machine', a fireship packed with powder and stones and metal fragments, which was exploded at the entrance to the harbour. As an attack it was only moderately successful, since it had been intended to be sent right into the harbour, but blew up while still outside. St Malo was a major naval harbour, and as the source of large numbers of privateers it could certainly be said to be a legitimate target for attack, and the news of the attack was generally greeted enthusiastically in England. However, as other attacks of a similar sort continued to be made over the next years, doubts as to their utility, and of their ethical content, spread.

The real trouble was that, with no enemy fleet at sea, this was the only means of attacking France that the Royal Navy could devise, so other attacks were made on increasingly inoffensive small towns – and for decreasingly worthwhile results.

A more traditional attack was attempted next year, this time by a major part of the fleet. *Shark*, still under the command of Captain Durley, had been in the Thames for a time, at Blackwall, no doubt attending to supplies and repairs, and sailed early in May, reaching Spithead on the 9th. The ship sailed with the fleet on the 29th, called at Guernsey, and was off Ushant on 7 June. The aim was to attack – raid or invade or occupy, or simply destroy, is not altogether certain – the French base at Brest, and on 8 June *Shark* went in to land a contingent of soldiers in Camaret Bay. But the French knew all about the expedition, and where it was to land; the soldiers suffered 500 casualties in the process of landing; the whole expedition was instantly called off.

Suspicions as to treachery were, of course, rife, and John Churchill, Earl of Marlborough, was and is widely blamed, though there were many Jacobites in England willing to explain to the ex-King James in France what was being done. It was always difficult to keep such expeditions secret – too many people had to know something of them – and a large fleet carrying soldiers westward down the Channel was always likely to be going against Brest.[15]

The fleet returned to St Helens to repair damage. A new target was selected and the ships sailed on 5 July, *Shark* again carrying a contingent of soldiers; the ship would go in close to the target, and fire from the shore was expected; the soldiers would be for its defence, either against boat attacks, or, if they could, they would reply to fire from the shore. Dieppe was bombarded, then Le Havre, both being set on fire, with exaggerated claims for damage inflicted, though it was reported that Dieppe burned for three days. Captain Durley's written account of events between 11 July and 13 August in his journal/log is virtually illegible, but by the latter date *Shark* was once again in the Downs, and a month later, with the main ships of the fleet already laid up for the winter, it was off Gravelines.

This time the target was Dunkirk. In his excitement Durley forsook the conventional third person detached style of the naval captain's log. 'I have orders to go with Captain Benbow to sound, they firing from Dunkirk about thirty guns at me', Durley commented, 'there being some ships in Flemish roads that fired several guns at me and our boat.' That is, Benbow took *Shark* in close to Dunkirk to gauge the chances of an attack like that at St Malo, and even rowed closer, using *Shark's* boat. The reconnaissance was successful, in that Benbow did locate a usable channel to get his explosive machines into the approach canal heading for the harbour. The approach, as this preparation suggests, was even more difficult than at St Malo, and a suitably intricate plan was devised.

Before the town and its harbour could be attacked, the defending forts at the seaward end of the canal had to be silenced, then the machines would need to be taken along the canal into the harbour. The defending fort of Rhysbank, at the entrance to the canal, was the target for *Shark* and the group of four small boats it was leading, plus a machine and a fireship. The idea was to get the machine and the fireship close to the fort, using the boats to cajole them into position, and then, the fuse having been lit, to evacuate the machine's sparse crew in the boats. It was intended to explode the machine at the Rhysbank fort so as to open the way for the other machines to reach the harbour. Nobody was in the least optimistic.

As usual, it proved impossible to place the machine and the fireship close enough to the target, and they respectively blew up and burned without causing much damage. The only success of the day was the recapture of a Dunkirk privateer's prize by the 32-gunship *Tiger,* an old vessel originally built by the Republican Admiralty in 1647. For a week after the attack *Shark* cruised along the nearby French coast, but on 4 October it was back in the Downs, and by the 25th was once more laid up for the winter.

III

Another new captain, Edward Cole, took command on 25 March next year (1695), and rigging and recruiting took until 8 April.[16] After a brief visit to the Nore, the ship went back to Sheerness for ten days, then spent a month cruising back and forth in the Downs. Exactly what the ship was doing in all this is never explained, but at last it was ordered to Spithead, and on 20 June it sailed out with the fleet, first to Guernsey, and then back to St Malo. Benbow had planned another bombardment of the place, though this time it was more costly to the English than before. The French were clearly better prepared. There had by now been several of these attacks, and the appearance of the English fleet was no doubt a clear signal of a coming bombardment. The French put up a strong defence, though the mortars did successfully bombard the town. Benbow did not this time use *Shark* as his reconnaissance ship, but the *Charles Galley*, which he could control more easily and which could manoeuvre in the difficult approaches. The attack 'which was performed with an abundance of bravery', Cole states in his journal, had the usual result. 'The town was on fire', so he reported, but the damage was not inflicted on the French navy, or on the Malouin ships.[17]

Shark received eighteen men from the line-of-battle ship *Shrewsbury* in the next days, as a supplement to its crew. After a conference of the flag officers the ship was 'detached to go with Mr Benbow to the bombing of Granville, which [passage] was performed without opposition', as Cole recorded. The achievement was less costly, and, given that the town was small and undefended, even less worthwhile than attacking Dieppe. 'The town was burned almost down when we left it,' according to Cole, though this, and similar judgements, were formed from a distance, and it is certainly considerably exaggerated.

The fleet retired to Guernsey, and the men from *Shrewsbury* were returned to their ship; their function is never explained, but it may be that they were intended to supplement *Shark's* crew in some enterprise, or as a defence, like the soldiers at Dieppe, or possibly just as a reinforcement to help cope with the dangerous waters around Granville, which has one of the greatest tidal ranges of this dangerous coast. *Shark's* sides were pierced for oars, and in such a dangerous navigation situation, where the oars would come in handy – as with *Charles Galley* at St Malo – extra hands would be very helpful.

Cole cleaned his ship at Spithead on 12 July, then waited at Portsmouth for several days before being sent back to the Downs. Another brief stay there was followed by a trip across the Strait of Dover to lie off Dunkirk, which it had been decided to attack once more. This raid was as unsuccessful as the one the year before at St Malo, or as the previous attempt at Dunkirk, no doubt in part because France had been well warned of the possibility by the events at St Malo and Granville, and by the fact that the English fleet lay off the port for three days before beginning the attack.

This attack was finally made on 31 August. It was expensive, with four fireships expended, and a Dutch ship went aground and was presumably lost. Three bombs and a brigantine were also lost. The difficulty of the approach was again the basic problem. The ships withdrew, and *Shark* waited off Gravelines for a decision from the commanders on what to do next.

On 2 September, 'At a conference held on board the flagg, [*Shark*] was ordered to sail for the Downs', Cole recorded. But then, as he was 'hoisting in my boats came a Dutchman of war of 50 guns on board, carried my bowsprit away, tore all my foreshrouds, cut my cable, and [I] lost the major part of her furniture.' The fright of the moment is emphasized by Cole's descent into the first person singular in his journal once more. The catalogue of damage sounds worse than it apparently was, and he managed to sail back to the Downs next day, no doubt under a jury rig.

IV

It was now too late in the year for the fleet to undertake any further operations, but *Shark* was retained in service for the winter. Between returning to the Downs on 4 September and its next assignment on 17 February next year the ship patrolled back and forth along the coasts of Kent and Sussex, calling at Dover and Rye, anchoring in the Downs and off Dungeness and at the Nore.

Cole records no events of this time in his log, which is rather strange, for he was one of the captains named by a government warrant on 6 November to 'observe and follow such instructions as they shall receive' from Captain William Rinard. This captain, an army man, it seems, not Royal Navy, was instructed in another warrant of the same date 'to search such houses as he shall think fit and apprehend persons suspected of dangerous and treasonable parties'. No doubt the actual work was done by the crews of *Shark* and *Discovery* (a ketch) whose captains are named in the warrant. Only three days later Cole reported that he had 'clapt all my men on board the *Ruby Prize*', leaving only his steward and clerk on board *Shark*. This must be an attempt to hold on to the men while in or near London, either to prevent them from deserting, or to keep them quiet. It is an indication of the nervousness of the government that such searches were undertaken – but then it was a revolutionary time, and there was a war on – and it was close to the opening of Parliament. It is also a mark of the versatility of the crews of naval ships.[18]

V

Captain Cole's journal, as noted, is particularly sparse during the winter of 1695/1696, and he makes no mention of the curious activities in London in November. However, the Admiralty agent at Deal wrote to London on 1 January (1696) that *Shark*, along with the *Henry Prize*, *Maidstone*, and *Wrenn* pink, had been forced back by the weather from Dover; ten days later he reported that they had sailed again, heading westwards, though *Shark* was then anchored off the South Foreland; the implication is that the others had managed to sail on. This group of ships was presumably a convoy escort, and was then to bring another convoy on from Spithead. The force was two 24-gun ships, and two brigantines. (*Wrenn* was even smaller than *Shark*).[19]

For the next campaigning season *Shark* was given a new assignment, but only briefly. On 17 February 1696 it had crossed to the north side of the Thames Estuary, to patrol the Wallet, one of the channels bounded by sandbanks which made the navigation of this area so difficult. This was the innermost channel along the Essex coast, stretching from Harwich to the mouth of the River Colne, and used by coasting vessels heading for London in preference to the open sea, where privateers were active – though the privateers followed them into the inshore channels. From later events it seems clear that this was intended to be *Shark's* station during this campaigning season, but within five days it was recalled to the fleet, and on 28 February it was sent across to Gravelines, where the fleet was lying; there it waited. It was back off Dover on the 16th, where a few days before it had been nominated to be the bearer of the final orders for the expedition, and on 31 March Cole went on board Benbow's ship to brief him – 'give an account of my proceedings', as he put it – and then *Shark* went with the fleet across to Calais for another one of Benbow's bombardments.[20]

Cole explained in a letter to the Navy Board that he had been ordered to join the expedition which Benbow was preparing at Dover, which suggests again that this was a fairly sudden summons, and one which the Board had not previously authorized. He also said he needed sails, which he had evidently been attempting to buy himself, but he needed Admiralty permission to do so, and forwarded a note of the prices he had been quoted.[21]

On 1 March, having joined Benbow's expedition, *Shark* sailed for Gravelines once more and there reported to 'the general'. There was no activity for a month, during which *Shark* returned to Dover for a fortnight. It is during this time that Cole decided he needed new sails. On 31 March he reported to the vice admiral (probably Benbow, only in fact a rear admiral, though he was effectively second in command of the expedition under Lord Berkeley and so *vice*-admiral), then sailed for Calais, which was bombarded in the usual way, and with the usual uncertain and exaggerated results, on 2 April. *Shark*, and the fleet, was back in the Downs on 6 April.

There followed another summer for *Shark* of sailing to and fro across the Channel. It is clear that Benbow was pleased with the ship and with its captain, and seems to have asked for the ship each time – hence probably the abrupt removal of the ship from its station in the Wallet to serve again with the fleet.

Cole was a much more persistent correspondent with the Admiralty's Navy Board than any of his predecessors as captain of *Shark*, none of whom had generated any correspondence which survives, perhaps because, as a new ship, little (apart from the non-leak at Brixham) went wrong with the ship in its first couple of years. But Cole repeatedly wrote letters to the Navy Board, mainly in pursuit of supplies. This may be due to the fact that the ship was, after the summer of 1696, no longer part of the fleet, and could not rely on being resupplied as part of the general attention paid to it. On the Essex and Suffolk coasts *Shark* was essentially alone, and Cole had to do the gathering of supplies himself. Even so during 1695, in his first period in command, he had asked for more slops (working clothes), for tallow, and for various other items, and had issued a bitter complaint about the 'insolant rascal', James Wotton, a pilot of Harwich.[22]

After the attack on Calais there was a month in the Downs. From there Cole wrote on 22 April that he needed supplies for the sick.[23] Then the ship sailed to Spithead, and returned to the Downs with a 60-gun fourth-rate and a convoy. *Shark* was anchored close to Benbow's ship, and so it was handy when a Danish ship came by; *Shark* was sent to check its cargo, which turned out to be ballast. The English were becoming very particular about trade between France and other countries in wartime, compiling a varying list of goods which they declared to be 'contraband', which was not something any other states accepted; this led to repeated conflicts with other mercantile powers, as did the demand for respect they felt was due to their fleet from neutral ships; the Strait of Dover in particular was now being taken and treated as English territorial waters. A neutral warship which failed to acknowledge this was liable to be attacked; in the same way, a neutral merchant ship, like the Dane, was liable to be inspected at least, confiscated at worst.

Benbow aimed for another attempt at Dunkirk, in which *Shark* joined. On 22 May the ship was sent to Chatham with a letter from Benbow, presumably for the Admiralty. *Shark* had been described as a 'messenger advice-ship' in the warrant of the previous November, and that was obviously one of the ship's primary uses. At Dunkirk the privateer Jan Bart had escaped from the harbour, evading the English ships which were preparing to attack the town, and Benbow took the main fleet off in pursuit; this was presumably the burden of the letter carried by *Shark*.

Shark was used as a convoy escort next, under the command of the 60–gun *Pembroke*, and with the *Dispatch* brigantine in company;[24] the convoy consisted of twenty-three coasters, and was carrying stores for Shoreham.[25] From Rye on 23 May the ship's muster was sent in, and then *Shark* was returned to its original task for the year. It was in Yarmouth roads from 29 May until 7 June, and was then stationed in that area, off Yarmouth and Gorleston, for a fortnight. On 17 June Cole was ordered to go into Harwich for the ship to undergo a refit, and by 22 June it was refitting when surveys of the stores and of 'the particulars belonging to the boatswain' were taken.[26]

Just before going into Harwich for the refitting Cole sent a long list of defects and requirements to the Navy Board.[27] He was unhappy at the sailing qualities of the ship, and he wished to replace the lugg sail with a square sail. He also complained that some of his beef and pork had been stolen, though he did not accuse anyone. A note on the letter by someone in the Admiralty pointed out that the ship had been built for a lugg sail, and that it should not be altered; Cole's requests otherwise would be met.[28] (But the Admiralty did not use the lugg sail in later ships; Cole's comments were not ignored.)

Shark's refitting in Harwich took three weeks. On 15 July it was on patrol again, this time in the Wallet, which had been its original station at the beginning of the year. This, as explained, is a channel which stretches from Harwich to the mouth of the River Colne at Brightlingsea. It was the channel closest to, and parallel with, the coast, one of several channels all trending the same way, and was clearly a favourite route for coasting vessels, who could feel they were protected by the barriers of sandbanks between them and the open North Sea, a sea which was a lair of privateers and other enemy ships in wartime, and where the victims had several ports, large and small, within fairly easy reach if they faced trouble. The channels were too shallow for large vessels, but the colliers from Newcastle which supplied London regularly used the Wallet or its neighbouring channel the Swin; another brigantine was usually stationed in the Swin. Because of the substantial traffic, the area was therefore also a favourite haunt of privateers, many of which were small shallow–draught vessels which might well be able to approach across those very sandbanks at high water. (*Shark* had done this on occasion in the past.) Dunkirk was a prolific source of these privateers; at this level the war was in part a contest between the men of these small ports.

Shark's task was not so much to protect the coasters as to chase the privateers when they were seen – at least that is what Cole recorded doing in his journal; it is unlikely that he would have been able to get any of the independently-minded skippers of the coasters to sail at his behest. It is not always clear that the ships he chased were really privateers, and it is quite likely that he recorded as such almost any ship which came to his attention – lone ships of any origin, English, Scottish, French, and so on – rather than convoys or hordes of coasters or colliers. He began by referring to every ship he 'chased' as a 'privateer', but later he referred to some as simply a 'snow' – a type of small ship which might be of any origin, and was quite likely to be English and local. But he was certainly kept busy: between 17 July and 4 August – nineteen days – he recorded chasing fourteen ships, almost one a day; some of them at least were probably privateers.

On 4 August the ship lost its topmast (again) and went into Harwich for a replacement, coming out again on the 16th. It was perhaps in this time that six men deserted, taking the ship's boat to do so. We only know of this because the Admiralty's man in Harwich, J. Hearne, reported that he had hired a Norway yawl for the moment as a replacement, because the boats he had in store were too large – then he added in a postscript to his letter to the Navy Board that the original boat had been found two miles away, and could be recovered. Evidently the escaping men had got clean away.[29]

The same routine as before was then followed. The ship stayed out on patrol, except for a brief call at Harwich, until 23 September (when it presumably received a new mast, recorded as having arrived on 3 September),[30] and next day Cole wrote to the Navy Board asking for some 'trifling' small stores.[31] In that time, *Shark* was out for 37 days, during which twenty privateers or snows were chased. Two of the privateers were identified as French, as were a pair of snows, and one of the French privateers was 'engaged', without result; no details are stated.

The visit to Harwich in late August had been in order to clean the ship, and it was out on patrol again on 1 October. Privateers were now less frequent, but on 1 November a fleet of colliers was spotted being attacked by a privateer a little way to the north of *Shark's* regular patrol beat. It fell dark before *Shark* could reach the action, and the ship ran aground during the night; but by the morning it had been refloated and was able to engage the privateer and 'put him to the run, chased him into the sea'.

This was the ship's final performance for this season. Two days later, on 4 November, the ship returned to Sheerness and was paid off a week later. In January it was proposed to clean the ship, but the agent quoted a cost of £336 for cleaning *Shark* and three others; it is not known if the work was done.[32]

Shark was recommissioned four months later, on 3 February 1697, when another new captain, William (or Will) Jones, arrived and took command.[33] But it was another month before he received his last two crewmen, transferred from other ships, and was then given orders for the ship to cruise once again in the Wallet.

Either Jones was less diligent in his record keeping than Cole, or the privateers were less active than the year before, but it was not until the end of April that *Shark* met, or rather saw, an 'enemy' ship. Jones identified it as a 'pirate', and attempted to chase it, but the wind was calm and the privateer, which it presumably really was, got away. During the rest of his cruise Jones spotted only three more privateers, two of them in the Swin, the channel which ran seaward of the Wallet, where the *Dispatch* brigantine (with only two guns) patrolled. Possibly Jones' (and Cole's) earlier vigilance had been so successful that the privateers stayed clear; possibly there were fewer privateers; possibly Cole had exaggerated the number of his encounters.[34]

It was also the case that everyone involved in the war was by this time exhausted, and that no military or naval victory was in sight for any of the states which were at war. Peace talks were being held for most of the year, and in October and November a series of treaties was finally signed, collectively known as the Treaty of Ryswick, bringing peace to most of Europe for a few years, though the basic problem, French predominance and ambition, was not solved. On 10 November *Shark* was sent to London for orders, and ten days later 'the Clerk of the Cheque at Woolwich came on board and discharged officers and men'. Hearne at Harwich sent in the ship's muster book on 16 December by post 'there being no passage to London at the time by water, by reason of the frost'.[35] Only the boatswain was retained on the ship until it was sold. It was still included in a list of Royal Navy ships on 31 December, and the sale was not completed until November of 1698; it was bought for only £44.[36]

It is a mark of governmental financial desperation that a ship which was only six years old, and had proved to be an exceptionally useful vessel during its brief life, should be so unceremoniously removed. (It was, of course, not just the proceeds of the sale, meagre enough in all conscience, which were considered, but the reduction in expenditure on the crew and the maintenance of the vessel as well.) The ship had been shown to be versatile and useful, especially in the shallow waters of the coasts of France and Flanders and amid the sandbanks of the Thames Estuary. It had fought in a few actions – or maybe it was just present – perhaps rather more than might be expected of such a small and presumably vulnerable vessel. Its sale was probably for financial reasons, in that it was not needed in peacetime – but at the same time its design, and especially its lugg sail, was not liked by the Admiralty, any more than by Captain Cole. A year's pay for the crew was between £400 and £500, even discounting the non-payment to men who had 'run', and even noting that it usually took three years to pay the men finally (some of whom probably never received the last payment). For a small ship this looked to be expensive to the Admiralty and to the parliamentary money-counters.

It had been the first of the set of eight brigantines of similar design to be built. The others were all larger, though no better armed, but perhaps more robust, and those which survived the war were retained in service. It was therefore *Shark* itself, not the type, which was thought unsatisfactory. Perhaps Captain Cole's complaints – and those which may have been voiced orally by other captains – had some effect after all, even though rejected at the time they were made.

Chapter 2

Shark II, a Sloop, 1699–1703

I

E ven as the first *Shark* was being sold off, the second was being planned and built. This time the ship was classed as a sloop, with up to fourteen guns, and with a single large sail plus a smaller foresail. Precision is hardly possible since the term 'sloop' was as loosely used as a term for a ship at this time as 'brigantine'. It was a somewhat larger ship than its predecessor, which, given its larger number of guns, is not surprising.

The ship was in service, in a technical sense, by 6 September 1699, under the command of John Carleton.[1] He reported to the Navy Board on 11 September that he had a crew of twenty so far (though his muster book counts only eighteen by that date, plus himself), and he was busy installing the rigging. He wanted to replace the guns he had been given, which were of bronze, with others of iron. A week later the ship was out of the dock and he had 'got my complement of stoute saylors'; he needed sails still, but he now expected them to be provided within a week. However, on 25 September he still needed another suit of sails, and had not yet acquired powder and small arms, and he needed cables.[2]

No doubt most of Captain Carleton's deficiencies were supplied and on 28 September the ship was at Blackwall, then out at sea by 1 October. He had a crew of forty-four men by then, recruited perhaps fairly easily, for this was still peacetime and the press was not available; there would be numbers of unemployed sailors in and about London and Chatham. On the other hand, it seems likely that he was still undermanned, for he actively recruited at every port at which he called, though this might have been deliberate Admiralty policy.[3]

This first cruise was down-Channel, but the ship took a curious course, first following the English coast as far as Beachy Head, which was reached on 4 October, but then Carleton ran south and anchored off Guernsey for the night of the 10th/11th. Five men were enlisted from the island during that brief call. From there he visited St Malo, where he again anchored offshore, though, not surprisingly, no recruits were forthcoming here, and it is unlikely he even tried to recruit. These overnight stops can no doubt be explained because he was in awkward waters, but to flaunt an English ship called *Shark* off St Malo was cheeky, to say the least. No doubt he had been told to take this course, for peace may have existed, but it was still an uneasy condition, and from his anchorage off St Malo he could make an estimate of how many French warships were in the harbour.

By 19 October *Shark* was in Plymouth Sound. In the next two weeks, six men took the opportunity to desert, and one was discharged; on the other hand, three men were recruited. The net result of this first cruise so far therefore was a minimally larger crew than Carleton had started with (5 + 3 recruited, less 7 lost).

Shark sailed from Plymouth on 4 November and was off Strangford in Ulster three days later, a very speedy passage. From there the ship went on to Lough Larne. The *Bonetta* sloop was already there (as new a ship as *Shark*, and of the same type), and soon after *Shark* arrived another vessel left for Liverpool; *Shark* was its replacement. Carleton wrote a brief report to the Navy Board, reporting his arrival at Carrickfergus, and asking if Londonderry was the only place at which he could clean his ship, suggesting a considerable ignorance of the area. More importantly, he said that the ship sailed well, though he decided he would like a little mizen mast, which he thought would improve the ship's sailing qualities.[4]

From Lough Larne *Shark* sailed west into Lough Foyle on 1 December, and called at Londonderry, arriving on the 5th. After staying there a month (possibly cleaning the ship, as he had requested) it sailed back eastwards, calling at several ports and loughs along the way – some of whose names are not locatable – and reached Belfast Dock on 13 February. (It is not always easy to decide the places at which the ship called, for they are written down in Carleton's version of the English version of Irish names, and in handwriting not always easy to read – but the ship's general course is clear enough.)

This voyage from Strangford to Derry and then back to Belfast was to be *Shark's* regular beat. The Admiralty produced a memorandum for King William III a year later, dated 18 March 1701 (a year after *Shark's* first visit to Belfast), setting out the ships and their stations in Irish waters. In effect these were patrol lines for a set of small armed vessels, to which *Shark* had now been added. There were seven other sloops and four larger ships involved, plus a yacht, each of which patrolled a section of the Irish coast.

The four bigger ships had longer or more difficult areas to cover. There were two 32-gun fifth-rates, *Bridgwater* and *Looe*, which between them covered south-west Ireland, from Ballycotton, a little east of Cork, round to the Blasket Islands at the north end of Dingle Bay. Two 24-gun 6th rates, *Swann* and *Solebay* – what would later be called frigates – covered the northern coast from Rathlin Island westwards to beyond Londonderry. The eight sloops each took shorter or easier sections of the coast, and between them they filled the gap between the larger ships' area, from Ballycotton to Derry. It is these ships which did the detailed visits to ports and towns and harbours of the smallest size.[5] (Oddly, the west coast appears to have been ignored, probably because its lack of arable agriculture and thin population made it an unlikely target for an invader; this would change.)

The main purpose of these patrols is not stated in the Admiralty memorandum, probably because it was not necessary, though it is noted that the ships should recruit men as and when they could and they were available. In 1701 it was only ten years since Ireland had been reconquered by the English king after yet another great Catholic rebellion. The places to which French and Jacobite arms had come during that war included Bantry Bay (in *Bridgwater's* area), Belfast (in the area covered by both *Solebay* and *Shark*), and Dublin. The patrols were clearly designed to watch this entire coast, seeking out every small port – *Shark* looked in at nine places in its initial there-and-back cruise along the northern coast. Ireland could hardly be said to have been properly pacified, and large numbers of Irishmen had left with the last French ships, while there was still a constant leakage of emigrants leaving – or fleeing, or escaping – the island. Ulster, a region then as now of bitter Catholic/Protestant discord, was one of the prime sources of this migration, which until 1700 went mainly to England or to the European lands, particularly France and Spain; from 1700 an increasing number went to North America.[6]

Those men who went to France generally became soldiers, though between 1697 and 1701 there were precious few military employment opportunities while Louis XIV's government went through a period of financial retrenchment. But for the English government the existence of several thousands of trained Irish soldiers just across the English Channel was obviously a standing threat. The sudden landing of, say, 5,000 of these men in Ireland could well spark a new rebellion. So, although the journals of the patrolling ships do not give any hint of the purpose of the patrols, it may be conjectured with some confidence that they were there to watch for, and intercept, or at least report, any possible invasion.

   The one purpose which is clearly stated in the Admiralty memorandum for the king was that it was hoped that the ships would be able to recruit men into the navy. This *Shark* at least succeeded in doing this. A pay-book of July 1702 records that thirty-eight men had been recruited in Ireland, and this could be set against the twenty-eight men who had deserted. Two men died and eight had been recruited before reaching Ireland, a net gain of sixteen men. It was clearly a good notion to open the ships to Irish recruits.[7]

   Shark's patrol area was largely confined to the north-east coast of Ireland – the visit to Londonderry was not repeated for over a year. Larne, Carrickfergus, Bangor, and Carlingford were the regular places of call for the ship. However, one visit was made to Lamlash on the island of Bute in the Firth of Clyde between being anchored off Larne and going into Belfast Lough. It is certainly a curious distraction, and was quite possibly due to being driven there by the weather – there is no indication of the cause in the log. (On the other hand, the Clyde did become part of *Shark's* patrol area later.)

   This visit to the waters beyond the island (in April 1700) was only the first of these sideshows. After six months prowling the coast of north-east Ireland, *Shark* went – was sent, presumably – to the Isle of Man, where it called at Ramsey and then sailed to the northern tip of the island, the Point of Ayre. (This was technically within the patrol area of *Martin* – a 10-gun ketch – and *Swallow*, a 6-gun sloop.) But then the ship went to 'Blue Morris', which is Carleton's rendering of Beaumaris in Anglesey. Probably this was again due to the weather, since the voyage to the north point of the Isle of Man would suggest an intention of returning to Ireland. As it was *Shark* finally returned to Lough Larne on 4 November, where it stayed until late in January next year.

   In 1701 the first routine was much the same as the year before. An early visit to Lough Foyle and a return to the north-east coast was followed by patrolling between Larne and Carrickfergus, but this was varied by a brief cruise off the Mull of Galloway on 31 May, and another cruise to the Isle of Man in June. Then there was a patrol all the way down the east coast of Ireland calling at Dundrum and Wicklow, and then on to Kinsale, where a week was spent gathering replenishments for the ship's stores.

   The ship returned north along its course, calling at Wicklow and Dublin Bay, Donaghadee, and Lough Larne, where it stayed throughout the rest of July. Then on 1 August it sailed back to the Firth of Clyde, and this time the weather cannot be blamed, for it clearly went with purpose, and stayed at Greenock for a week. This marks a considerable extension of the ship's patrolling area, for, though it did not again sail along the eastern Irish coast, it did return later to the Clyde, to Greenock and to Glasgow, where it was tied up to Glasgow pier for three weeks in October. In between these visits *Shark* patrolled as far west as Lough Foyle once again, suggesting that the patrol areas for the ships had now been redefined. Finally on 14 October it entered Lough Larne, and stayed there for the winter.

This year, 1701, was one of increasing international tension, as the question of the succession to King Carlos II of Spain and the Spanish Empire agitated the diplomatic dovecotes ever more strenuously. It was not a new problem, having been the subject of discussions and intrigues ever since the sickly king succeeded to the throne in 1665. It became urgent in November 1700, when the king finally died. He made a will leaving all his dominions – Spain, much of Italy, the Spanish Netherlands (i.e., Belgium), and the Spanish overseas empire in America and the Philippines – to the grandson of Louis XIV, the Duke of Anjou – with the clear intention of foiling all the several European schemes aimed at partitioning his inheritance which had been aired and planned for thirty years. This upset all those previous arrangements, probably quite deliberately, since the Spaniards were distinctly displeased at the prospect of their kingdom and empire being dismembered by a coalition of their friends and enemies. (Not that there was much prospect of any of those many earlier arrangements being carried out, but the deceased king's new will now allowed everyone to blame the dead king for the war which resulted.) The legatee, who became King Philip V of Spain, was not in the direct line of succession to the French throne, and Carlos' will forbade him to inherit both kingdoms, but this did not stop several Frenchmen from King Louis XIV down, from remarking that 'the Pyrenees had ceased to exist'. This characteristic French pleasure and arrogance comprehensively annoyed the Spaniards, and scared much of the rest of Europe.

The crisis had several other dimensions. The war, which began in Italy in 1701, is generally called the War of Spanish Succession, but it was equally a war of French Succession, since, although by his will King Carlos had specified that the duke of Anjou should not inherit the French throne as well as the Spanish, there was no guarantee that this would not actually happen sometime in the future. It also was a new episode in the problem of the succession to the English and Scottish thrones, and this made it a problem in English politics, since the Parliament which was constituted during the development of the crisis was dominated by Tories, who were preoccupied with restricting the spending by the government and the powers of the king. The Tories disliked King William, and the members contrived for some time to disregard the growing threat across the Channel.

Louis XIV took a series of measures which were seen as hostile by several other rulers, and this, along with some successful diplomacy by King William and the Earl (later duke) of Marlborough in the Netherlands, eventually united much of Europe against France and Spain. Louis announced in February 1701 that his grandson accepted the Spanish throne, but carefully avoided accepting Carlos' prohibition of the union of the two thrones. He then sent French troops into the Spanish Netherlands, where they disarmed and expelled the Dutch forces which had been occupying a series of forts by treaty as a defence against just such an invasion. This persuaded William to set about the intricate diplomacy of creating a new Grand Alliance, which occupied much of the summer of 1701, but was accomplished by September. (The Tory-dominated parliament complained at not being consulted, and even impeached some ministers who were involved; it was not consulted, of course, because the Tories would have objected and would have set up barriers to any diplomatic conclusions.)

By that time even the Tories in Parliament had become convinced that a war was now probable. Parliament had just passed the Act of Settlement, which regulated the English succession. This had become a matter of some urgency, since William's health was poor, and he was not expected to live long. His heir was Anne, his sister-in-law, whose children had all died; it was therefore necessary to select a new heir to inherit from her. But at almost the same time the ex-King James VII and II died in Paris. Louis XIV, possibly in an attack of emotion, but also possibly as a direct reply to the Act of Settlement, immediately recognized his son, James, called in Britain 'the Old Pretender', as King James III of England and VIII of Scots. Within a year, therefore, Louis was claiming the right to regulate the royal succession in both Spain and England (and Scotland).

The English Parliament had been reluctant to contemplate another war, but William dissolved the former Tory-dominated assembly, and had the satisfaction of seeing that the elections eliminated quite a number of his Tory enemies, particularly several obstreperous Jacobites. This election result was, had Louis understood it, an English reply to his gesture of recognition. The merchants of the City of London were increasingly angry at the prospect of being shut out of large areas of the world by the French succession to Spain, and Louis' inept recognition of James 'III' roused many in the country to anger and to a vociferous defence of the Protestant Succession, or at least to be able to regulate their own system without French interference. There is no evidence that Louis ever understood what had happened in England since 1688.

Parliament may have been slow on the uptake, preoccupied as the Tories were with internal arguments, feuds, and problems, but the officials of the Admiralty were more alert. The memorandum to the king which set out the patrolling areas around Ireland was dated to March 1701, not long after the French king in effect claimed to anticipate the unification of France and Spain. Further, the discussions in Parliament about the succession in England also affected Scotland, which had its own Parliament, and had the right to regulate its own royal succession, though the English Parliament carelessly made the assumption that it could regulate both. (It was not only Louis who was tactless and blundering; the Tories in Parliament were good at that too – some things never change.)

It is perhaps in the light of these considerations in this lengthy digression that *Shark* went to Greenock in August 1701, and back again to Greenock and then to Glasgow in October. Scotland was still recovering from the disastrous attempt to develop a national South Sea Company by planting a colony deep within Spanish Caribbean waters, and unrest was quite possible, for the royal government was widely blamed for its failure – the Scots being unwilling to see the issue at all clearly. On top of this came the insensitive English Parliament's assumption in the Act of Succession that it could regulate the Scottish succession as well as the English. Sending a small Royal Navy ship to Glasgow was a reasonable precaution, a reminder of the power at the disposal of the united government, yet such a small ship that no obvious threat could be apprehended; no doubt Captain Carleton was able to gather intelligence, and perhaps to gauge the local temper – not that Glasgow could ever be taken as a clear indicator of the temper of Scotland as a whole.

By the time the ship re-emerged after its winter in Lough Larne, in March 1702, the international situation had worsened. There had been open war between France and Austria in Italy for nearly a year, and Austria was now a full ally of England by treaty (though war had not yet broken out between England and France). Furthermore, King William died on 19 March, two days after *Shark* was revived from its winter slumber. *Shark* began its usual patrol along the north-east coast of Ireland in April, visiting Donaghadee and Carrickfergus, but then in mid–May it was called back to Spithead.

II

War was declared on France on 15 May, and this was clearly the occasion for bringing a useful small ship back into English waters. *Shark* called at Plymouth and then Dartmouth, and reached Spithead on 27 May, a voyage from Lough Larne of almost three weeks. At Spithead Captain Carleton noted in his journal that the joint English and Dutch fleets were present. The day after its arrival *Shark* was reprovisioned at Portsmouth and the next day, 29 May, it received fifteen men from the *Royal William* line-of-battle ship, and sent twelve soldiers of Lord Dungannon's Regiment, whom *Shark* had evidently brought from Ireland, into *Royal William* in exchange.

That day *Shark* sailed again, and within a day it was off the Lizard. It was apparently sent on a reconnaissance mission, for Carleton estimated his position for the next several days by reference to Cape Finisterre, the north-west cape of Spain. On 8 June he was in sight of land near The Groyne – that is, Corunna; then he turned back and was at Spithead again on 13 June. Quite probably he had been checking on the possibility of a Spanish fleet being gathered or gathering in Corunna harbour, or that the Spanish treasure *flota* had arrived there. He could report that there seemed to be no unusual maritime activity there.

III

The journal Captain Carleton had kept for the past three years ended on 7 July. He was replaced as captain of *Shark* by George Fisher, who had been a lieutenant since 1691.[8] He had been part of William Dampier's exploring voyage in the *Roebuck*, but during this he had quarrelled with Dampier, who put him ashore in Brazil. When he returned to England Fisher brought charges of cruelty against Dampier, which he proved at a court martial. The command of *Shark* was therefore his first independent command.[9] (Dampier, found guilty at his court martial, was fined his pay for the exploring voyage, but he was also soon re-employed.)

At Portsmouth, *Shark* was nominated as one of a small squadron to be sent to Newfoundland, under the overall command of Captain John Leake. Leake was another of the coming men of the navy, who would be active in Spanish waters for much of the war. He was given seven ships, three of which had been part of the Irish patrol – the sloop *Woolf* (2 guns) and the 5th rate *Looe* (32-

guns) as well as *Shark*. The others were of somewhat greater force: the 60-gun *Exeter* and the 50-gun *Assistance*, both relatively new ships; *Reserve* (42-guns), was fifty years old, but had been rebuilt in the last year, and *Charles Galley* (32-guns) had been a busy ship – it had been Benbow's command ship at St Malo, for instance – during the last war. (The Irish patrol had been withdrawn, replaced by five frigates, which were more likely to be able to interfere with an enemy arrival than the small, poorly armed, sloops.)

The purpose of Leake's expedition was to damage the French fishery in the Newfoundland area. There had been a long dispute over rights and powers between French and English fishermen, which had gradually involved their home governments. The squadron Leake was taking is listed in a letter of 26 June, before *Shark* had returned from Corunna, but it was presumably able to reprovision quickly and join the rest.[10] The squadron convoyed a group of ships for New England and Virginia before attending to matters in Newfoundland waters. Leake was to collect two other substantial ships, *Montague* (52-guns) and *Lichfield* (48-guns) at Plymouth. This was a very substantial force for Newfoundland, indeed overwhelming, and was clearly designed to suppress the French activities in these waters without encountering much resistance.

The expedition left St Helens on 16 July, collected the Plymouth ships on the 21st, and the merchantmen were all present next day. *Shark* was part of the convoy escort until 1 August, when Leake detached the ship to convoy the merchantmen to New England (and the Virginians would presumably make their further way alone.)[11] The rest of the expedition spent a month or so off Newfoundland. It called first at St John's, and cruised at the mouth of Placentia Bay, on the south of the island, where it captured two dozen French boats, destroyed others, and burned the French fishermen's camps on the shore.[12]

Leake was congratulated by Secretary of State, the Earl of Nottingham, on his return, though he may well not have much enjoyed the work.[13] It had little effect on deterring the French, but a greater effect in stirring them to campaign to recover their position. It was not only the English who were stimulated by opposition and atrocity.[14]

Captain Fisher's journal has not survived (for a good reason – see below), so we do not know the details of the work of escorting the convoy to New England. The ship probably returned to England independently, unless a return convoy was available. Fisher was retained in command of *Shark* through the winter of 1702/1703, and the ship was kept at Plymouth for that season. It was now to be refitted, but the place for this was changed from Plymouth to Dover, and then changed again to Portsmouth.

This series of changes was to be *Shark*'s and Fisher's undoing. He took the ship to Dover, where he met his wife, who had arranged to meet him there, the assumption being that the refit would be at Dover and would take some time, so that they could live together for that time. But the change to Portsmouth upset their plans, and Fisher decided to take his wife with him in the ship to the new place for the refit. On 30 March 1703 he was chasing a French merchant snow near the Isle of Wight in hazy weather (only a couple of hours from his destination) when he encountered a French 40-gun warship, which caught up with *Shark* and carefully and skilfully manoeuvred to windward so that the wind was taken from *Shark's* sails. Menaced by a possible broadside of twenty guns, Fisher had no option but to surrender.

The result was French possession of *Shark*, and for Fisher two courts martial. In the first he was tried for having lost his ship, and was acquitted because of the overwhelming force of the Frenchman. In the second he was accused of having had his wife on board at the time, and the implication was that this may well have affected his judgement in a possible conflict. Taking into account the verdict of the first court martial, the court inevitably decided that his surrender of his ship had not been affected by the presence of his wife – after all, the presence of women on English warships was hardly that unusual. One may, however, convict the court of extreme leniency in this, for his wife's presence surely affected his judgement, if not in the particular case of the surrender, then it surely would have in any other circumstances. Had the two courts occurred in the reverse order the verdict might have been different.[15]

Shark was in fact the fourth of the set of small ships which had been patrolling along the Irish coast in 1699–1702 to be taken by the enemy. *Swift* (a 4-gun sloop) had been captured in the previous August by the privateer *Duc de Bourgogne* off the Scilly Isles, quite possibly as it was returning from Ireland as *Shark* had done a couple of months before. Four days earlier, *Prohibition* (also a 4-gun sloop) had been similarly taken by a privateer, off Land's End. The ketch *Martin* fell to three French privateers off Jersey at the end of August. These were all small ships, each with very few guns; against an even moderately armed French privateer they were probably as helpless as *Shark* facing a 20-gun broadside, unless they could escape by speed. But it was surely careless of the Admiralty to allow these small vessels to be so easily taken.[16]

Shark's capture was thus the fourth of these ships to go, and the toll was not yet over. *Swallow* was captured by a privateer off the Maas in April 1704; two months later *Woolf*, which had been part of the Newfoundland squadron, fell to a French ship – though it was retaken four years later. Of the nine small ships on the Irish patrol only *Bonetta* (a 4-gun sloop) and the yacht *Soesdyke* (8-guns) survived the war untaken.

Fate was no kinder to the captains of the first two *Sharks*. Three of the captains of these first ships, Jedediah Barker, Edward Durley and Edmund Cole, all died within a year of each other in 1702–1703; Cole, indeed, had been admitted to the Bedlam Hospital. George Fisher died in 1705, having survived the battle of Malaga in command of a fireship, and Will Jones was drowned in 1708. Of the first captains, therefore, only George Stepney lived on, though he was court-martialled and dismissed his ship in 1703 – which may have allowed him to live on, dying in 1738; the fate of John Carleton is not known (the record of his death in 1698 is clearly an error). It could mean that *Sharks* wore out their captains.

Chapter 3

Shark III: a Sloop, 1711–1732

I

The Admiralty waited another eight years before naming another ship *Shark*, just possibly put off by the fate of *Shark* II and the decision to abandon *Shark* I's experimental sail-plan. Once again the ship was a sloop, and again with fourteen guns, but it was substantially larger than the second of the name. Built as before at Deptford, it was afloat by April 1711, and was at sea by June. Its first captain was Francis Legh, who was transferred from *Lancaster*, and *Shark* was his first independent command, so far as we know.[1]

This ship proved to have a very different history from its previous namesakes. For a start it lasted much longer than either of them, twenty-one years, and its captains tended to be in command of it for several years, rather than just for one or two campaigning seasons, at least until towards the end of the ship's life. Of course, one good reason for this change is that the ship was operating mostly in a time of peace. When it was launched on 20 April 1711, built by Jos. Allen, Britain (now a United Kingdom since the Act of Union of 1707) was on its way out of the War of Spanish Succession, to the dismay and anger of its allies, though this was the trigger for the rest to make peace as well, and the treaty was finally signed at Utrecht in the Netherlands in 1713.

For the first year or so, then, the new ship was necessarily on a war footing, and its first task was as part of convoy escort with the pink *Rose* (or *Rosepink*) and *Monck's Prize*, the latter a French ship captured two years before, both somewhat better armed than *Shark* (often spelled '*Sharke*' in the Admiralty).[2] They were gathered at Spithead with the eighty ships of the convoy by 20 June, but it was another two weeks before they all got away; the delay was perhaps largely due to *Shark*, which had its flying jib boom carried away, and then, soon after the convoy sailed, it had to collect more ballast; despite these delays, it was reckoned to be on the coast of Ireland by the Admiralty on 1 July.[3]

The complement for the ship was forty men, though it seems unlikely that this figure was ever attained. Seventy-six are listed in the first surviving muster book, of late 1711; of them, twelve had deserted by 31 May and five were discharged. In a later muster, of December 1714, only thirty-three names are listed – though this has the look of a fair copy, and it has no annotations of service; it cannot be taken as reliable. A pay list of 1711 suggests that a large number of men deserted at the very beginning of the ship's existence. While in service, on the other hand, only seven men are listed as 'run', three at Deptford, while the ship was still being organized, three in Spithead before it began its work, and one at Chester; once it settled into its routine voyages, therefore, only that one man deserted.[4]

The destinations of the ships in the convoy were several places around the Irish Sea. The ships stayed together along the south coast of England and across the Bristol Channel as far as Milford Haven. At this point *Shark* took charge of twelve of the merchant ships and sailed for Dublin, while the rest went to other destinations. Dublin was in fact *Shark's* own destination, and when it delivered the ships of its convoy it was on its assigned station.

The work of the ship for the next two years and more was to sail back and forth between Dublin's port ('Polebagg' in the captain's journal) and various ports on the east coast of the Irish Sea. There were two main destinations, either Holyhead next to Anglesey, or Danpole, near Chester. Occasionally, until early in 1712, the ship was used to escort convoys to England or back to Dublin, but this stopped after April 1712, presumably because the war was now all but over and convoys were no longer necessary. From then on, the main purpose of the ship was to act as a sort of taxi service for important people, and for groups of soldiers going to or leaving Ireland, and perhaps to carry some goods. Of the passengers only the titled people are noted, perhaps because the ship had to fire a salute for them. The Bishop of Ossory crossed more than once, Lord Bramblestone, the Duke of Ormonde, the Countess of Meath, and others used the ship to make the crossing. After ceasing to escort the convoys, the ship made crossings of the Irish Sea twenty-four times between 1 March and 30 November 1712, a crossing on average every eleven days; it then ceased its crossings until March 1713, when the routine resumed until January 1714.

The ship was one of three engaged in regular government traffic across the Irish Sea: there was also the packet which went regularly between Holyhead and Dublin Bay, and the 'Dublin yacht' which tended to transport the more exalted travellers, probably because it was a particularly fast sailer, though *Shark's* normal destination of Chester would have saved them the effort of an uncomfortable ride through North Wales. The more or less regular passages by the packet were largely predictable, and the yacht and *Shark* were always available if the packet was not. *Shark's* voyages were so routine that only occasionally did something happen to merit inclusion in the captain's journal, such as when *Shark* hit a rock near Great Orme's Head on 19 August, due to the 'ignorance of the pilot', according to the writer of the journal.

The journal was kept not by Captain Legh, but by his lieutenant, George Speight. In fact, there is no trace of Legh in any of the records of the time, except that he was certainly listed in the muster of *Shark's* personnel in 1714. Further, only there, and in his signature at the end of several sections of the journal, is there any indication of Speight's existence; neither man's name appears in any of the lists of naval officers, contemporary or modern. This is also the case with Henry Longridge, who is recorded as the lieutenant of the ship in the muster of 1711, and seems to have been Speight's temporary predecessor. It is distinctly odd that all three men on the same ship at the same time are missing from the lists.[5]

The repetitive cross-sea patrols continued until June 1714, at which time the ship departed for Portsmouth, which it reached on 26 June, after a voyage of only seven days. The ship went into dock at Portsmouth for a fortnight, presumably for a good clean, repairs, tallowing, and a refit, but was then sent back to the Irish Sea to resume its tedious voyages. On the way, at Dartmouth on 9 August, the ship fired a salute of twelve guns to mark the death of Queen Anne, and then eleven guns for the accession of King George. This, though the crew could not know it, was an early warning of the next stage in the history of the *Shark*.

II

The visit to the Irish Sea left the ship idle in Dublin Bay and at Polebagg from August to December 1714. Whatever the purpose of stationing the ship there, it does not seem to have required much seamanlike activity, and the transfer of people between Ireland and England was presumably now being accomplished by the other vessels involved; the packet in particular made regular crossings, and for those of a more fastidious disposition the yacht was available. In December *Shark* was ordered back to the English Channel. It sailed from Dublin on 6 December and was in the Downs on the 10th, a remarkably speedy passage, no doubt assisted by the winter winds and its recently cleaned condition. From the Downs *Shark* went round to Deptford, where it stayed until 5 March. In that time a new captain, George Warren (or 'Warrin') took over the command (recorded in office on 1 January). He had been a lieutenant since 1701, and so enjoying a slow career, which does not suggest either sparkling ability or influential connections.[6]

It was now the spring of 1715, and the British political situation was becoming steadily tenser, with the Strait of Dover and the North Sea at the geographical heart of the problem. The speedy proclamation of King George I the previous year had not been universally welcomed. The Tories were generally in favour of the accession of James III, but were now undecided whether to challenge the new king by working for his replacement by James (who would have to become Protestant, even for the Tories), or to accept George because he was a Protestant. Their problem was made more difficult because George was inheriting by the will of the Act of Settlement, and had been legally proclaimed, two factors which were serious obstacles to any attempt to set James on the throne. The Tories' indecision stemmed mainly from James' continued adherence to Catholicism, which he steadfastly refused to renounce. Nevertheless, moves began to be made in James' cause by individuals and groups in both England and Scotland. One of the government's responses was to gather its naval power to interdict any possible expedition on James' behalf from France.[7]

Admiral Sir George Byng was placed in command of the Channel Fleet, and given the task of preventing James and his supporters from crossing. It became clear that a group of ships in Le Havre had been allocated – either chartered by James' supporters or simply provided by the French government – for the expedition to put James into Britain, and that this intended expedition had French government approval, though only of a passive sort. During the summer of 1715 Byng hovered off Le Havre so that the Pretender's ships could not safely leave. They were investigated by agents of the British ambassador in Paris, Lord Stair, and found to be conveying arms rather than troops – so that the aim was evidently to raise a rebellion and then use the munitions to arm the rebels.

Shark was in the Downs in the middle of March, and it sailed west as far as Dartmouth and Torbay and Portland during that month and April. This seems to have been a precautionary move. It was in March that Parliament met, and, among others, the Duke of Ormonde – *Shark's* erstwhile Irish passenger – had been plotting to raise the West Country in rebellion, for there had been trouble in Devon and Bristol earlier, and it seemed to be useful Jacobite territory. But the original disturbance had been easily suppressed and there was no more desire in the West Country to make more trouble; then the two main conspirators, Bolingbroke and Ormonde, both fled abroad in the summer, and this was virtually the end of any Jacobite possibilities in southern and midland England. *Shark* returned to the Portsmouth area and stayed there until the end of July; on the 30th it was once again in the Downs.

The secretary of the Admiralty, Josiah Burchett, reported to Admiral Byng on that day that all the small ships in the Thames and the Medway had been ordered to join him; *Shark's* presence in the Downs was noted in a postscript.[8] For the next two months the ship was at Byng's disposal, and he used it, and other relatively small vessels, to patrol back and forth along the French coast observing Dunkirk and Calais and Boulogne, and later Dieppe as well, looking for Jacobite activity, and investigating any ships which came out of these ports;[9] meanwhile Byng was able to reduce French government support for James – never very strong – after the death of Louis XIV at the beginning of September, by simply enquiring if the Jacobites' ships were officially supported by the French government. This provoked the French regent, the Duke of Orleans, to back off; he withdrew whatever support the French had been providing. There was still much support for the Pretender amongst the French, but the uncertainties of French politics – the new King Louis XV was only five, and a minority regime was always unstable – led the regent to look to Britain for support internationally; this support Britain was glad to supply – once the threat of James and his rebellion was removed, of course. French official encouragement for James' expedition became much muted, though it was never eliminated, and he could still rely on semi-official help from many levels of French society.

Byng kept his eye on *Shark*, and on *Swift*, a fellow sloop which was also being used to watch the French ports. On 19 September he spotted them both in Rye harbour, which he did not expect, and sent his boat in to get them back to work. They had been given new orders by the Admiralty to go to Great Yarmouth to defend the fishery there against Dutch and French harassment, but Byng pre-empted the Admiralty's scheme, and sent both ships back to France. *Shark* was ordered to return to Dover every week or so to provide reports on possible Jacobite activities, but it could only repeatedly report no action.[10] This was, of course, good news, implying that the blockade was tight. But then the autumn gales caused damage to several ships and *Shark* had to refit at Dover.[11]

None of this, other than the movements of the ship, was recorded in the captain's journal. And now the references to the ship in the surviving Byng correspondence cease, because the Channel Fleet stood down for the winter while *Shark* was being refitted. That refit had been completed by the end of October, and on 1 November the ship was reprovisioned from Dover and then sailed north: the smaller ships were too useful to be allowed to rest for long. It was known that James had not given up his attempt to reach Britain, despite the winter weather, and by now the only region where it was worth his while to land was Scotland, even though the rebellion there was not prospering, thanks to inept generalship and the unreliability of the highlanders, who were in effect the only men to come out in his name. So *Shark* and other ships were redirected towards Scottish waters. The ship moved north in a fairly leisurely way, first to Gorleston in Suffolk, then to the coast of Yorkshire and Lincolnshire – the north of England had been disturbed earlier – where it waited until December. By the beginning of that month *Shark* was off Berwick and on the 6th was in Leith roads in the Firth of Forth.

This progress northwards was parallel to the destruction of the weak and ineffective rebellion in northern England, which eventually collapsed in the confrontation – it cannot be called a battle, or even a fight – between the rebels, consisting of a small highland army and a few northern Englishmen, and the royal army under General Wills at Preston in November. It was therefore no coincidence but a response to events at Preston, that on 2 December the *Shark* left Grimsby roads, first for Berwick, then for the Forth. For the next ten weeks it patrolled in the Firth of Forth, as news arrived of the landing of James at Peterhead in the north-east early in December (having sailed from Dunkirk), more or less at the time *Shark* set sail for Scotland. Further news was of his steady failure to attract any real support at Aberdeen, Dundee, and Perth. The Highland army had fought a drawn battle at Sheriffmuir with that of the Duke of Argyle on the same day as the non-battle at Preston, but its men had then collected what loot they could find and had largely dispersed to their homes soon after.

The *Shark* called at Leith and Prestonpans, and at Kirkcaldy, and then went back to Leith, patrolling the firth in case James found enough strength, and the will, to attempt to cross the water towards Edinburgh. He was close to the firth for most of January, and at Perth from the 9th. The men in *Shark* may have been able to see the smoke rising from the Fife villages, Auchterarder and others, which James had ordered to be burnt, but they caught no clearer view of him. The presence of the Royal Navy ships along the coast of eastern Scotland, even a ship as small as *Shark*, was an effective deterrent to crossing open water in small boats. James' delaying and equivocation, and the destruction of the Fife villages, did the Pretender no good, and he gave up his attempted usurpation. On 4 February he left Scotland in the *Marie Therese*, a small ship of Dieppe. There were two Royal Navy ships nearby when the ship sailed, but with its shallow draught the ship sailed close along the shore, and they failed to realize its significance, or to intercept it. *Shark*, which might have been able to do so, and had practice in this from its time off the French coast, was not present.

Shark stayed at Leith until 13 February (1716), then sailed northwards. Clearly it was understood that the danger of a Jacobite advance southwards was now over. The ship moved north in slow stages, as before, stopping at the main east coast ports, searching for Byng's squadron. Off Montrose it 'spoke with a fishing boat which gave us an account of the men of war stood to the northwards about four or five days ago'. It was off Stonehaven for two days, then Aberdeen for two, where on the 18th it finally caught up with the squadron – *Royal Anne Galley* (42-gun), *Pearl* (42), *Portmahon* (20), and *Deal* (probably *Deal Castle* (24)). The whole group now returned to Leith. There a salute was fired for the Duke of Argyle, and another for Admiral Sir John Jennings, who now succeeded Byng in overall command. And then this part of the captain's log ends on 7 March with the notation 'Captain Warren departed this life', and the comment that it was not signed 'by reason of the indisposition of Captain Warren, since dead'. The captain's indisposition may be the reason why the ship had been moving slowly, even hesitantly, for the past two or three months.

A new muster had been taken on the arrival of Captain Warren in 1715. This had listed fifty-six men in the crew, of whom five had been discharged under Warren, and ten more were marked as 'run', though seven of these were actually on detached duty. (There seems to have been no category between desertion and presence on duty – 'absent on command', or simply 'on command', would be the correct designation in the army.) None of the men had died – at least until Warren himself. On the other hand, a later pay list, of February 1716, listed 115 men, but twenty-one had deserted, and one had died. The new captain countersigned this, Warren being the man who had died.[12]

The new captain was Edward Mansfield, appointed from the *Royal Anne Galley*.[13] He signed himself as 'master and commander', a description which was now rather out of fashion. By the time he took command it was clearly known where and when James had gone, and, rather late in the day, a small squadron led by *Oxford* (54-gun), and including *Shark*, went in chase. Of course, James was long in France by this time, but the little squadron followed in his tracks to Texel in the Netherlands. It has all the appearance of a show chase, to indicate that the navy was doing its best, even if it was late by more than a month. *Shark* anchored for a time off the Texel, and then separated from the rest of the squadron and sailed for the Thames, arriving at Deptford on 27 March. James had been in France for two months by then. No doubt there was plenty of relief in Britain's government circles that he had escaped, since if he had been captured something would have had to be done with him, and the best was perpetual imprisonment, where he would have been a permanent target for internal plots and international reproaches. (One wonders if the admirals knew this, and carefully avoided catching him – as opposed to defeating him.) *Shark* was then paid off.

III

Shark was left out of commission for a year and a half, being remanned in February 1718. Presumably in that period it was tallowed, refitted, and made, once again, as good as new. The new captain was George Pomeroy, who was promoted to commander on 8 January, presumably in preparation for his appointment to *Shark*, which had been selected to form part of an expedition.[14] Two months later, *Shark* was in Galleons' Reach, and on 16 March at the Nore. Ten days later it reached Spithead, staying there until 1 May.[15]

Captain Pomeroy regularly wrote to the Admiralty Secretary, Josiah Burchett, on the ship's progress and condition, and these letters are collected in the 'Captain's Letters' file of Admiralty correspondence.[16] Only Captain Cole had been as assiduous a correspondent among *Shark's* captains so far, but his letters are distributed in the Navy Board's correspondence, being mainly requests for equipment. Pomeroy, however, reported regularly to Burchett on where the ship was, and on its state. For example, he wrote on 6 February that he expected the ship to receive its guns, and that it would then move to the Nore; four days later he reported that *Shark* was out of the wet dock and was about to go into dry dock to be sheathed; he had a full complement of men.

This is a curious correspondence by a captain reporting such relatively minor matters to the Admiralty Secretary. There is nothing personal about the letters; they are all businesslike. It must be presumed either that Burchett had specifically asked Pomeroy to send these regular reports, or that Pomeroy was doing so to curry favour with the Secretary. Unfortunately from the point of view of this account the letters are scarcely more informative than the captain's log, of which indeed they seem at times to be no more than extracts or summaries. Pomeroy was not usually a descriptive correspondent.

Shark's new destination was the West Indies, at first as part of a small squadron whose first task was to install a new governor for the Bahama Islands. The governor was Captain Woodes Rogers, famous already as a circumnavigator and privateer; the islands had become a notorious pirate base, and, despite a previous visit by a Royal Navy captain, who had been sent from New York with the royal proclamation promising pardon to any pirate who surrendered, and who persuaded over 200 of the men to accept the amnesty and leave the islands, there was still a considerable number of pirates in the islands. It was not therefore at all clear what the reception of the expedition would be. Indeed, it could be assumed that those who had surrendered were the unwilling pirates, and therefore those who had remained were likely to be the more determined to continue their racketty lifestyle.[17]

There may be another explanation for the letters. This was an unusual expedition. Captain/Governor Rogers had been a notorious privateer in his earlier career, and was now going up against an even more notorious pirates' nest. It would seem reasonable in the Admiralty to solicit independent reports of what he was doing, for one fear must have been that Rogers might be using an official expedition as a cover to join the pirates rather than to suppress them; indeed, the idea had surely crossed Rogers' mind. Pomeroy's letters might thus be a means of checking on Rogers' own reports.

Rogers' expedition was small enough. Besides *Shark*, the smallest ship in the group, there was *Milford* (32), under Captain Peter Chamberlain, who had the temporary rank, or perhaps position, of commodore for the occasion, and *Rose* (20), under Captain Thomas Whitney. (This was the successor to the *Rose* 'pink' which *Shark* had been associated with several years before.) These three ships were in fact the escort for the colonizing and anti-pirate expedition which had been organized by Rogers. He had recruited 100 men to form a garrison for a fort whose dismantled parts he had in store, and there were three armed merchant ships in the convoy – the largest of these, *Delicia*, a former East Indiaman, had as many guns as *Milford*. If he chose to join the several hundred pirates already in the Bahamas, Rogers would be in a very strong position.

Pomeroy's ship came out of dry dock, sheathed, on 21 February, so he reported, and by 17 April he was at the Nore, where he reported – as if Burchett did not surely already know – that the complement of the ship had been increased from sixty to eighty men; he now as a result wanted more small arms for the larger crew. The ship was in Portsmouth on 24 April, and the voyage of the expedition finally began on 1 May; Madeira was reached on 2 June; from there *Rose* was sent ahead to find a pilot in Barbados, if one existed there who knew Providence Island and the Bahamas generally. The other ships left Madeira on 11 June, and arrived at St Kitts on 7 July. Two days later Pomeroy reported to Burchett that *Shark* had lost a mast on the voyage from Madeira westwards, and had had to be towed by *Milford* for part of the distance to the West Indies.

The whole fleet came to Nassau on New Providence Island in the Bahamas on the 25th, having met *Rose* with the pilot a few days before. The sloops went into the harbour next day and the bigger ships a day later. In a letter of 3 September Pomeroy reported that *Rose* had been fired on by the pirates, and that the two sloops had then driven the contumacious pirates out. Some of the diehard pirates had therefore escaped in a couple of ships, but most of those still there were welcoming – with 'a great deal of seeming joy', Pomeroy wrote. He noted in the journal (but not in a letter to Burchett) that two ships laden with sugar were taken in the harbour; it is not clear if these were regarded as pirate ships, or were seized because they were trading with pirates. Rogers persuaded the pirates of New Providence either to enlist with him, or to go away; he built his fort, and settled in to be a strict governor.

Shark waited at Nassau until mid-August, when it was clear that Rogers was more or less firmly in control, and then it sailed to New York, probably to report to the governor there on these events; he had been the origin of the news of the royal pardon to the island in the first place. Pomeroy stayed in New York for two months, until December, then sailed for Jamaica, another two-month voyage. A sign of the naval tension in American waters came when *Shark* fell in with a squadron of five French ships, who prepared their broadsides. *Shark* bore away but was fired at for several hours, 'as long as their ship would reach us'. His explanation was that 'I believe they took us for pirates', which seems likely, and is an indication that pirates' and Royal Navy ships were essentially indistinguishable. *Shark* had left New York in company with *Milford*, but they had become separated. They met up again at Harbour Island in the Bahamas, then both went on to Kingston in Jamaica.

Kingston was to be *Shark's* base for the next two months, though it then only went on a single brief voyage on 21 March to Port Morant, still in Jamaica, and then returned to Kingston. Finally *Shark* sailed on 28 April back to Providence. Governor Rogers regularly complained to the Admiralty that he ought to have ships based there to support him, suggesting that two sloops would be suitable, though the Admiralty did not comply; indeed, it probably did not have the ships to spare, certainly not to be permanently stationed in such a minor place as the Bahamas. Perhaps a visit by *Shark* was the best the Admiralty could do. *Shark* stayed a month, and we know that another ship, *Flamborough*, was there next year, 1720.[18] Its presence helped to prevent an attempted Spanish landing, though the weather was probably of greater effect.[19] Rogers was not quite as forgotten as he supposed and complained, and the fact that the Admiralty did not feel the need to send him more support suggests that it was well understood that he was doing a good job. And, after all, Royal Navy ships were not intended as garrisons, but were supposed to sail. Surely Rogers, circumnavigator and former privateer, understood this.

For the next three years *Shark* did sail, back and forth, quartering the Caribbean, staying days or weeks at a whole variety of ports and islands. From Providence it returned to Port Royal, then east to Barbados, returned to Port Royal, then spent six weeks cruising with no particular destination, and back to Port Royal. In February 1720 it sailed west to Bluefields, still in Jamaica, then back to its main base at Port Royal. In each case the ship stayed in port for a few days, or for two or three weeks, before moving on. This was clearly a presence later described as 'showing the flag', an intermittent reminder to those in the islands that the Royal Navy was ever-present; it was both an encouragement to the law-abiding and a menace to others.

Shark went to Barbados, then to Antigua and Montserrat. It was at this time that the Spanish expedition menaced Nassau, as part of an undeclared war in Europe which nevertheless involved a full-scale battle off Sicily – the battle of Cape Passaro – and a siege of Gibraltar. Presumably *Shark* was sent to assist in any necessary defence of Antigua in particular, in case of a Spanish attack there. The failure of the attempt on Nassau, coupled with the wreck of one of the Spanish ships in a storm after their withdrawal, probably reassured the British.

In this period Pomeroy's correspondence with Burchett ceased. There were no letters between 30 January 1719 and 18 April 1721. This suggests that it was the expedition to the Bahamas which was the main concern of the Admiralty in these letters, and that once Rogers was in control, and was seen to be loyal, Pomeroy's reports were no longer needed. And since he stopped writing, he knew this.

Shark left the islands on 27 July 1720 and spent the summer in Boston, Massachusetts, no doubt to avoid the hurricane season; the ship stayed in the north until December, and from then on was more or less permanently stationed in the Leeward Islands. It returned to Antigua on 20 December and between then and July 1722 it visited Antigua, St Thomas, St Kitts, Nevis, and Montserrat repeatedly, and Barbados twice, on each visit staying for a few days, or even a few weeks. The pirates of the Bahamas had been pushed out of Nassau, and were now substantially reduced in numbers, but there were still several bands in the area, particularly in the outer Bahama Islands, not far to the north of the Leewards.

Pomeroy resumed his correspondence with Burchett on 18 April 1721, reporting that on 28 March he had taken two French ships which had been trading illegally 'in our islands'. A privateer had taken a captured ship to Barbados and had sold it and its contents there; another was taken by a French ship out of St Martin. Pomeroy was clearly assuming that his correspondence could be resumed to report such awkward events, which were really international problems. But he then followed up this letter by one on 10 May, explaining that the ship's condition was bad. He no doubt hoped to be recalled. But it clearly had no effect; he wrote again in December from Antigua saying that if the ship stayed much longer in the West Indies it would need a great – and expensive – repair.

On *Shark* it must have seemed, if there were any sailors on board who might have recalled the time in the Irish Sea, that this constant patrolling was just as tedious a life as that had been, despite the warmth, the rum, and the scenery. What, if anything, *Shark* had to do during these visits is not recorded, other than in Pomeroy's single letter to Burchett in April 1721. Perhaps the ship's mere presence ensured that it had nothing to do. The ship at last returned across the Atlantic in July 1722, once again avoiding the hurricane season, arriving at Spithead on 9 August 'according to orders' as Pomeroy reported, and went on to Deptford once more on 16 August; there it was laid up for a refit.

There are two muster books surviving from Pomeroy's time in command. The first covers the two months the ship was in English ports during 1718, before it sailed to the West Indies. This muster lists ninety-seven men, of whom eleven were discharged in that time and seven deserted. This was a fairly normal percentage of loss in an English port at the beginning of a ship's cruise, and it left the ship with approximately its new official complement of eighty men.

The other muster book covers the rest of the voyage as well as those first months. Apart from Pomeroy, who remained in command all through, three other officers are named, two midshipmen, James Brown and Francis Scott, and a lieutenant, Roger Martin, who held the post from 21 August 1721. Further, this second muster is signed by Daniel Wiseman, and the first one lists the mate as Walter Curve. Scott is listed as commissioned as a lieutenant from 4 April 1720, though no other details of his career are known – this presumably means that his predecessor Brown had died or been promoted or transferred; Martin is listed as lieutenant only from 1723, after the ship's return, so his appointment in 1721 was probably a temporary promotion, and no doubt Scott (who is not listed as present in the first muster), had either died or was also transferred.[20]

On the second muster, taken in 1722, no men are recorded as having deserted, but six men had died. The record of no desertions is highly unlikely (though maybe in the islands there was little opportunity to desert at this time, which required the men to vanish from sight – a new white face would be instantly noticed; on the other hand this never deterred other deserters); New York and Boston were places very attractive to deserters; it seems likely that the record in the muster is wrong. If only six men died during four years spent largely in the Caribbean, it was a remarkably healthy cruise, no doubt largely due to the ship having been kept at sea for long periods, and so well away from the land's infections.[21]

IV

After four years mainly in the Caribbean, *Shark* needed a dockyard's serious attention. Between its arrival at Deptford and the following April it went through a process which may be termed a rebuild. It will have been badly affected by the *teredo* worm, prevalent in the Caribbean, and much of its hull would need replacing. (The 'sheathing' it had been given at the start of its life was another layer of wood, not the later copper sheathing.) That this rebuilding process took only six months or so to carry out is a function of the relatively small size of the vessel – rebuilding a larger ship might take years. This new *Shark* version lasted for another nine years, several of which were once again passed in tropical waters.

It was, however, a procedure which was hardly worth doing. The six months spent, in effect, in taking the ship apart and then reconstituting it, using any good wood which had survived and replacing the rotten wood with new, could have been used to build a completely new ship. And in fact, with only one other ship of this size subjected to this sort of rebuild, this was clearly realized in the Admiralty. *Shark* III was thus a pioneer of naval work just as was *Shark* I.

V

The ship was ready for sea in April 1723, virtually a new ship, though still *Shark*. A new captain, George Sclater, took command. He had been made commander on 9 April, and so, like more than one of his predecessors, had presumably been promoted expressly to be given this command.[22] The ship was manned and provisioned – the complement was now ninety men – rigged and equipped, during April, and by May it was off Galleon's Reach. The first muster book of Sclater's captaincy lists no less than 270 men. Of these ninety-four were soon discharged, and thirty-one quickly deserted, almost all at Deptford or at Plymouth before the ship's work had really started. One man was recorded as having died, at Plymouth in November 1724.[23] The ship's first voyage was to move by stages down the Thames Estuary, the stages – Greenhithe, Sheerness, Sheppey – are marked in the journal.[24] No doubt this was relatively slow progress, and if not simply due to the weather, it probably was in order to test the soundness of the dockyard's work.

The new assignment for the ship was to patrol along the coast of Devon and Cornwall. Once again this was to be a policing role, which involved liaison with the customs officers in the several ports; that is, the ship was to catch, or just deter, smugglers. Cornwall was a notorious smuggling area, as was indeed much of the English south coast. For the next two years *Shark*'s ports of call were Plymouth, Dartmouth, Fowey ('Foy'), Falmouth and the other small ports along the coast from Dartmouth to Land's End. But first there was a cruise from Sheppey (left on 20 May) to Pendennis Castle, next to Falmouth (reached on 3 June) and then back to the Downs, presumably as a shakedown voyage; from June onwards *Shark* sailed back to the West Country and got to work.

Within a month Captain Sclater had to deal with his first problem. On 7 July between Mounts May and the Lizard he sent his lieutenant, John Jackson, in the ship's boat to intercept a merchant ship. It was dark and the boat was fired on from the shore; one man was hit. The next day the Customs House boat came out, presumably from Penzance, in response to the incident. The customs officer explained that they were suspicious of two French ships, a sloop and a galliot hoy, and they had fired on the former, or so they thought, and had hit *Shark's* boat instead. Both of the suspicious ships had 'escaped'.

Shark went into a series of ports and harbours, probably at first largely to display its presence, and so as a warning to potential smugglers. Ten days after the encounter with the sloop and the customs men it went into Falmouth for several days, and back to Plymouth, then to Dartmouth and Falmouth and then to the Helford River. The galliot hoy – or another like it – was encountered again on 18 August off Eddystone. *Shark* fired three shots at it, but it got away, probably by using its oars. Such conduct clearly made it an object of increased suspicion. A month later off the Lizard, Sclater fired at a sloop, which stopped. It was carrying brandy and tobacco, prime smugglers' goods; it was towed into Mounts Bay and then sent into Penzance for the customs officers to investigate it. They sent it on to Plymouth, and *Shark* towed it there.

The winter of 1723/1724 was spent in several harbours, Fowey for two months, Falmouth for ten days, Plymouth for ten weeks, then Falmouth again. There was perhaps little point in patrolling in the winter, but at least the ship was not wholly idle, and its presence reminded the local smugglers that they needed to be careful, if not lawful. From early March 1724 the coastal patrols were resumed: Falmouth to Plymouth – having fired at a Dartmouth coaster on the way – to Penlee and Plymouth, Dartmouth and Plymouth, to Mounts Bay. In early April Sclater stopped a sloop said to be a notorious smuggler, and took it into Falmouth for the customs to inspect. On 30 May a French sloop was found at anchor in Mounts Bay, loaded with brandy, wine, and salt, said to be bound for Ostend: it was sent in for examination. A coaster was examined on 4 June, and a brigantine on 10 July between Fowey and Plymouth; a sloop sailing from the Isle of Man to Rotterdam with cloth was stopped on 16 June; five days later a sloop and a brigantine conveying salt to 'Menagazie', wherever that was, was stopped; two days later another sloop carrying wine was sent into Plymouth, and the day after he sent two more sloops, also with wine, into Falmouth. Next day a ship with cloth for Lisbon was examined, and one from 'Mengerzie' for Plymouth, and one with salt, cloth, wine and brandy for Guernsey – this last was the only one of these three sent in for examination to Plymouth.

Shark went into Plymouth for two weeks, and when it came out again the work resumed at once. A brigantine from Nantes with brandy for Ostend was sent in. A French sloop with wine, brandy, and cloth for the Isle of Man was sent into Falmouth; *Shark* itself went in there next day, and had to act to stop the sloop when it attempted to get out without permission – a fairly sure indication of guilt. A ship from the Ile de Bas (or Batz) for Guernsey with salt, wine, and brandy was sent into Plymouth – its route was certainly curious and will have raised suspicions, as would its cargo. *Shark* went into Plymouth itself that day, and came out on 20 July and immediately intercepted a sloop off Rame Head bound from Bordeaux to Rotterdam with wine and brandy. When stopped it was noticed that a 'fishing boat' put off from the sloop; Sclater sent his lieutenant in the *Shark*'s boat to investigate, and the fishing boat was found to contain four hogsheads of wine; the sloop, and presumably the boat and the wine as well, was sent into Plymouth.

Curiously, after all this activity in June and July, no more ships are recorded as being intercepted for the rest of 1724, and then from October to January *Shark* lay at Plymouth. It had continued its patrols between August and October to Falmouth, Fowey, Plymouth, and Salcombe. Then in January 1725 the ship came out again, intercepted and fired at two local sloops off Falmouth almost at once, and fired at a bark from Mounts Bay off St Anthony on the 4th, before going into Fowey on the 15th for two weeks; one wonders if there had been an assumption by the smugglers that *Shark* would stay in harbour throughout the winter, or perhaps there had been a gathering of intelligence by the customs. The harvest of suspicious ships in a short time in winter was certainly unusual. The ship stayed at Fowey and then at Plymouth until the end of March.

Late in March the ship was evidently being surveyed to judge its condition, and the masts were found to be 'defective' (this, only two years after the rebuild). It was moored beside the *Thunderbolt*, a French fifth-rate captured in 1696 and converted into a hulk three years later. *Shark's* masts were taken out and new ones inserted; the ship then went through a full programme of tallowing, cleaning, painting, and maintenance.

In a new muster of April–May 1724 the complement of the ship was said to be eighty, but when it went into Plymouth in February 1725 this was raised to a hundred; between February and May, while it was being renovated and repaired, Captain Sclater successfully recruited the extra men, in fact to more than 100 – he clearly assumed, rightly, that there would be some 'wastage' in the ship's next assignment.[25]

VI

The Admiralty had evidently decided before the maintenance began that the ship would be used once more in American waters where sickness and desertion were much more likely than in British waters; hence the ship's increased complement. The rebuilding and refitting work was completed, it appears, by the end of April 1725, and the ship sailed from Plymouth on 17 May, for Madeira initially. In company with the 32-gun *Tartar* frigate, *Shark* left the island on 10 June, arriving in Hampton Roads, Virginia, on 22 July. (Compare the ship's much swifter passage to Nassau, not much further, several years before.)

The reason for the sudden dispatch of ships to the American colonies was that growing difficulties were once again developing with Spain. Sending *Shark* and *Tartar* was, of course, a minimal gesture, but it was the sort of move which might impress in a diplomatic quarrel, and in North American coastal waters, an extra Royal Navy ship was a powerful symbol of power. Later, in 1726, Britain sent a fleet under Admiral Hosier to the Caribbean, and then Spain eventually responded to the crisis by laying siege in 1727 to Gibraltar, which was one of the items in the dispute – the Spaniards wanted it back. The active quarrel thus lasted about a year, though it had been building for much longer. Then Spain's policy suddenly switched and a new treaty (the Treaty of Seville, 1729) was agreed. In the meantime, however, it was necessary to be on guard wherever Spanish and British territories and interests intersected, and one of these places was the south-east coast of North America.

Shark waited in the area of Hampton Roads for two weeks, then sailed south to the Cooper River at Charleston, South Carolina. With a crisis in Anglo-Spanish relations approaching this was a point where conflict might arise, since Charleston was the centre of the southernmost settlements of the British colonies, and was in almost continuous dispute with the governor of the Spanish fort at San Agustin in Florida. They argued over a wide variety of issues, including Indian relations, the flight of black slaves to Spanish freedom, piracy by both sides (the pirates of the Bahamas were a constant nuisance); British occupation of Nassau and other Bahama islands was equally a source of conflict, for Spain continued to claim exclusive right of possession for all the islands of the New World. Above all, Spain and Britain disputed over the location of the boundary between South Carolina and Florida, which had been pushed repeatedly southwards by the British settlers for the past half century and more. These disputes were collectively one of the elements which fed into the undeclared war of 1727, though no real attempt was ever made to settle these matters in the final discussions – in many ways it suited both sides locally in America not to have matters settled. Neither of the metropolitan governments really knew much about the problems of the area – nor did they very much care – and so it was largely left to the local powers in Charleston and San Agustin to pursue or solve the quarrels themselves.[26]

The presence of *Shark* probably had little direct effect either to restrain the Carolinians, who were notably aggressive in their demands and ambitions, or to deter the Spaniards from retaliating. On the other hand, the ship was present in the area while the dispute went on. It stayed in the Cooper River from the middle of August until late October 1725, then made a visit to Providence Island and Nassau. This was another Spanish concern, for between Charleston and Providence ran the Bahama Channel, used by the Spanish treasure fleets on their voyages from the Caribbean to Europe. Having well-founded and aggressive British colonies on either flank of that route was very uncomfortable for the Spaniards, and was clearly one of the reasons for their resistance to the Carolinians' advances south along the mainland coast. A British armed sloop stationed more or less permanently in the region might perhaps be intended as an assistance to the Carolinian and Bahamian defences, but the Spaniards could see that it was also a threat.

After Nassau, where the ship stayed for five weeks, *Shark* returned to Charleston and the Cooper River for the winter. Into the area also came the 32-gun frigate *Scarborough*, and another sloop went to Bermuda. *Shark* remained at Charleston until the beginning of May 1726, then moved north to the York River in Virginia once more. The summer was spent at New York, and in October the ship came south to the York River again, and for the winter of 1726/1727 to the Cooper River once more. This was the time when the Spaniards in Europe began their lethargic siege of Gibraltar. By appearing regularly at Charleston *Shark* was clearly being used to impose some control over events on the Florida-Carolina boundary, though in fact the Carolinians were much more active than perhaps the government in London would have liked, or, indeed, than it may have realized.

In this period of the 1720s more regular muster accounts for *Shark* were drawn up than before, and a series of quarterly lists survives. Captain Sclater was actively recruiting men in North America, mainly in South Carolina, where he recruited twenty more recruits. Two men died in the year 1725/1726, and five others deserted almost as soon as the ship arrived in Virginia, but at the end of 1726 *Shark* had a full complement of men, and more. During 1727, however, the total number gradually declined from 105 to 89, and by July 1728 the ship was short of twenty-two men. The casualty rate was serious in that year, 1727/1728: seven men died in Virginia, one in South Carolina, and two were drowned; but desertion, perhaps influenced by the deaths, which were clearly mainly from disease, became even more serious, especially so considering that it had been a relatively minor problem earlier; nine men deserted in South Carolina, seventeen in Virginia, and three in New York. By the time of the muster of July 1728, the last muster before the ship returned to Europe, the ship was down to only fifty men, half the stated complement.[27]

Shark spent almost a year from May 1727 at the York River, which was perhaps the reason for the death rate in that time, for Virginia was a source of malaria; then, after a call at New York, it returned to Britain. The heavy desertion rate in the last year may well have been due to the knowledge that this was the men's last chance, and that, once the ship was gone, retribution was unlikely. *Shark* arrived at the Downs on 17 July 1728, the time of that final muster, and moved to Deptford on the last day of that month. The ship was then paid off.

VII

There is another gap in the sequence of the captains' logs between the return of *Shark* to Deptford at the end of July 1728 and the first entry in the next log in December 1729. But since that new log commences with the ship once more at Port Royal in Jamaica, we can make some obvious assumptions about the events in the interim. The ship will have needed a general refit when it got back in July 1728. The crew had been paid off at Deptford, and after several months, perhaps in the spring of 1729, and no doubt once the general condition of the ship after years in American waters was determined, it was decided in the Admiralty to send it off to American waters again. A new captain was appointed and a new crew recruited.

The new captain's log was being kept in December 1729 by Lieutenant William Thomas, though the new captain was Commander Foot Pike, whose earlier career is not known. He took command in October 1728 along with Lieutenant John Pocock, and so there is a year or more missing from the history of the ship.[28] The complement of the ship was again eighty men, but of the ninety-five enlisted by the end of November 1729 eleven had 'run'. By 3 June another muster had increased that deserter total to twenty-seven, and two had died 'at sea'.

These musters can give some idea of where the ship was in the time of the missing captain's log (October 1728 to December 1729), though not what it did. It is only in the musters of 1729 that men are recorded as having died in Jamaica – four men – so presumably the ship had sailed from Britain late in 1728, arriving in Jamaica early in the following year. It seems likely that it spent a good deal of 1728 at Port Royal, where the four men who died did so in the hospital there and five more died elsewhere in Jamaica. The steady toll of deaths went on into the rest of the year, with eight more men dying in the summer. A total of fifteen died in that year; in addition sixteen men deserted in Jamaica.[29]

The absence of a log before December 1729 means that we do not know exactly what the ship did between its recommissioning and that time. It is listed in November 1729 as present in the West Indies, and in that month Lieutenant Pocock died while the ship was at sea. It was this which led to the opening of a new log which was kept by Lieutenant Thomas – no doubt the former log had been kept by Pocock, but it has not survived. Pocock's death occurred while the ship was escorting a Spanish packet boat to Santiago da Cuba. In reporting this to the Admiralty, the new commander-in-chief at Jamaica, Commodore Charles Stewart, also remarked that this had been arranged before he arrived, and that the new governor at Santiago was someone who, he believed, hoped for an end to the 'depredations'. By this he meant the illegal (to the British) capture of British merchant ships by the Spanish authorities, making use of their *guarda costa* ships.[30]

Stewart reported only a few weeks later that *Shark* had again gone to Santiago and had successfully recovered a captured and detained British ship. He also explained that he intended to send the ship to Providence, from which he had received melancholy news, which he did not detail, but he hopes the ship's presence coming among the islands will have a good effect.

Stewart reported on the ships he had available. At Port Royal, he had seven vessels. Others were sailing on various duties. *Plymouth* (60) and *Seaford* (24) were escorting convoys, three others, *Tartar*, *Dursley Galley* (20), and *Tryal* (14), were patrolling along the three sides of Hispaniola to frustrate Spanish and piratical activity, and *Shark* was passing through the Windward Passage on its way to Providence.

On 17 December *Shark* had sailed from Port Royal, east and then north-east, to pass through the Windward Passage between Cuba and the French sugar colony of St Domingue (western Hispaniola), noting in passing Cape Tiburon and St Nicolas on the way. (Cape Tiburon, of course, translates as 'Cape *Shark*'.) It is possible that the ship was escorting a convoy, though this is not mentioned in the log or by Commodore Stewart, but the destination of the ship was then the Bahama Islands, and the log shows that the ship turned north when it reached the southern end of the line of the islands, which is usually where convoys were detached to make their own ways across the Atlantic, at least in peacetime, the open ocean not being the haunt of the Spanish harassing ships. It then made a gradual passage from south to north along the line of the outer Bahama Islands. This was clearly an inspection cruise, and a show-the-flag exercise. Several of these outlying Bahama Islands had been, or had become, pirate bases after the cleaning out of Nassau by Woodes Rogers, and no doubt *Shark's* presence was intended to inhibit their activities. Ending or at least inhibiting piratical raids would also diminish the excuses adduced by the Spaniards for their harassments, as well as increasing the general security of the British islands, both in the Bahamas and in the Leewards to the south.

The first island named in the log is 'Heneage Island', which must be Thomas' rendering of Inagua, which would be the first place to be reached after exiting from the Windward Passage. The cruise is then marked by the islands visited, if only briefly – Crooked Island (where convoyed ships were generally freed to travel on their own), Long Key, 'Little Island' (probably Little Exuma), Rum Cay, Long Island (probably Long Bay on San Salvador), Catt Island, where the ship stayed a day or so. Harbour Island at the north end of Eleuthera was visited on 20 January and then the ship sailed by way of 'Royal Island' (unlocated) to Nassau on Providence.

The ship stayed at Nassau for two weeks, partly no doubt for the captain to visit the governor of the islands, and to report to him what had been seen in those islands, partly to replenish the ship's water supply, and partly, according to the log, due to the weather. The governor by this time was once again Captain Woodes Rogers. He had been ousted by his subjects in 1722 and had been succeeded by George Phenney, who had let the town's defences decay, in part because of the difficulty of raising taxes from the obstreperous settlers – who, after all, were not very numerous. Rogers was appointed for the second time, and had arrived at Nassau on 25 August 1729.[31] This was therefore the third visit of *Shark* to this place, each time under a different captain and crew. When *Shark* arrived on 23 January 1730, HMS *Aldborough*, a 6th rate with 20 guns, was in the harbour, so, with two Royal Navy ships present, Rogers was well supported. However, neither of the ships stayed for long, though no doubt the visit was one of the prime purposes of *Shark's* cruise. *Aldborough* had trouble with its anchor and in the end had to slip the cable and leave without it; *Shark* towed a longboat out and recovered the anchor later.

Shark's cruise continued from Nassau, first north to Abaco Island, then back the way it had come, calling at Long Key Island (Long Island) and Acklins Key, and then back through the Windward Passage, arriving at Port Antonio on the north-east coast of Jamaica on 13 February. At this place Admiral Stewart was organizing the construction of the new base, and *Shark* was detailed to supervise the work – that is, to supervise the slaves doing the work. The ship stayed there until June, apart from a brief visit to Port Royal in May. It then returned to Port Royal on 18 June, but for only six days.

The visit of *Shark* to Providence and the Bahamas was partly an inspection, but it was also a cruise to demonstrate the continuing British interest in the islands in the face of the continuing trouble with Spain. The quarrel which had involved the siege of Gibraltar and had brought *Shark* to North America between 1725 and 1728 had been officially resolved in the Treaty of Seville in 1729, but in West Indian waters a subdued conflict continued. Spain in effect claimed that the Caribbean Sea was a Spanish sea and thus insisted it had the right to inspect all non-Spanish ships there, for which it used *guarda costa* ships, some of which were more like privateers, at least to the British. This claim was resisted by the British and at times reprisals were licenced against Spanish vessels. (Note that the British were claiming similar 'rights' in the waters around Britain.) The whole matter was complicated by the legal trade carried on by the British South Sea Company at Porto Bello in Panama, though here the British had expanded and distorted the rules to increase their trading profits – thus both sides in the continuing disputes had legitimate complaints.

Shark was sent on 24 June to Santiago in Cuba once more with an express from Stewart, now a rear admiral, promoted in December 1729, to the governor in the city concerning the detention of a British merchant ship and its cargo there. Stewart instructed Captain Pike not to go into the harbour but to send in his boat with the letter. Lieutenant Thomas was sent in and was treated, as Stewart reported, with 'civility', though the complaining merchant was said to be quite clear that he would never recover his ship or his goods.

This visit was one more stage in the low-level but continuous Hispano-British quarrel. A particularly unpleasant episode in early 1730, when a Liverpool ship, *Mary*, was seized by some privateers out of Porto Rico, roused Stewart to unusual anger, and the Admiralty told him to exact reprisals, which meant that he could use his ships to attack Spanish ships. He attempted first to gain compensation from the governor of Porto Rico, but failed. He then proposed to send out his ships, and the message *Shark* took to Santiago was a further stage in this process of escalation. But at that point Stewart received a petition from the South Sea Company, which warned that Stewart's proposed reprisals would trigger a Spanish seizure of their annual trading ship which was then at Port Bello in Panama.[32]

Stewart pulled back and restricted his reprisals to attacks on the Spanish *guarda costas*, as the Company men had suggested. One result was that *Shark* was employed for the next several months shuttling back and forth between Port Royal and Port Antonio and Anotto Bay on the north coast of Jamaica, presumably acting to deter any Spanish raids – reprisals perhaps for the British reprisals – on the coastal settlements, or on the coastal shipping.

Captain Pike died on 19 September. Curiously this is not mentioned in the log, though the muster list and the pay list make the change of captain clear. But perhaps this was because of a new and more exciting local event.

The new captain for the ship was Cornelius Mitchell, appointed on 20 September.[33] Mitchell began his own log on his appointment on 30 September, while Lieutenant Thomas continued his own version until January 1731.[34] (They more or less coincide, though with slight discrepancies which do no more than demonstrate the different authorships.) Thomas' log effectively ends on 15 December with a final comment that he was 'ashore from this day to the 2nd of January, which time the ship was out upon a cruise'. He had therefore been dismissed, though it would seem that he had taken his log with him (and later sent it to the Admiralty). Thomas eventually rose to commander in 1744.

Mitchell's first task was to attend to a wrecked ship on Pedro Shoal, south of Jamaica, which was marked by a boat sent from Port Royal. The wreck was of a Spanish 50-gun ship, the *Genovese*, which had been carrying a considerable quantity of treasure to Spain. Rear-Admiral Stewart sent out two small local vessels and *Shark* to attempt to rescue the crew and the treasure – he mentioned them in that order. It turned out that the crew had plundered the ship even before attempting to escape, and the British recovered only a fraction of the treasure. The estimates of the violence involved when the ship struck were of course wild. One casualty was the President (that is, governor) of Panama, who was going home to Spain to face trial for some sort of suspected malfeasance. He had got onto a raft with a dozen others, but this had drifted away, and had disappeared. One of Stewart's tasks after this was to send the treasure his men had recovered on to Spain.

Shark then visited Milk River and after that Savanna Key, areas west of Port Royal, the first time the ship had been along this part of the coast. It was probably searching for survivors – and for the treasure, of course. At least one group of Spaniards had got ashore at the west end of the island, and had 'borrowed' a small ship from a local man – with his permission – but were then never seen again, at least not in Jamaica.

Shark spent the next five months once more moving irregularly between Port Royal, Port Antonio, and a few other Jamaican ports, again apparently on guard against raids. Mitchell remained in command until 14 June, when he was transferred to command the 42-gun ship *Lark*, having been promoted to captain. At the end of 1730 Lieutenant Thomas had been replaced by Lieutenant Alexander Stewart, transferred from *Lyon*, Admiral Stewart's flagship. We may assume that they were father and son.[35]

Mitchell's place as captain of *Shark* was taken by Commander the Hon. Charles Craufurd, who also remained in command for only four months.[36] During this time he took the ship once more through the Windward Passage, and towards the Bahamas. This was part of Admiral Stewart's modified reprisals policy, which had been approved by the government in London. For once, we have a record of the orders Craufurd was given, though he did not adhere to them, and they were a little ambiguous. He was to patrol the Windward Passage, and escort the convoy north-east and then past Hispaniola and Porto Rico to the release point beyond the Bahamas. He was to treat any Spanish ship whose activity he thought suspicious as a pirate, and to detain it. It was this last part which produced the ambiguity, since pirates would scarcely allow themselves to be 'detained', and the elasticity of the definition of a pirate was obvious, and was presumably intended.

In the Passage he stopped four ships, presumably for examination. In effect, Craufurd was searching for Spanish ships which were regarded as encroaching on British rights and territories, just as the Spaniards sought out British ships which they claimed to be illegally in the Spanish sea. He escorted his small convoy as far as Crooked Island in the Bahamas, and left it there. On his return he anchored in Tacco Harbour in Hispaniola and there surprised and captured a Spanish sloop fitted with guns and 'granados'. The ship was not a Spanish warship, but probably one of the private hired vessels which were being used by Spain as supplementary *guarda costas*. These were even less respectful of such rules than were the official coastguard men, and were wholly ignorant of any international agreements between Britain and Spain; they generally acted more as privateers than as coastguards; such ships were the precise targets of Stewart's reprisal campaign.

This was the beginning of the British response to the Spanish methods, to the 'depredations'. Any private *guarda costa* was now liable to 'arrest'. It was in this year, 1731, which was the time when Captain Jenkins claimed that one of these private *guarda costas* cut off his ear, which he then preserved in spirit, and exhibited in the House of Commons in 1739. (The story may not have been correct in all its details – he wore a wig, and underneath it he probably had both ears – but it was correct in essence, since there had been plenty of similar incidents in which greater hurts had been perpetrated.)

Craufurd sank the Spanish sloop, no doubt after looting it. He then sailed to loiter off the Mole at Cape St Nicolas, the north-west cape of Hispaniola, and on 7 September *Shark* captured another Spanish sloop. In fact the ship attacked *Shark* first, 'charging' the ship at night; its manoeuvre failed and it was closed with and captured by *Shark*'s men. This time Craufurd made it a prize, and sent his lieutenant and ten men on board to take it back to Jamaica.

Admiral Stewart was annoyed. Craufurd is said to have brought two Spanish sloops back to Jamaica, though the log implies only one. Perhaps the admiral was glossing over the violence involved. But how Craufurd was to 'detain' a Spanish ship without violence is not clear. Stewart put on a show of anger and claimed that Craufurd had acted 'quite contrary to my orders', but then he sent him out on another cruise into the same Windward Passage, 'by way of punishment'. This was surely obfuscation of the same sort as Nelson's use of his blind eye at Copenhagen.

Stewart's anger was partly feigned, of course, as a sop to Spanish official opinion, but he was surely conscious that Craufurd's attacks on Spanish ships were going beyond what the home government expected; he must also bear in mind the fears of the South Sea Company. He could at least hope to sow doubts in Spanish minds – the Spaniards were obviously aware of the liability of some of their own captains to exceed their orders, and could easily imagine it in British captains. In that case Spanish reprisals for British reprisals were perhaps less likely. On the other hand, he surely also knew that this could well have a salutary effect in the Caribbean generally, and sending out the violent captain on a new cruise in the same area no doubt carried a clear message for the Spaniards. (It is noticeable that the orders Admiral Stewart says were given to Craufurd are undated; were they composed retrospectively?)[37]

In fact, Craufurd, taking out the new convoy, went only as far as the White Horse Cliffs at the east end of Jamaica, where the convoy was left on 24 October, and *Shark* was back in Port Royal next day. But the message was out; no doubt the ship's return was done very quietly. In the interval between these voyages, there was another change of lieutenants, Alexander Stewart being replaced by Henry Stewart – presumably another son of the admiral.[38] Then, when the ship returned from the second, brief, foray, the news had arrived of Craufurd's promotion to captain. (The news of this may well have been broadcast as another hint of official approval of his activities, though it was probably an automatic promotion.)

Craufurd's log continues until 15 October.[39] He had been promoted to captain from commander on 6 September, and presumably he heard of this when he returned to Port Royal late in October, since the news would take at least that long to reach Jamaica from London. He was thereupon removed to a command more suited to his rank. He left a note which was inserted into his successor's log, to the effect that 'Lieutenant Henry Stewart had acted as lieutenant on the *Shark* from 24 September to 18 October 1731'. A second insert by the Admiralty notes that Stewart should have the wages for this period.[40]

However, the acting captain from 6 September 1731 (and so backdated to the date of Craufurd's promotion – more obfuscation?) was Lieutenant Bagnall Owen, transferred, once again, from *Lyon*. He makes only one appearance in the log, which was kept by Henry Stewart, who started his own journal from 3 October, thereby overlapping Craufurd's for a fortnight; they agree. Owen appears not to have kept a log himself, or at least none has survived, and the only evidence of his work in command of *Shark* is in a few letters in Admiral Stewart's records.

The ship was soon sent on another convoy escort as far as Mayaguana Island ('Morapavona'), the easternmost of the Bahama Islands. The voyage was slow, taking three weeks from Port Royal on 24 October to leaving the convoy at Mayaguana on 13 November; Stewart reveals nothing about the ships they were escorting, but he does note that the boatswain, James Devron, committed suicide by cutting his own throat, on 28 October. (The change of captains had not been noted in the log.)

The return voyage to Port Royal was interrupted by a long wait off Cape St Nicolas, and then by two other brief delays in St Domingue waters in the Windward Passage, no doubt in hopes of repeating Craufurd's feat of seizing a Spanish ship. But that exploit may well have warned off any of those ships, and

Owen had no luck; at the same time the presence of *Shark* clearly underlines British determination to combat the depredations of the *guarda costas*-cum-privateers, as did the regular use of convoys for the vulnerable merchantmen. And it clearly had an effect: whereas there were ten seizures of British ships in 1731, the year of Craufurd's captaincy, there was only one in 1732, and numbers remained low until 1737.[41] *Shark* finally returned to Port Antonio, then to Port Royal on 26 December.

A brief visit to Titchfield, a new settlement in the east of the island which was troubled by raids by Maroons, escaped slaves, was followed by a new cruise for two months, once again in the Windward Passage, without any success, if the capture of Spanish privateers was the aim. From this cruise Owen wrote to Admiral Stewart a brief report on his activities, which were innocuous enough. The main purpose of the letter seems to be to report the news that a particularly notorious Spaniard, 'Ferdinando', had been at last taken into 'confinement at Havana', possibly one of the results of Stewart's assertiveness. *Shark* returned to Port Royal on 26 March 1732, then on 24 April it was dispatched back to Britain.

Henry Stewart continued to keep the ship's journal. Captain Owen died on 28 May, during the voyage to Britain. *Shark* was off the Scillies on 11 June and at the Downs on the 17th; it arrived at Deptford on the 26th, and was paid off on the 29th.[42] The ship, now over twenty years old, was now finally decommissioned; it was sold on 3 August 1732.[43]

Chapter 4

Shark IV: a Sloop, 1732–1755

I

The next *Shark*, being built while its predecessor was still cruising the Atlantic, was another sloop. It was once again larger in all dimensions than the third, 80ft long and 24.5ft in the beam, though it was technically built for the same number of guns, fourteen. For the first time, however, this *Shark* was not built at Deptford, but at Portsmouth. Its first captain was Commander Richard Symonds, who stayed with the ship for seven years, longer than any other of the several *Sharks'* captains.[1] He arrived while the ship was still on the stocks in the dockyard, and therefore took over the command even before the ship was launched. Meanwhile, Commodore Richard Hughes, the supervisor of the Portsmouth dockyard, was organizing the appointment of the crucial first crew members, the boatswain, the carpenter, and the gunner, for whom warrants were ready on 10 September.[2]

The ship was launched on 7 September, but this of course was only the beginning. Symonds' log details the stages of the work done on the ship from then on. On the day of the launch the masts were stepped; next day, the rigging of the standing masts was installed, and more ballast was added to that already acquired. On the ninth the fireplace was brought on board, and bricklayers set about placing and building it. More rigging and the topmast yards were added. The carpenters from the dockyard worked all through this and beyond, building cabins and the internal structures. Supplies of beer arrived, water casks were filled on the 13th, and next day more work was done on the rigging and the topmasts. The rigging work was finished on the 15th, when the spritsail and the jib boom were installed. Next day the lower masts and foremast shrouds were set, and during the next week supplies and smaller items of equipment were loaded – butts, puncheons of beer, firewood, anchors, cables, and so on. The ship's bottom was tallowed. And at last, after two weeks' hard work, the ship sailed on the 23rd.[3]

Commissioner Hughes reported to the Admiralty on the experience of the ship's first brief voyage. 'I have only to acquaint you His Majesty's ship the *Shark* sailed out of harbour early yesterday morning. I stood out with the yacht and busy boat to try her sailing, almost as far as Dunmore Point, with a fine gale of wind at WSW. She out went the yacht very much, both by the wind and large, and observed I could scarcely see her to heel, notwithstanding all her sails were set upon a wind, altho' the yacht almost plunged her guns in the water, so I hope she will prove a complete vessel in all respects, and answers your expectation.'[4]

Commissioner Hughes may have been enthusiastic in the light of one brief sail, but Captain Symonds, the ship's first captain, was not. This early brief sail was the preliminary to one to the east, to Dover, the Downs, and on to Great Yarmouth, where the ship was under orders to protect the fishery. After only a few days, however, Symonds brought the ship back to the Nore and then to Sheerness where some refitting took place, no doubt as a result of this early sail.[5] He then sailed west to Plymouth in company with four other sloops and the *Terrible* bomb. In the meantime the oars were tried out and as a result the oar-ports needed alteration; Symonds said the carpenter could do this.[6] In November, out of Spithead, *Shark* and nine of its contemporary sloops were sailed as a testing group from Plymouth to Eddystone; Hughes, still evidently pleased with the ship, reported that *Shark* had sailed best of the ten. However, on the same day Captain Symonds also wrote to the Board and asked for several changes to be made to the ship: a longer foremast and bowsprit, a larger foretopsail, and improvements to the jib boom, amongst several other details. Hughes passed all this on to the Board, and, evidently accepting the captain's assessment, he recommended that his suggested changes be carried out. The Board noted that the ship was due to sail and could not wait for the changes to be effected; the Master Shipwright agreed that they could be made, at least eventually. Clearly the captain's recommendations carried great weight (unlike those of Captain Cole with the first *Shark's* lugg sail).[7]

The ship sailed for Jamaica on 26 November, taking a package which Hughes reported having been handed to the captain the day before; it also had a passenger, James Addams, headed for Port Antonio.[8] The ship was clearly a good sailer, even before Symonds' improvements were included. It reached Madeira on 6 December, and Carlisle Bay in Barbados on 1 January 1733 – a transatlantic voyage of just five weeks. By way of a brief stop at Antigua it was at Port Royal, Jamaica, on the 24th. Its return was equally speedy: from 25 January, by way of the Mona Passage (east of Porto Rico) and passing Watling Island in the Bahamas, the ship was back at Spithead on 16 March – five weeks again.

Symonds reported to the Board on his return, in a letter of 26 March, that he had not set a main topsail at all on the voyage westwards, and had to keep a reef in the mainsail all the time. But he concluded that it was a good sloop and sailed well.[9] The work on Symonds' suggested alterations did not begin straight away, but on 3 April the officers – which must be Symonds, his lieutenant, and the warrant officers (the boatswain, the gunner and the carpenter) – listed the changes needed: the bowsprit should be lengthened by 4ft, the foremast lengthened by the same amount, but the mainmast did not need altering. Hughes sent this to the Board next day, and two days later a warrant arrived for the changes to the bowsprit to be made – a decision clearly only waiting for the return of the ship to be implemented. The ship went into the Great Dock at Portsmouth soon after, and was brought out on 12 April.[10]

The ship was being used as a swift message–carrier, just as the original *Shark* had been, on occasion. After its docking and the delivery of its pay books, it sailed again, returning to Spithead on 11 May, and again on 15 May to Plymouth and back on the 21st. The ship was clearly being favoured by the Admiralty, for the crew were paid up to 31st December on 26 May, an unusually speedy payment – perhaps they were keen to keep the crew in existence, though Symonds had lost nine men to desertion in the first cruise, at Barbados and Port Royal.[11] After another brief voyage in July it was sent round to Sheerness to be docked and for the main alterations to be made. Symonds pressed for the alterations to be carried out quickly, pointing out that he was ordered to the West Indies again (and so it would not be possible to make the changes for another six months). Two days later the ship was in the dock.

The dockyard officers at Sheerness recommended different, or rather additional, changes: raising the quarterdeck several inches, making the steward's room into the bread room, and adding a new steward's room. But Symonds' own original suggestions had themselves also been changed: instead of increasing the height of the foremast as he had wanted, the mainmast was to be reduced by 4ft, something the officers had not wanted. At the same time the complement of the ship was increased from eighty to a hundred men.[12]

II

After all the busy excitement of swift voyages and the flurry of docks and alterations, *Shark* was now sent back to America. Its enlarged complement was no doubt instituted in the knowledge that a long stay in American waters was liable to be expensive in manpower, both in deaths from disease and in desertions, as *Shark* III had already demonstrated, and that replenishment by new recruits was difficult in American ports. Some men had already deserted in various English ports – eleven for certain, while the records of four others are ambiguous, being marked as 'never mustered' – and nine had 'run' in the first West Indian voyage; one man had been drowned. Symonds also had difficulty with his surgeon, the perennial problem. In June 1733 he reported that the surgeon's mate had been drowned (this was the death already mentioned) and that his surgeon was 'very indifferent', so he needed a new surgeon's mate; three months later he wrote that he needed a surgeon – and since he was intended for a long stay in American waters, this was probably both important and urgent by this time.[13]

His first destination in America was Nassau on Providence Island in the Bahamas – yet another visit by *Shark* to that island. He was to take out the new governor, called in the log 'Williams', but actually Richard Fitzwilliam; Governor Woodes Rogers had recently died. Symonds pointed out that with the governor and his suite on board, and carrying six months' provisions, he had no room for the slops he was also to carry, as he had no place to put them. He suggested that a merchant ship should be employed to carry them to Providence. He had also been ordered not to take either goods or passengers on this voyage, except by specific order from the Admiralty. This suggests that it was a normal practice to do so, as with the passenger Addams in the previous voyage. At last, after all the alterations and loading of provisions *Shark* finally sailed from Spithead on 5 October 1733.[14] The ship was still without a surgeon, according to a letter to the Board from Portsmouth two days later (though it certainly had one next year). By way of Madeira the ship reached Providence Island on 29 November, collected supplies of wood and water, delivered the new governor, then sailed on to the Cooper River at Charleston ('Charles Town') in South Carolina, arriving there on 11 December.

Symonds' instructions, according to a letter sent by the Secretary of the Admiralty, Josiah Burchett, to Alured Popple in Nassau, were to exercise command over the security and defence of the islands. It was also noted that captains had recently been in the habit of staying in port for much of the time; Symonds had been cautioned against such a habit. But these were only the part of his instructions relating to the Bahamas, and he was also required to make regular visits to Charleston, and to act in coordination to some degree with other ships in the area. The partial quotation of all this to the correspondent in the Bahamas, whose people considered that they should be protected before all other colonies, caused Symonds a problem later.[15]

His presence in South Carolina was just as essential – more so from the Carolinians' point of view – and a letter of three years before from the then governor there, Sir Alexander Cuming, had stated quite firmly that only the presence of His Majesty's ships had prevented the colony from descending into chaos.[16]

So this was the new 'beat' for the new *Shark*. Between arriving at Providence in November 1733 and having to return to Britain in June 1739, the ship stayed twelve times in the Bahamas and twelve times in Charleston. Each stay was different in length and in the season of the year in which it took place, though in fact *Shark* did tend to stay in the Cooper River during the winter months, and its early visits to the Bahamas were usually only for a few days. This changed later.

There were two basic reasons for stationing an armed vessel in this area. Charleston was a busy port, and the pirate menace was not yet finally overcome. The South Carolinians had successfully organized a profitable trade with the Indians of the interior, and they had used their slave labour to develop the production of two valuable products, rice and indigo, which were in demand in Britain but which had earlier been imported from other countries. These crops were good examples of the mercantilist system in action, which provided protection for producers against foreign competition and a guaranteed market for exotic goods – plus, of course, the possibility of earning foreign exchange from re-exports. An armed vessel would be a useful deterrent to piracy.

The second reason for a naval presence was the continuing quarrel with Spain. This was no doubt for the Admiralty and the British government the more compelling reason. Providence Island since Woodes Rogers' time had become a better-founded colony, but it was still small, with a population of no more than 1,300 in all the Bahamian islands in 1731 – half white and half black. Controlling all the Bahamian islands with such a small population was impossible – hence the continuing piracy problem in the outlying islands – and they had been the targets for Spanish raids several times over the past century. Only three of the islands were populated, at least officially. Providence Island had a little over 1,000 people, but only 375 were adult whites, Harbour Island had less than 200, of whom only fifty-six were adult whites, and the rest of Eleuthera only about 150. This, to be sure, was an increase on four years before, but most of the islands were still uninhabited, except possibly by pirates and escaped slaves.[17]

This was a time in fact when the incidence of slave insurrections was increasing. There had been occasional risings and conspiracies in the previous two centuries, and a series of revolts in the British islands – Jamaica, Barbados, Antigua – occurred in the last quarter of the seventeenth century. Now in the 1730s there was another series of outbreaks – Antigua in 1729 and 1735–1736, Jamaica from 1730 until the 1740s (the 'First Maroon War'). The Spanish island of Cuba and the French island of Guadeloupe were others which were affected in that decade. It seems clear that the news of one rebellion helped spark off others.[18]

Admiral Stewart's Jamaica had encountered raids made by escaped slaves near Port Antonio about 1730, and that had been the beginning of the First Maroon War, during which small numbers of slaves fought the British army to a standstill in the Cockpit country, and where they maintained an effective independence for much of the rest of the eighteenth century. There was another slave rising in Antigua in 1734, and one in South Carolina in 1740. And almost as soon as he took office at Nassau in 1734, Governor Fitzwilliam faced the threat of a slave rising in the Bahamas, though it did not happen when the probable leader was caught.

This was clearly a situation in which a disciplined force of sailors would be a great help to the governor, and *Shark* arrived at Nassau during the crisis – which in fact was much inflated by white fears, and largely consisted of the activities of one determined escaped slave. There was little fertile land to cultivate in the islands, and the main reason for the existence of the colony, at least in London's eyes, was still strategic, as a possible base against the nearby Spanish territories. It therefore needed its naval presence, intermittently at least, as a defensive measure.

On the nearby American mainland the issue was still the expansion of the British settlements along the coast south from Charleston, an expansion to which the Spaniards of Florida took exception. In 1732 a new colony, to be called Georgia, and to be planted south of the Savannah River – which then became South Carolina's southern boundary – was chartered in London. It was organized and developed with some vigour under the leadership of General James Oglethorpe, one of whose early measures was to found a series of forts along the coast from his new capital at Savannah as far as the St John River.[19] This brought British occupied territory to within fifty miles of San Agustin. As

Oglethorpe's military rank suggests, the British presence was overtly military in nature, and was backed up by a fairly rapid settlement in the colony of several distinctly Protestant groups. This British advance, as the Spaniards saw it, of course reignited the long dispute about control of the coast which had theoretically been settled by the Treaty of Seville in 1729.

Negotiations took place between the two parties in America in 1736, but the result was seen as a diplomatic defeat by Spain and the Governor of San Agustin was recalled and put on trial; the treaty was repudiated.[20] Meanwhile *Shark* had settled into its regular round of visits, winter and summer, to Charleston, and relatively brief visits to the Bahamas (see chart on p.94). The ship stayed in Charleston from its arrival in December 1733, until late February 1734, then paid another visit to Providence Island, staying for five days, after which it sailed south to Exuma Island and Stocking Island, where it stayed until early May. This was a source of salt, acquired by simply scraping it up into heaps and storing it in barrels in the ships, which were then exported mainly to the British ports of North America. The camps were unregulated most of the time, and had been raided by Spaniards and pirates in the past; it was part of Symonds' instructions to visit the island and provide visible protection – and some control.

Providence, that is of course Nassau, was visited for nearly three weeks in May 1734, then the summer (June to September) was spent in the Cooper River. The ship was back in Providence in October, then spent three months at Charleston, until February 1735. The captain's log gives no indication of what was done in any of these visits, and his correspondence with the Navy Board is sparse to a degree, consisting only of notices of bills to be incurred, and his careening accounts, or his requirements for equipment which could not be had locally. But 1734 was the time of the possible slave insurrection on Providence Island, and *Shark's* presence and that of its disciplined crew, were no doubt reassuring.

This was the period when the Spanish annoyance at Georgian encroachment on the Floridian borderlands brought on the negotiations which were in the end unsuccessful. The presence of a British armed vessel so obviously sailing back and forth along the Florida coast, and passing San Agustin several times a year was no doubt one of the matters constantly in the background in the talks. These took place during 1736, at first at San Agustin and then at one of the new Georgian forts, Frederica, on St Simon's Island, about halfway between Savannah and San Agustin. Oglethorpe put on a show for the edification of the

Spanish delegates, implying an alliance with the local Indians, and exaggerating the strength of his forts. When the treaty failed, Oglethorpe persuaded the government in London to send a regiment from Gibraltar to bolster the defences in Georgia, which until then were entirely in the uncertain hands of the local militia.

This military reinforcement, being from Gibraltar, could hardly be hidden from the Spaniards, and it may be one of the sources for *Shark*'s unusual movements during the next year, 1737. It set sail on 17 February from Charleston, more or less as usual, but instead of going to Providence Island, it sailed only as far as San Agustin, and evidently made sure it was seen; a Carolinian ship had also investigated the ships in the harbour; a Spanish launch came out towards *Shark*, probably to identify it, but then returned to the harbour.[21] *Shark* turned back on its tracks and waited outside the bar of the Cooper River for three or four days, either unable to get over the bar, or just in case the Spaniards sent a ship to do to Charleston what *Shark* had done at San Agustin. Finally it went into the river and stayed there for a month.

It would seem likely that these movements were due to the apprehension of a Spanish attack. The fact that Britain and Spain were technically at peace had not prevented repeated minor conflicts in the Caribbean, and in 1737 the number of Spanish seizures of British merchant ships in the region had suddenly increased, from none the previous year to eleven in 1737.[22] This, combined with rising annoyance in Britain at the Spanish harassment at sea in the Caribbean, and the movement of troops, made it evident that a war was becoming very likely. *Shark*'s moves were defensive, if you were a Georgian, or provocative, if you were from San Agustin. On 14 April the ship was once again off the Spanish city, at anchor, no doubt with a view to establishing if any more preparations were being made, or if there were serious naval forces in the harbour. In the event, it did not go to Nassau until September, and was back in the Cooper River in November.

The visit to Nassau provoked an argument between Symonds and James Scott, the Chief Justice, when Symonds took a man accused of some local crime on board his ship and landed him at Charleston. Another argument about a boy he had on board the ship, whose mother complained about his absence, was also aired. These seem to have been as much the product of the increased political tension with Spain as anything else. Scott's complaint about the release of his prisoner shifts without a beat into a parallel complaint that Symonds 'spent a good deal more than half of his time at South Carolina' – that is, the Bahamians were frightened, and felt they needed defending.[23] Of course, the facilities at Charleston were much better, if not up to British standards, and the ship was regularly careened there each winter. Also the provision of supplies from the vestigial agriculture of Providence Island was always difficult.

Next year, 1738, matters returned to normal, so far as *Shark*'s movements were concerned. Symonds made a more than usually detailed inspection of the ship in February 1739, and reported to the Navy Board that although the bottom of the ship was in bad condition – probably referring to the sheathing which protected the main hull – despite repeated careenings and tallowings over the past five years, 'the worm has not gotten into the plank'.[24] This was just as well because South Carolinian and Bahamian fears had come close to being justified the year before. *Shark* moved back and forth between Charleston and Providence rather more frequently in 1738 and 1739, and made a visit to Stocking Island in April. In Havana, however, an expedition had been prepared in 1738, to be launched against Georgia, though in the event it was called off on instructions from Madrid. It is not clear if anyone in Georgia knew of this, but it is quite possible that *Shark*'s provocative actions the year before had some influence on the Spanish plans.[25] *Shark* continued on its oscillating voyages until June 1739, at which point the ship was ordered back to Britain, and was to be replaced at Nassau by *Spence*, another small sloop. *Shark* arrived at Deptford on 20 July.

It was perhaps not before time. The upkeep of the ship in Charleston was not easy (though easier than in the Bahamas). The sloop was regularly careened and Symonds could ask for supplies from Britain, brought out by merchant ships (such as *Mary Ann*, which arrived in November 1737), but in February 1739 Symonds had reported the unpleasant state of the ship's bottom. Quite possibly it was the receipt of this report, which will have reached the Board by April, which triggered the decision to replace *Shark* with *Spence*, and bring the former back to Britain.[26]

The return of the ship also brought the compilation of a pay list for the six years since it had sailed from Spithead. In fact it covers the ship's foreign travels from early 1733 to its paying off in late 1739. The early voyage to the West Indies had cost the ship two desertions at Barbados and seven in Jamaica, and suggests a fairly unhappy experience. But the toll in the years in the Bahamas and South Carolina is staggering. First of all, fourteen more men died. The sequence of these deaths suggests accident or natural causes rather than some sort of disease, for they occurred singly and at intervals of several months, and are spread from March 1734 to August 1737. Nine men died while the ship was in South Carolina, and four at Providence. Nevertheless this is a substantial toll: fourteen men were 14 per cent of the complement.

But it is the desertions which are so astonishing. Four men ran at Providence Island, which is a surprise since in such a small white population their identities must have been known to almost everyone almost at once. But in South Carolina no less than sixty-four men deserted. In a complement of 100 men, therefore, deaths and desertions accounted for eighty-two men. Captain Symonds had obviously succeeded in recruiting some replacements in America, though a good proportion of these new recruits rapidly became deserters themselves. He retained a core of his original crew of experienced seamen, otherwise he would not have been able to sail his ship; even so his crew had added fairly substantially to the white population of Charleston. In January 1739, before the ship returned from America, the required complement was reduced to ninety; perhaps the Admiralty understood what was happening, though a reduction of ten hardly dented the problem.

Symonds himself survived only a little over a year after his return to Britain, dying in October 1740; his lieutenant, Henry Dennis, however, who had been a lieutenant since 1727, was made commander in January 1741 and captain in June of the same year. He rose to be a rear admiral by seniority in 1757 and died in 1767.[27] Not all those who went to sea in *Sharks* died young.

III

Shark was refitted over a period of six months at Deptford between July 1739 and January 1740, when it was relaunched; this refit cost £2,372 (compared with the £1,750 which the ship cost to construct in the first place).[28] A new crew was being recruited by October when the original crew – or the survivors, at least – was recalled. They had apparently been held in two ships, *Colchester* and *Newcastle*, at Chatham. Both of these vessels were old and were soon to be broken up; they were being used as virtual prisons to ensure that the men of the navy of freedom-loving Britain could not leave – or escape. The ship was reckoned to need only two months for a refit after a survey at Deptford in August 1739.[29] A new commander, Thomas Limeburner, was in post as the new captain by 1 January 1740, but the refit took much longer than expected. A new survey was taken in January, but in March it was predicted that the ship would be 'ready to receive men by 15 May'.[30] Limeburner was transferred to

HMS *Seahorse* in July. He was replaced in *Shark* by Henry Swaysland; it is from his time that the next captain's log begins.[31] The speed of the original recommission means that Symonds' report on the ship's condition as being relatively good had been accepted, but the more serious investigation which could be carried out at a big dockyard had clearly revealed that much work remained to be done. Limeburner's term as captain had been only nominal; he had hardly taken the ship out of the dockyard.

Shark was thus still at Deptford when Swaysland 'took possession' as he puts it, and he then spent six weeks refitting and gathering the necessary stores; evidently Limeburner had done little in this regard, perhaps not being expected to do anything when the refitting time was repeatedly extended. (This re-equipping included supplying a new copper pot for the surgeon, for which he was charged 16s. 6d.) Before they sailed Swaysland found that his boatswain had disappeared. Bitterly he reported that 'my boatswain, where always neglectful of his duty and guilty of many faults, left me at Deptford without leave', and he had taken his warrant with him, so that the replacement now needed a new one. The boatswain was one of three warrant officers on a sloop of this size, and his disappearance would be very disruptive.[32]

The ship was then sent to Milford Haven in south-west Wales, with the mission of pressing men for naval service, though it took a month to get there. It chased a privateer in the Channel and went into Plymouth briefly, where some of the company were paid. It only reached Milford on 21 September. The ship was in effect being used as a slaver, but confining its attentions to British men, specifically sailors, who were seized by force to serve, without the option, in the Royal Navy. On the voyage down-Channel, it had pressed four men out of a ship on 21 August, and another at Plymouth.

The pressed men were held on the ship as supernumeraries 'for victuals only', that is, even though they were being held for naval service, they were not entitled even to the meagre pay allotted to ordinary sailors. Every ship which *Shark* encountered, either in Milford Haven harbour or on its occasional cruises in the Bristol Channel, was liable to its unpleasant attentions. Many of the ships had some sort of legal protection, as did considerable numbers of individual sailors, not that this always did protect them. The log frequently remarks, almost in a plaintive tone, that the ship which was intercepted was 'protected'.

The reason for this deeply unpleasant activity was, of course, that while *Shark* had been returning to Britain from North America, war with Spain had finally begun (the 'War of Jenkins' Ear'). This was largely a naval war in which British expeditions to the West Indies were supposed to be the means of getting wealth and victory. But for this to happen sailors were required, and the West Indies was already notorious as a deathly station. The only way to man the Royal Navy was by forcing sailors – and landsmen where necessary – into the service. The press was proclaimed and *Shark* became one of the instruments of it.

Shark steadily collected men from many ships. Those arriving from the West Indies and North America were particularly targeted, since none of the men on board had any sort of protection. The press gangs took only a few men from any particular ship, but no doubt their choices were always the fittest-looking seamen. The pattern was that *Shark* stayed in Milford for a few days, then sailed out into the Bristol Channel for three or four days. Occasionally other ports were raided, notably Bristol, a major seaport. Any ship which came into Milford was visited, and any ship encountered at sea was examined. Gradually the hold filled with these new slaves (though some escaped – to be regarded as deserters, of course, in the perverted logic of the situation).

At the same time, the crew of the *Shark* itself gradually decreased. Men deserted at every port at which the ship stopped – Galleons Reach in the Thames, Deal, Portsmouth, Plymouth, Bristol, Falmouth, and, of course, Milford itself, and three men died in the six months of Swaysland's captaincy. Altogether thirty-seven men deserted and three died in his period, while in June 1741 sixty-eight men were discharged into four other ships at Portsmouth, a net recruitment of twenty-eight men in nine months.[33]

At Milford the crew also had policing duties. Under the captain who succeeded Swaysland in January 1741, Samuel Goddard, a detachment had to be sent across to a ship called the *Charming Molly* which was threatened with being looted of its cargo of corn by the men from a number of colliers.[34] The officer Goddard sent met with resistance, and he ordered his people to fire, 'by which one was killed and two wounded'. Next day, 15 February, he had to send men into the town itself to prevent the infuriated colliers rioting and 'robbing the town'; men from two of the Royal Navy tenders in the harbour were also used in this.[35]

At times the enthusiasm for enlisting men by means of the press gang was counterproductive. Thirty men were pressed on shore on 4 June, but two days later the masters of twelve ships from which the men had gone ashore all turned up on *Shark* and required that they be released. Quite possibly it had been hoped that the men, when missed, would be presumed to have deserted; the men, once on board, were effectively invisible from the shore.

Before he was transferred Swaysland had complained about the foretopmast, on which he said he could set little or no sail; he wanted a bigger one, or as he put it, 'with equal bigness of the main'. This was one of the issues Symonds had highlighted at the start of the ship's career, and here it was returning. By December when the ship was at Plymouth 'her bottom being cleaned and tallowed', as the commissioner there so delicately explained, the new foretopmast was being installed.[36]

This was, once more, a fairly minor refit. From now on to the end of the ship's life, there were ten refits over a period of less than ten years. It seems clear that the ship was by no means in a good condition. Most of these refits were fairly brief, but one, in 1745, took four months. Each of them cost several tens of pounds, or a couple of hundred; the investment in the ship was thus another £2,000 or thereabouts on top of the major refit in 1739.

The new captain, Goddard, took over on 22 January 1741. The ship was driven to Cork by a north-easterly storm, having escorted a convoy of six ships from Plymouth for Milford.[37] It seems that both Swaysland and Goddard were on board – the former's log continues until the ship finally reached Milford, though Goddard's begins on the 22nd with the statement that he received his commission to command the ship, though that is not, of course, the same as actually being in command.

Goddard commanded for the whole of 1741. The work was much the same as under Swaysland, though it did include such variations as the fight with the colliers over food, and the incident of the thirty men released by their captains. In June the ship sailed to Portsmouth to unload its cargo of men, some of whom had been kept on board for nine months by then. The ship was ordered into dock for a clean and tallow 'with all possible despatch'.[38] At the same time, Goddard dealt with the foremast problem by cutting the top 4ft off it, then the rigging had to be put right. The unpleasant work then resumed, until October, when fifty-two men were discharged at Spithead. Again the opportunity was taken to take the ship into dock for care and attention: it sailed from Spithead on 9 November.[39]

The ship returned to Milford in the middle of November, but on 1 December it sailed again as escort for a convoy to Cork. This more congenial work (one assumes) was interrupted almost at once by another storm in which the ship was damaged by grounding when trying to get back into the harbour when the storm was seen to be too bad. The rudder was broken. The next two days were spent extemporising a replacement, but the full repairs took another month.[40]

When the ship, repaired, returned to Milford the captain's log records no pressings of men, but occasional notes imply that it was now being used as a convoy escort between ports around the Irish Sea – Milford Haven and Dublin – and round into the English Channel. It certainly took a two-ship convoy from Dublin to Falmouth in March, and another from Falmouth to the Downs later that month. In the process it fired at a 'Salcombe snow' which it thought was a Spaniard, and chased a supposed smuggler, which escaped when dark fell. A return convoy took the ship back to Dublin, then to Danpole (near Chester) and to Holyhead and Milford again. In July the ship returned to the Thames, being given a period of maintenance at Sheerness, then it was employed in the North Sea, escorting convoys between Holland and the Thames, including the royal yachts. Another refit at Sheerness came in December, then in January 1743 it was employed in the Channel again; on the 22nd it sent a boat on shore near Boulogne in search of intelligence; early in February it went into Spithead, where Goddard's captaincy ended.

IV

Another new captain was appointed early in 1743, when Commander Blumfield Barradall took over the command from Goddard at Spithead on 13 February.[41] There had been little delay in his replacing Goddard, who relinquished command on the 10th (having been promoted to captain on 1 February), and almost as quickly the ship was off on its new assignment. It sailed on 22 February escorting a convoy for Gibraltar, was driven back from Falmouth to Torbay, but set off again on 4 March. *Shark* arrived at Gibraltar on 16 March.[42]

This was to be *Shark's* base for the next two years. Its task was partly convoy escort and partly patrolling in search of enemy ships; at times it was sent with messages. In other words, the ship was employed in much the same tasks as before, both by this ship and by its predecessors, though this was the first time in or about the Mediterranean. Rather more unusually it became involved more than once in actual fighting.

All this became clear within a month of the ship's arrival at Gibraltar. On 1 April it sailed as escort to a convoy westwards, the convoy heading for Britain. The escort was only required to get past the Spanish bases to the west of Gibraltar, principally Cadiz, as far as Cape St Vincent or thereabouts; the merchant ships sailed independently from there onwards, for the Portuguese and French coasts were neutral. *Shark* went into Faro, a Portuguese port. When the ship came out next day it encountered a schooner which was stopped by a warning shot, then found to be Portuguese. Then another ship was seen to the west, and after a four-hour chase it hoisted Spanish colours. *Shark* fired two shots at it, which were returned, and about noon the two were close enough for *Shark* to be able to fire several shots with effect, at which the other ship, a *settee*, struck.[43] But the ship proved to be going to Lisbon with a cargo of tobacco snuff. It is not clear what Barradall did with it, but he possibly made it prize and sent it into Gibraltar, depending on its actual origin.

These, in other words, were busy seas, with ships from a variety of countries to be examined. To add to the complications the lands were ruled by a similar variety of powers – British at Gibraltar, Portuguese about Faro, Spanish along the main part of the European coast, including Cadiz and Algeciras and the several ports east of Gibraltar, and also across in North Africa were Ceuta and Melilla, and the Moroccan sultanate and the Barbary state of Algiers in Africa. There were enough Spanish vessels at sea to keep any patrolling British craft alert and busy. In addition, the Gut, as the sailors called the narrow strait between Africa and Spain which was now dominated by the British naval base at Gibraltar, was liable to storms, and had a powerful current from west to east which could easily neutralize an easterly wind and leave a ship unable to advance westwards – or it could be blown well past any local destination. The difficulties of the region, meteorological and political, were thus great; the opportunities were just as appealing, but just as likely to be foiled.

An example of the latter came in *Shark's* second local cruise. The ship sailed from Gibraltar on 6 May after three weeks spent on maintenance; within a day it encountered a ship which evaded examination and got into Ceuta; there the Spanish batteries fired on *Shark* as it approached, and *Shark* veered off. Three days later, it found a Spanish *bacalayo* which had clearly been plundered by Barbary corsairs (there were two Algerine ships moored in Gibraltar Bay at the time).[44] When the ship's boat was lowered to go to investigate it was stove in; *Shark* had to go into Gibraltar for it to be repaired.

Shark sailed again on 12 May, this time eastwards, and spent nearly three weeks stopping, examining, and chasing a variety of ships. One chase lasted three days, until the ship – presumably a Spaniard – took refuge under the guns of Ceuta. Thus the pattern was established, with just occasional variations. On 9 June, for example, it came across a brig and a 'sloop brig' being attacked by privateers, and rescued the victims; on another occasion a Spanish *xebec* towed a captured British ship into Algeciras harbour – just across the bay from Gibraltar – but *Shark* was unable to catch up to rescue it before the Spanish batteries provided protection for the Spaniard.[45]

The dangers and difficulties were clear and numerous, from Spanish warships, from privateers (presumably Spanish, possibly others), and from Barbary corsairs (though Britain had a treaty with Algiers which supposedly protected British ships from molestation). On 12 July, while escorting a convoy, *Shark* had to assist the sloop *Mary* by towing it; three days later a distant firing was noticed and *Shark* went to see, but then had to return to guard the convoy; at Faro later Barradall heard from the Portuguese coastguards that the fight had been between a victim and corsairs. Next day *Shark* ran aground on a shoal, but got off as the tide rose.

Barradall took *Shark* into Gibraltar to check for damage, but all was apparently well; he was then charged with taking a 'packet' from the governor of Gibraltar, Major-General William Hargrave, to Faro. The undeclared war in Flanders, in which British forces were engaged with French even though the two countries were not formally at war, meant that a certain harassment of French ships seemed possible – *Shark* took one French *tartan* into Gibraltar on the 28th and chased another into Algeciras on the 29th.[46] At Faro he found the sloop *Mary*, which he had assisted a month before, and escorted it across to Tangier. There it anchored, but did not come out. Barradall found it still there two days later, and sent in a boat to investigate. It was stormy and the captain said the sloop was not able to 'keep the seas'; at that point, apparently no longer anchored, the ship was driven on shore, and stove in. Barradall could do nothing.

However, his presence in the bay was noted, and the British consul, Pettigrew, came on board; he said that the *bashaw* (i.e., the pasha, or governor) of the city had recently been killed by the Moroccan Sultan Moulay Abdalla, who was still in the area; Barradall fired a salute in recognition of the sultan's victory. Any British warship captain had to be a diplomat, even obsequious, as well as a sailor. He took a convoy out of Tangier and had to drive off four *xebecs* which had come out of Tarifa to attack the ships.

And so the work went on, sailing west to and beyond Faro, east to and beyond Malaga, in and out of Gibraltar. Then in September *Shark* escorted a convoy of seventeen ships further into the Mediterranean than usual. The first destination was the British post at Port Mahon in Minorca, but then *Shark* sailed on alone to Genoa, hindered by a split mainsail but driven on by gales. The ship reached Genoa on 8 October where it stayed until the 18th, then sailed west along the coast to Villafranca where the British Mediterranean fleet under Admiral Thomas Matthews was based. *Shark* arrived on 15 October and sailed to return to Gibraltar on the 17th.

Barradall does not explain the purpose of this voyage in his log, but it was clearly urgent, even if the opportunity was taken to have *Shark* escort a convoy to Minorca as well as deliver a message to Admiral Matthews, though it was the message which was eventually the more important of these tasks. This was, in fact, a key moment in the European wars which had been spreading over the continent since Britain and Spain began fighting in 1739. In September 1743 a new treaty had been agreed between Britain, the queen of Hungary (Maria Theresa, later empress) and the king of Sardinia, whose main territory was in north-west Italy, the area called Piedmont (of which Villafranca was the only port). This treaty, concluded at Worms in Germany, bound the three states, already fighting on the same side against France, but not all formally at war, into a much firmer alliance. One of the prime fronts in this alliance was in the Alps, between France and Piedmont, where a Spanish army had been menacing Piedmont for some years, and where the British Mediterranean fleet under Admiral Matthews had been hindering Spanish movements.[47]

The British fleet in the Mediterranean was involved in helping to interfere with any Spanish land attacks directed at Piedmont or Austrian Milan, for which the coast road was the easiest route, and which could be dominated from the sea. The fleet had to watch Toulon, which the French allowed the Spanish fleet to use as its base. The base at Villafranca had been chosen because it was the one port along the coast which belonged to King Charles Emmanuel of Sardinia-Piedmont, and so it was an essential element in alliance communications. Admiral Matthews had sent repeated complaints to the Admiralty and to the Secretary of State for the Southern Department in the past year, and had several times asked to be allowed to resign his command – he was certainly ill, and even driven by gout collapsed at times. On 9 September the Admiralty Secretary, Thomas Corbett, had written a testy reply to Matthews' letters, and it is quite possible that *Shark* was conveying this for delivery to Matthews.

The call at Genoa is more difficult to account for. The city was neutral (though the Worms treaty envisaged despoiling it of some of its territory for Charles Emmanuel's benefit). It may be that *Shark* also carried messages to the

British ambassador in Turin concerning the treaty, for he would be most easily reached by way of Genoa.

Shark returned to Gibraltar, which was reached on 30 October, but by this time the ship had twenty of its crew sick. On 5 November, when the sick numbered twenty-six, it was patrolling as far as Cape Trafalgar. The disease, whatever it was – quite likely malaria – had clearly been picked up at Genoa, or perhaps at Villafranca, though no one went ashore at the latter place. The ship continued its work, which was evidently to patrol to the west of Gibraltar. It was driven through the Gut by westerly gales and the strong current on the 15th, but was back at Tangier on the 21st. By then the sick still numbered twenty-four, but this included all the officers except the gunner. Barradall took the *Shark* to Gibraltar where the lieutenant, the master, the purser, and eight of the seamen were sent on shore to recover; one of them died in the Gibraltar hospital.

December was spent cruising back and forth between Cape Spartel and Tangier Bay. The only incident was *Shark's* failure to prevent a Spanish bark taking a captured snow into Tarifa, even with the assistance of boats from the *Lowestoff* (22), the local flagship of Captain John Crookshank, the chief naval officer on the station.

The occasional incidents, the patrols and convoys, the examinations and intermittent returns to Gibraltar, continued until April 1744.[48] On 8 April *Shark* captured a Spanish ship loaded with molasses and on the 16th met the *Solebay* (24), which brought news that open war had now begun with the French. Next day a French ship was captured, and over the next three weeks on a convoy *Shark* captured two more. This busy period was then followed by more routine patrolling until the end of June, when Captain Crookshank of *Lowestoff* gave Barradall an order to go into Faro to tallow his ship.[49] Without a dock this would take some time, and it was only after nearly a fortnight that the ship's activities were resumed – and then the ship spent another week in Gibraltar.

Shark was next sent to Lisbon. On the way it met a *xebec* and a brig wearing 'English' colours, but these were hauled down on *Shark's* close approach; Barradall seems to have been suspicious of the vessel from the start. *Shark* was fired on and the two ships manoeuvred to approach it from both sides, but Barradall was able to reply at once with the starboard guns firing at the *xebec* and those on the larboard at the brig. These two then put up Portuguese colours; *Shark* sailed off, though the attackers followed for some distance.

At Lisbon the ship carried out convoy escort duties for a month. One morning in thick fog it suddenly found itself close to a large warship at which Barradall, 'judging there to be a part of a French squadron' all around him, put on sail and got away smartly. But next day it turned out that the ship had been British, and that the British fleet under Admiral John Balchen had arrived. At this point, on 26 September, probably as a result of the arrival of the fleet, Barradall was transferred to the recently commissioned sixth-rate *Phoenix* (24).

He was succeeded in *Shark* by Commander Robert Hughes,[50] whose first priority, as it was with every new captain, was to inspect his new command and set about putting right that which he found was wrong, tallowing, caulking, acquiring stores.[51] Then it was the same work as before, with the added danger and opportunity of being at war with France. On 3 November *Shark* captured a French ship bringing supplies of fish from Newfoundland to the Mediterranean, a ship which had obviously set out before hearing of the declaration of war. Hughes took no less than seventy-five prisoners from the ship, and three days later took, along with *Guernsey* (48), another such ship. Then there followed visits to Tetuan Bay and Port Mahon and several cruises in the Gibraltar region. On one occasion, however, the ship met a Spanish privateer bark out of Cadiz and they fought. The privateer's captain was killed and sixty-one of his men were wounded; nobody on *Shark* was hurt.

The log of Hughes' captaincy ends on 3 April 1745, and there follows a short log kept by Blumfield Barradall once more.[52] Hughes and Barradall were near contemporaries and entered their first commands within a few days of each other. What seems to have happened is that Hughes was removed from *Shark* to a larger ship at Gibraltar just as Barradall had been earlier, and now Barradall was to take over another ship which was still in Britain. Sensibly he was given *Shark* again, which was also to be returned to Britain. He took command again on 16 May and arrived at Falmouth on the 27th. The opportunity was also taken to send two other men, Bartholomew Smith, a surgeon, and Robert Savage from HMS *Neptune*, to Britain, together with various muster books and letters to the Admiralty. Already on the day before *Shark* arrived, Commissioner Hughes at Portsmouth had acknowledged to the Navy Board that the ship was to be refitted for foreign service.[53] Barradall was at once transferred to his new ship, and was promoted to captain on 18 July.[54]

V

The new captain for *Shark*, the third (or fourth) in a year, was Christopher Middleton, who had had the rank of commander since 1741, and so was unusual among *Shark's* captains in not having arrived as a newly-minted commander or lieutenant.[55] He was also unusual in the long line of captains of *Sharks* in other ways. He was originally a captain in the Hudson's Bay Company, making frequent voyages in command of its ships, and he became an officer in the Royal Navy in 1741, being commissioned directly into the rank of commander, when he was recruited by a man called Arthur Dobbs to command a voyage in search of the Northwest Passage; the Admiralty agreed to sponsor the voyage, whence Middleton's naval rank. He failed to find the passage, of course, and described his subsequent disagreement with Dobbs in a pamphlet, and the voyage itself in another. He was therefore a much more experienced sailor (as well as more literate) than other *Shark* captains, older, more loquacious, and more alert; his log is more extensive and literate than any other. His appointment to *Shark* was undoubtedly made because of his own particular qualities.[56]

On appointment, of course, as usual, his first task was to make the ship ready for 'foreign service'. Before he took command the ship had been docked and cleaned and tallowed, and a long list of its defects was compiled, including the fact that the false keel was worm-eaten, as were several planks.[57] It seems probable, though no log says so, that the crew had been paid off, or perhaps their numbers were much reduced after two years and more at Gibraltar and at sea, for on 12 June it received a draft of sixty men from *St George*, which was being used as a holding pen for sailors. The orders came from Vice Admiral James Stewart, commanding at Portsmouth. Captain Middleton immediately sailed his ship the day after receiving these men, which would prevent any escapes. It seems that it was once more to be based at Gibraltar, but after a month there it was sent back to Britain – for it was at home that small ships such as *Shark* were now required.

The ship had clearly revealed more defects on its short voyage to the south, and it stayed at Portsmouth for another six weeks after its return. This was the major refit, which is recorded at the Admiralty as lasting from June to September.[58] A warrant was issued on 22 August for the ship to be fitted for foreign service, cleaned, tallowed, and provided with adequate stores. Clearly there was more wrong with the ship than had been discovered in the earlier docking, and this had no doubt been revealed in the short cruise to Gibraltar.

Another list of defects was compiled on 24 August and it went into dock three days later; altogether it remained at Portsmouth for almost three months (June to September).[59]

Middleton asked that the master be replaced because 'Philip Pope Master is much afflicted with rheumatism, and is not in condition to perform his duty especially on board these ships which are generally wett as often as a sail is set' – one of the few comments on conditions in these ships that we have.[60] Commissioner Hughes also asked that the ship be given 'a proper top gallant mast' – the old problem once more – and a new middle staysail. He reported the appointment by warrant of a new carpenter, a new gunner, and a new boatswain.[61]

Shark sailed at last, after all this attention, on 30 September, in company with *Eltham* (44) and the newly built sloop *Tavistock* (14), and next day was in the Downs.[62] From there *Shark* was sent across to the French coast to look into Ostend and Dunkirk, and to note the shipping there, and discover the readiness of any ships for sea. For, once again, *Shark* was being used to frustrate the plots of the Pretender, just as its predecessor had been in 1715–1716; this time it was the expedition of his son, Prince Charles Edward.

This was, of course, rather late if the intention had been to prevent the prince from sailing and landing in Scotland, for he had been there for two months already when the *Shark* looked in at Dunkirk, and he had taken Edinburgh a month before, but the real danger was of a French invasion across the Dover Strait, and this was what *Shark* was studying. *Shark* was blown back and forth in the southern North Sea in early October, moored at the Downs briefly, then went across to Schouwen in the Netherlands. There a brigantine from Lynn claimed that 'the Romans were rising in Norwich', a good example of the sort of unsubstantiated rumours which were spreading in the nervous atmosphere in an England subjected to a land invasion from Scotland once again and simultaneously threatened with an invasion from France; a Dutch ship passed on another rumour that there was a French privateer operating at the Dogger Bank, and that it had taken five British prizes already.

Clearly the centre of attention had to be in the north, and *Shark* was sent to the north-east English coast in late October – Hartlepool, Whitby, Flamborough Head – then south to Great Yarmouth.[63] In November it escorted a convoy of twelve ships to the Humber and then on to Tynemouth and Leith. Prince Charles Edward may have taken Edinburgh but the city had rapidly reverted to loyalist control, with some relief, as soon as he left, and the Royal Navy was easily able to make use of Leith, and its ships were free to sail anywhere along the Scottish coast.

The traditional view, that the navy was decisive in preventing French intervention in support of the Pretender, has been criticized.[64] But the criticism brings together two problems: the threat of an invasion of England across the Strait of Dover directly from France, and the blockade of the Scottish coasts to deliver or intercept smaller maritime interventions and incursions. The first was prevented, as is admitted, by a combination of the presence of Admiral Vernon's squadron in the Downs and French dithering. The Scottish blockade was fairly porous as, given the length and intricacy of the coasts and islands to be blockaded, must be expected but some vital captures were made. Above all, the real task of the navy in Scotland was to support the army's advance along the east coast so as to outflank the Highlands, where ambush and surprise were possible, even likely, and Highland charges could be sudden and decisive. This was *Shark's* main activity. It is obvious that, given the extent of the coast, and its intricacy, and the unreliability of the weather, the navy could not prevent all the connections between France and Scotland, but it could certainly make them difficult, and its presence and potential presence clearly deterred plenty of the French attempts to reach Scotland.

Shark was one of a whole series of small vessels which picketed the east coast, all under the command of Admiral John Byng – another curious coincidence, for *Shark* III had been under the command of his father thirty years before, doing the same job.[65] *Shark's* objective was to both prevent the arrival of French reinforcements or supplies, and to harass the rebels anywhere along the coast. These tasks evolved into intelligence gathering and convoying supplies forward for the army. *Shark* sailed north on 15 December with a small squadron looking first for Admiral Byng. Off Girdle Ness, by Aberdeen, a ship carrying French colours was seen but it and a fishing boat thought to be French could not be intercepted because 'it began to blow'.

It proved difficult to locate Byng's ships, but *Shark's* group went into the Moray Firth, and *Shark* collected from Frazerburgh a pilot for Cromarty. Finally on 23 December came the news that Byng had probably been driven north; supplies among *Shark's* companions were now short and they returned to Leith on 25th January 1746, where Byng arrived on the 28th; he was reinforced by several other ships soon after. By this time it was probably known to Byng that the prince and his army had reached Derby and then turned back northwards.

The threatened French invasion of the south-east and London was still possible, though the French had dithered too long over setting out, largely because of the very obvious presence of British warships in the Narrows when the Channel Fleet under Admiral Martin had joined the Downs fleet under Admiral Vernon. Gradually the will of the French to set out onto the Strait of Dover, never very strong, wilted further; by the end of January this was clear even to the most fearful in England. And by then the Highland army of the prince had returned to Scotland.

A warning of continued difficulties came on 3 January (1746) when a watering party ashore near Inverkeithing was surprised by a rebel force and taken prisoner; one of the men was from *Shark*. The ship stopped a snow in the Firth of Forth which was loaded with goods which Middleton eventually decided were probably 'contraband' – a term which in this context probably covered war supplies for Prince Charles; he sent the ship on to the admiral for a decision. At Leith 6,000 Hessian soldiers hired by the government were landed, an event recorded by Middleton in his log. (These soldiers were not used in the fighting, but they provided a firm garrison base for the campaign of the army under the Duke of Cumberland.)

Shark sailed north again, stopping and investigating ships and hoping to find news in each port. It looked into the Tay Estuary, and sent a boat into Arbroath, without success; two intercepted ships were sent into Leith on suspicion. Back in the Tay Baillie Lyon of Dundee and several of the magistrates of the city came on board, explaining that the rebels had left the city two or three days before. Several of the small ships in the harbour had been got ready for sea, they reported, but these preparations had been discontinued when *Shark* had come in. This may or may not have had a connection with the rebellion, but chances could not be taken. Middleton sent his lieutenant and some men in to render the ships unserviceable – they unhung the rudders, took down the rigging, and carried off the cables, anchors and sails.

Shark returned briefly to Leith, then sailed along the southern coast of Fife looking into the many small ports for other ships likely to be used by the rebels, making them unusable in the same way as at Dundee. The ship called at Leith, where Middleton collected a message from the Admiralty for Byng, so he sailed again to the north, looking into Montrose, where Byng was given the message, then on to Peterhead and Frazerburgh, and on to Cromarty along with the sloop *Vulture* (14). *Vulture* had brought another message from the Admiralty (possibly enclosed in that for Byng), which was apparently directed at *Shark* itself, or perhaps to the two sloops collectively. It is not clear what it said, but it seems probable from later events that it directed the sloops to cooperate directly with the army, and with the Duke of Cumberland, the army's commander-in-chief, when it and he arrived.

The strength of the loyal forces in the northern area, commanded by Lord Loudoun, had been much reduced by defeat and by the loss of Inverness to the rebels. (This is an aspect of the rebellion, the continued fighting in northern Scotland, which is too often ignored by both English and Scottish historians – most Scots, including many of the Highlanders, were anti-Jacobite all along.) The two ships carried parts of Loudoun's army across the Cromarty Firth, and by occupying the entrance to the firth they prevented rebel forces from pursuing them. Again, the use of local boats by the rebels was prevented by bringing them off – at Cromarty nineteen such boats were seized. This campaign against the boats was presumably conducted in the knowledge that Prince Charles' father had escaped in just such a small boat in 1716; the requisition and disabling of the boats would make another escape like that difficult – and so it proved.

News of 'five' French ships off Burghead induced Middleton to investigate. A second report placed a French brig at Findhorn; yet another report claimed that the rebels had evacuated Findhorn. Middleton sent a fellow sloop, *Hawk* (10), to Findhorn to investigate the situation there. By hoisting French colours the captain provoked a friendly demonstration, showing that the rebels were still present, but his ship was too large to get into the harbour. The French brig, carrying a passenger who was to report the defeat of Lord Loudun's forces, later got away to France.[66] In another similar encounter two ships came out, believing *Shark* was a French privateer which the captains were expecting, and the captains were captured. *Shark* and *Glasgow* (24) then found the privateer, but it got away, and *Shark's* foretopmast was brought down during the chase. After repairs, *Shark* went back to Cromarty, carrying a messenger with dispatches for Lord Loudoun. Eventually, after enquiring at several places, the messenger was landed at Tarbat Ness amid plentiful warnings of the dangers, and *Shark* returned to its patrolling along the coast of the Moray Firth.[67]

By this time the Duke of Cumberland had reached Aberdeen with his loyalist army and was about to advance further north. Progress was slow mainly because of the difficulty of acquiring supplies in a country over which the rebel army had already foraged and ravaged relentlessly. *Shark* found that Findhorn now really had been abandoned by the rebels; the news came by a boat from the town, whose passenger complained of ill-usage by the rebels – but then he was talking to a loyalist captain on his ship; such a sentiment is to be expected. Several Scottish noblemen were picked up, having escaped from the rebels, or so they said. (The French brig which escaped from Findhorn earlier had been, it was said, carrying loyalist prisoners to be held in France, perhaps as hostages to be exchanged for the prince if he was captured.) *Shark* took its rescuees to Aberdeen, where their stories could be verified and their information delivered, then escorted six supply ships northwards to lie in wait for the army; in calling at Findhorn again Middleton discovered the town was now 'full of rebels' – this was the main rebel army which was retiring towards Inverness in the face of Cumberland's methodical and relentless advance.

Shark returned to Aberdeen to report its findings 'with certain account of My Lord Loudoun and 7 or 8 hundred of his regiment being safe in the Isle of Skie, the rest dispersed, some in Sutherland, and some in Caithness', so Cumberland could not look for help there, either as an active distraction for the enemy, or as reinforcements. Instead he sent *Shark* back to the Moray Firth with another convoy of supply ships. While this was happening Cumberland began his march from Aberdeen towards Inverness. On 9 April *Shark* heard from a fishing boat that a group of rebels had invaded Orkney; the rebel forces were clearly as scattered as Loudoun's army, some in Orkney, others searching for or chasing Loudoun's forces – none of these were therefore available for the final battle.

Orders were now received that *Shark* should pace the army along the Moray Firth shore along with a provision convoy. The major obstacle on the army's route was the River Spey, a difficult crossing where the loyalist forces could have been held up by a determined Jacobite defence. *Shark* was off the mouth of the river as the loyalist army approached, and a party of rebels came down to the beach and fired at the ship – another pointless rebel dispersion. 'Briskly we returned 30 or 40 great shot', firing until it could be seen that the loyalist army was across the river four miles from the estuary. This, noted Middleton, 'had its desired effect, for a great part of our army made to the ferry before the rebels were apprised of it'. This is a factor not usually mentioned by the modern histories, which generally relate the defeat of the rebel forces as a land matter; *Shark's* bombardment was, along with the supply convoys, clearly of considerable assistance to the army. The fact that Cumberland could rely on supplies awaiting him, which could be landed at need, much lightened the supply train he had to bring along, and rendered his army much less vulnerable.

Next day supplies were landed for the army, and three days later *Shark* was near enough to the shore to see the rebels' defeat at Culloden Moor, noted by Middleton in his unusually detailed log. It was only next day, however, when he sent a boat ashore to ask for news from a party of cavalry – a safe enquiry since the rebels had little or no cavalry – that it was realized that Culloden had been a decisive victory. At Inverness Middleton reported to the duke and was instructed to convey Viscount Bury southwards. He was landed at North Berwick, in Lothian, and then rode fast to relate the details to the king.

Middleton had several times received orders directly from Cumberland, in the matter of the convoys, for example, and here again on the transport of Lord Bury. No doubt it was his ability, his maturity in comparison with the normal run of sloop captains, and possibly the fact that he was fairly well known, which would incline Cumberland to trust him to do these tasks, but mainly it must have been Middleton's natural authority and maturity which made him useful. There seems to have been no objection from Middleton's naval superiors, notably Byng, to this arrangement. (The Admiralty may have already arranged this, of course.)

The fleet was gathered at Leith roads, where *Shark* sent three sailors and eight marines to the hospital. Then it was back once again to the north. The prince was in the heather and a price of £30,000 was on his head – and so long as he was free and in Scotland the rebellion could not be said to be over; Cumberland's army was still hunting rebels, who had shown no signs of giving up, despite their decisive defeat. Nor was there any hesitation in hunting for the prince. The fright given to the loyalists by his adventure would justify almost any measures to capture and suppress him and his supporters. He also must be in fear of his life, for, if he claimed to be British, his invasion was an act of treason. Ships at Peterhead were still being prevented from sailing by the customs men, and off Girdle Ness (at Aberdeen) 'there was still a strict guard kept to prevent any vessels from going out without paper'. Clearly a careful watch was being kept for escapees heading towards France; this was much assisted, of course, by the previous disablement and confiscation of many of the fishing boats along this cost. A voyage by *Shark* south as far as 'Stonehive' was followed by a return to Cromarty. There the ship took on board forty-five marines and soldiers and sailed on past Caithness to Orkney.

This force and *Shark* had a clear objective, to find and arrest Sir James Stewart of Borough, who was the prime Jacobite in the islands. Middleton sent Captain Moodie of the marines and his lieutenant on ahead in the cutter to Orkney 'to prevent our alarming the inhabitants', as Middleton put it – but mainly to attempt to discover Stewart's whereabouts without alerting him by landing a more conspicuous force. *Shark* anchored in Scapa Flow.

Within three days Stewart and three associates were captured and brought on board by Moodie and his men; they were soon transferred to another ship to be taken to England. Then it was back to normal: on 29 May Middleton pressed three men from a Liverpool ship; on the 30th he fired a 21-gun salute in commemoration of the restoration of King Charles II – it is not clear if the irony of this anniversary in his present circumstances occurred to him.

The prince was known to be somewhere in the west of Scotland or in the islands. (He had made one attempt to reach Orkney, in which case he would surely have been taken by Captains Moodie and Middleton, or at least chased out.) It was therefore necessary to continue controlling and inspecting the shipping in Orkney waters. Ships coming from the west and passing Orkney were examined in case they were carrying the prince; those from the east were stopped in case they were intending to do so. Given the problems of fleets and a possible invasion, customs and smugglers and privateers, and the ubiquity of fishing craft around the English coasts, the numbers of ships sailing northabout past Orkney was substantial, and within a week Middleton had collected ten westbound ships, which he then took on westwards as a convoy, both for their own safety and to ensure they did not divert towards western Scotland. Six of the ships were for Hudson's Bay (Orkney was the major source of men employed by the Hudson's Bay Company) and two were heading in the same direction on yet another attempt to find the Northwest Passage – Middleton must have felt quite at home; one ship was for Antigua, and the other for Boston. *Shark* took them westwards past Rona Island, and there released them.

A call at Cromarty and then Leith was next. Middleton sent in a bill to the Navy Board for 'surgeon's necessities', a reflection perhaps of the sickness which had sent eleven men from the ship into the Leith hospital earlier.[68] From there *Shark* sailed south with a convoy of forty-five ships, of which thirteen carried Hessian soldiers returning to the continent, never having been used in the fighting. *Shark* stayed with them until they were taken across to Helvoetsluys, and then it brought the empty transports back to the Nore. The ship went to Sheerness and into dry dock for a clean and tallow and refit, no doubt something most necessary after the northern winters. The paint was to be 'refreshed' as well, and the crew paid up to the end of 1743.[69]

Middleton had also some points to make. He stated that he had been obliged to perform the duties, not just of captain, but of master, mate, pilot, midshipman, 'and all other officers' as well. This was perhaps something of an exaggeration, though no doubt based on his experience. For the ship he asked for a mast to be replaced (without specifying which, but no doubt it was that awkward foremast) and it needed more ballast.[70] There was clearly a good deal of work to be done on the ship. It was in dock at Sheerness for a week, suggesting a considerable amount of work was actually done.

VI

The work of *Shark* in helping to defeat the Jacobite rebellion in 1745–1746 is relatively well-known, but the ship's next work is one of those minor campaigns in which such small ships specialized, and which are, because they used these small ships, normally largely ignored. *Shark* returned to the Downs on 19 September 1746, as a member of the guard there commanded by Commodore Matthew Michell.[71] From there it crossed the Strait of Dover again and sailed along the coast of France and Flanders from Calais to Ostend, menacing, surveying, counting, spying, and then returned to the Downs.

After the first of these cruises Middleton returned to the issue of his duties and his lack of officers: he still had not been provided with a master; Michell took up the matter, with the result that an appointment was agreed. He also reported that Middleton was about thirty-five men short in his crew, which he would supply where possible. *Shark* was to cruise between Dunkirk and Boulogne, and call in at the Downs to report and resupply every fourteen days.[72]

From the Downs, with a master and an increased crew *Shark* sailed on its patrol, and this, or something like it, was repeated eight times in the next six months, visiting Boulogne and Dunkirk, Nieuport and Gravelines, Dover, Deal, and Dungeness. The result in intelligence acquired was, of course, cumulative, and the fact that the same ship was used for the service for a lengthy period meant that Middleton will have built up a body of knowledge of the condition of French naval forces in those harbours; the aim, of course, was to detect any preparations for an invasion. The toll on the ship of this work was large, and it went into dock again at Sheerness on 2 February 1747, when it was fitted for 'Channel service'.[73] Michell had a whole flock of small ships for his command; sloops, cutters, hired privateers. He corresponded in detail with all his commanders, and his accumulated letters constitute two enormous volumes in the 'Captains' Letters' files in the Admiralty archives.[74]

Then, on 14 April 1747, *Shark* was further north than usual, at Flushing at the mouth of the River Scheldt, and the oars were got out to row the ship upriver.[75] This was the start of a new task for *Shark*, none of which had ever campaigned inland before.

The French campaign in the Austrian Netherlands had suddenly made a major advance, and the ability of the Dutch to resist, or even to organize their resistance, was clearly failing. The French commander was the Marechal de Saxe, one of France's most eminent and intelligent generals, and at last, after being restrained by French efforts to negotiate a peace during 1746, he was given his head. By contrast, his opponents were a disharmonious alliance of Britain, the Dutch, and Austria (which was by this time the ruler of the former Spanish Netherlands i.e., Belgium). Despite a formal agreement to field a joint army of 180,000 men for the 1747 campaign, they had managed to do nothing of the sort. The Dutch were the weakest of the allies, and de Saxe aimed his new blows at them: one army invaded Dutch Flanders, a strip of land on the south side of the River Scheldt, also known as Cadzand. His aim was to seize the port of Sluys and thus menace or take a string of forts in the area.[76] Control of this coast would also open up several further possibilities for the French forces.

This French campaign interrupted the siege of Antwerp which the Duke of Cumberland had begun a little earlier. The Cadzand forts were picked off one by one and Sluys fell. The next stage was intended to be a crossing of the Scheldt and an invasion of the islands of Walcheren and Beveland, and so it was now a major threat to the whole Dutch province of Zeeland.

Control of the Scheldt and still more a French occupation of Walcheren would be unpleasant for the Dutch, but to the British this would produce French control of the whole Flemish-Dutch coast from Dunkirk to Walcheren (as well as of the French coast from Dunkirk to Brest), and the threat of a French invasion of England would be revived. Middleton and the other ships in Michell's squadron had reported that the French had been accumulating shipping, hiring cutters (in some cases from British merchants living in Dutch ports), and had hired French privateers in their own ports.

Michell, as commander at the Downs, was ordered into the Scheldt, partly to assist the Dutch defence, but also to establish British naval control of that estuary. He brought with him a flotilla of small ships, including *Shark*, and on 15 April, the day after its arrival, *Shark* sailed along the recently conquered

Cadzand coast 'to see if we could discern anything of the enemy's motion', as Middleton put it. Some French soldiers were spotted and fired at, and next day a group of '40 or 50' were also seen and fired at. There was, of course, little chance of hitting any of these soldiers, but the effort was clearly made so as to inform the French command that the British ships were present, and alert, and a clear threat to any attempt to ferry troops across the river. Next day *Shark* crossed to Flushing in Walcheren, which would be the main target of a French crossing, then went fifty miles up the river to Bergen-op-Zoom. Supplies were delivered to the Dutch garrison in the city (commanded by an octogenarian Swedish general) and the ship returned to the mouth of the river, between the (now French) Cadzand and Walcheren.

Michell had received a letter from the British consul in Walcheren, Charles Stuart, giving his assessment of French intentions and Dutch responses. It is dated 18 April, which would be 6 April in the (old-fashioned, unreformed) British calendar. 'As soon as Sluys is taken there will be a grand embarkation for this island', Stuart reported. The Dutch had asked for naval patrols 'for a few days'. By the 10th Michell was ordering more of his ships into the Scheldt; only the next day was he ordered to do this by the Admiralty, to whom Stuart had also written directly.

This naval intervention had thwarted any French advance further north. Meanwhile the British government was sending three regiments of foot to assist in the Dutch defence, and that defence was now likely also to become better organized. The danger had stimulated a rise in support inside the Dutch state for the appointment of a Stadhouder, an agitation beginning in the most endangered province, Zeeland, and a development which Michell reported on the 14th. By then he had fifteen ships under his command in the river, of which *Shark* was one of the smallest, with just twelve guns. But this was a shallow river, and it was only small ships which were useful. The largest of Michell's ships was *Sapphire*, with forty guns. By that date also, Dutch ships had begun to arrive, but were still off Flushing, not in the river.

More information arrived. At Ghent, connected to the Scheldt by canals, there were said to be 160 boats collected, which were to be rowed by 3,000 galley slaves who had been sent north from the French galleys in the Mediterranean. The Dutch ships had still not arrived – 'such dilatory proceeding I never saw', Michell complained.

But the Dutch had slowly realized that the crisis was over with the arrival of the British squadron, and that urgency on their part was no longer required.

(The 'few days' help they had asked for extended, as these things do, to over a year.) On 12 May both of the main allied developments came together, when the transports bringing the British regiments arrived in the Scheldt, and on Walcheren, where there were great celebrations to welcome the new ruling Prince of Orange, William IV, to power as Stadhouder.

The Dutch defence slowly improved, and in the Scheldt more British ships arrived. *Shark* and the other British ships patrolled in and out of the Scheldt, delivering supplies, but largely just being present as an obvious and constant deterrent to any French seaborne activity. The war became centred on the French siege of Bergen-op-Zoom, which fell on 16 September, amid notorious scenes of sack and rapine. In effect, despite some rather desperate diplomacy, this marked the moment when the Dutch decided that they must give up the fight; when they asked for an extra large subsidy from Britain as the price for fighting on, the British also decided that a serious negotiation for peace was now required.

Michell's squadron of small ships, having done their job, sailed for Britain in January 1748. *Shark* went into dock at Sheerness once more for needed care and attention. Then from March 1748 it was employed in escorting convoys back and forth between English ports and roadsteads – Harwich, the Nore – and Helvoetsluys. *Shark* was docked again at Sheerness at the end of May, by which time a list of its defects had been compiled. As a result of the docking it was evidently realized that much work needed to be done, and since the maritime war was winding down, it was decided that the ship should be laid up and the crew paid off.[77]

A pay list was compiled covering the whole period from 1743 to the end of this period of service. Deaths had occurred at most of the places the ship had visited – Gibraltar Hospital (one of the men taken ill at Genoa, probably), 'off Faro', at sea, in Orkney, in the Scheldt – seven men in all. The desertion rate, as the note by Michell of the ship's shortage of men suggested, was once again substantial, and like the deaths, the men had escaped wherever they could – Deal, Sheerness, and Portsmouth, which were the places the ship stayed at longest, Gibraltar, Port Mahon, Lagos in Portugal, Cromarty and Leith, London and Ramsgate, and four places in the Scheldt, two men even ran 'off Calais' when they took the ship's boat – ninety men in total, which, with the dead, counts more than the entire complement of the ship at the start.[78]

The negotiations for peace continued all through the summer, this time with clear prospects of success because every major power involved was near exhaustion. The Treaty of Aix-la-Chapelle was finally agreed in October. *Shark* lay at Sheerness, slowly refitting and waiting for more work.

VII

Shark's next captain was John Falkingham. He was commissioned as captain of the ship on 8 April 1749, having had the rank of commander since April 1747.[79] The ship had been refitting for six months, still at Sheerness.[80] On 22 March orders were given for the ship to be fitted for a voyage to the Leeward Islands, and four days later it was ordered to be sheathed.[81] When Falkingham was installed as captain, therefore, the ship was in preparation for the West Indies, and he was thereafter constantly involved in stating his requirements. On 12 and 13 April he wanted both sails and a sailmaker, and he asked for a 'Newman's water-engine'. This last was ordered to be supplied on 20 April.[82] The sloop went into dock for a week from the 15th. Boats were ordered, and surgeon's necessities – all the minor items for a long voyage, whose absence would at some point be crucial.[83] And while he was looking after such details, the ship's supplies of food and stores, water and beer and so on, were coming on board. The ship was ready to sail on 11 May, an advance on pay was made on the 12th, and a pilot was supplied on the 20th.[84] The ship finally sailed from the Nore on 21 May, destination Funchal in Madeira and then the West Indies.

Shark was once again being used as a patrol ship, its most suitable function, and it spent the next three years mainly in the Windward and the Leeward Islands, sometimes alone, sometimes with other ships, in fairly leisurely movements between the islands, though every now and again something dramatic or out of the ordinary occurred. The ship arrived at Carlisle Bay in Barbados on 11 July, after a typically swift passage – fourteen days from Beachy Head to Funchal, twenty-two from Funchal to Barbados. At Carlisle Bay Falkingham reported to Commodore Francis Holburne. The ship's first cruise was to Tobago, along with the commodore and the sixth-rate *Glasgow* (one of *Shark's* former colleagues off the Scottish coast.) On the way *Shark's* sail 'was blown all to pieces', and the sails and halliards had to be renewed. They stopped at Grand Courland Bay in Tobago briefly, no doubt to consider the situation in the island, for there was diplomatic work to be done there, then sailed north past the 'Granadillos' (the Grenadines, a string of islands between Grenada and St Vincent), as far as St Lucia, then back to Carlisle Bay. The cruise was partly to familiarize Falkingham and *Shark* with the area, but also no doubt for Holburne to observe both of them; apparently he was satisfied, for he used the ship and its captain on independent cruises repeatedly in the next years.

Shark, after two weeks at Barbados, sailed again to Tobago, only a day's sail away, though this time the island was more carefully inspected – Little Tobago (off the eastern point of the main island), Sandy Point, and Lowland Bay. After reporting in at Carlisle Bay again, *Shark* sailed north to Dominica (Prince Rupert's Bay) and then on to Antigua. It returned by way of Dominica (Roseau Bay this time) and St Vincent, arriving again at Carlisle Bay on 18 November. Thus Falkingham was now familiar with the islands and with much of the navigation. Unfortunately he is not anywhere near as verbose or informative in his log as his predecessor Middleton.

One of the purposes of these cruises was to estimate the degree of European settlement in what were called the Neutral Islands, which included Tobago, St Vincent, and St Lucia. These had been long disputed between the British and the French – and the native Caribs and Arawaks – and neither of the European powers had ever successfully occupied any of them more than briefly. (Annexation was also opposed by the existing plantation owners on the other islands, both British and French, since more plantations would mean the production of more sugar which, it was assumed, would result in a lower price for their product.) In the Treaty of Aix-la-Chapelle the neutrality of these islands had been reiterated. The voyages of *Shark* and the other ships under Holburne had clearly been aimed at seeing if that had been accepted locally, for such European decisions were often ignored on the spot in the West Indies.

This was the case in Tobago. The French governor of the Windward Islands – which essentially meant Grenada at this time – the Marquis de Caylus, was avid to increase his fortune during his term of office, and one of the places he was keen to acquire was Tobago.[85] A small French settlement had been put there either in 1746 or the year after. The British clearly noted this, and the *Speedwell* sloop (14) was sent to investigate, reporting that there were several huts, and a breastwork with guns for defence installed. *Shark*'s second visit, when the ship had sailed along much of the coast, confirmed this. In December 1748 *Shark* was sent back to the island; Falkingham had a royal proclamation, in which it was insisted that the French settlement be evacuated and demolished. A French brig, probably a local vessel, but carrying at least one French official, was also present.

The settlers were neither numerous nor resolute, and made no attempt to stay. Falkingham sent Lieutenant James O'Hara[86] with twenty men to see to the demolition of the buildings, and sent Lieutenant Patrick Drummond[87] and a French officer from the French brig to another small settlement to repeat the proclamation. O'Hara's barge was unable to make progress against the wind and current, but he and the men went ashore next day and succeeded in taking the French settlers off – no doubt they were put on board the French brig. The French guns were also put on the brig, and the trenches of the fort were filled in. Next day Drummond and his men set fire to the barracks.

It had clearly been an official French settlement in the sense that Caylus had promoted it, even though he was not authorized to do so, and had defied French government instructions in the matter; so the presence of the French ship and officers had been necessary to convince the settlers that their adventure was over. Without the French officers, it might have been necessary to use force to remove them, and the fort was probably strong enough to resist the attentions of a small British sloop. *Shark* then sailed to Sandy Point and to Man o' War Bay, posting copies of the proclamation on posts and trees just in case there were other settlers who were aiming to take advantage of the empty island (and could read English). The ship was back in Carlisle Bay by 3 January 1750, a small imperial task efficiently done.

There followed a curious voyage by *Shark*. Escorting five ships in a convoy they sailed near to the mouths of the Orinoco River, but without doing anything else, and overall the voyage seems to have been pointless. *Shark* sent the ships back to Barbados, then inspected Tobago, Grenada, and St Vincent before returning to Carlisle Bay. A week later it sailed towards Martinique for a few days, then returned to Barbados; this was repeated at the end of March, but the ship then went on to Martinique again. From there *Shark* sailed to the Leewards, visiting St Eustatius (a Dutch island), St Kitts, and back to Antigua, and passed Guadeloupe on the way back to Barbados. No explanation in the log is available for this or the earlier voyages, but the concentration on the Dutch and French islands is surely significant.

Another voyage to the north took the ship as far as Martinique and then back southwards, past St Lucia, St Vincent, and the Grenadines once more, noting the continued presence of French settlers on the neutral islands. In June the ship was sent to Guadeloupe to demand the release of the Guinea slave ship *King David*, which had been detained by a French sloop; the slaves on board had risen in rebellion when they reached the harbour; Falkingham by sheer persistence got the ship released, though it is not clear what had happened to the slaves; the French would hardly want them on their island, and returning them to the British was equally difficult. The whole affair, which included a prohibition which for a time prevented Falkingham from going ashore, along with the failure of the French to clear their settlers from St Vincent and St Lucia, was part of the continuing diplomatic cold war between the two states.[88] There followed another voyage for *Shark* to Antigua and visits to Montserrat, St Eustatius and St Kitts. Each of these local voyages took several weeks. Then *Shark* was sent to check on the conditions at Tobago once more.

This was still a neutral island, but it had in the past been known for its pirates, and *Shark's* new visit in December 1750 coincided with the arrival of a ship which came up from the Spanish island of Trinidad, described by Falkingham in his log as 'a quarter galley full of men, whites, blacks, and Indians, between 30 and 40 in number'. He sent his boats to intercept it, since the galley was in shallow water, but they failed to do so. The assumption may have been either that this was a pirate foray, or that it was a Spanish attempt to plant a settlement on the island, or even a private settlement expedition, to get away from all governments.

A different cruise followed, first from Tobago to Grenada, but then westwards along the coast of South America – the 'Spanish Main' – past Margharita Island (Spanish), and as far as Curacao (Dutch); from there the ship passed Bonaire (Dutch) and headed north-east to Puerto Rico (Spanish), and past Guadeloupe (French) and Dominica before returning to Carlisle Bay on 4 February 1751. The purpose of this cruise can only have been to show the British flag to the French, the Dutch, and the Spaniards – and to gather information.

The ship stayed within the Windward and Leeward Islands for the next five months, visiting Antigua and St Kitts, St Eustatius and the Virgin Islands, and went on to 'Spanish Town' on Puerto Rico, where Captain Falkingham called on the local governor. The return journey took in St Croix, a Danish island, where the local governor came on board, and St Thomas, another Danish island.

The ship then went back to Puerto Rico, this time evidently on an official mission. He went to the main Spanish port on that island, called 'Porto Rico harbour', that is San Juan. The ship stayed there for most of July. It is not clear what the purpose of the visit was, but a Spanish flag of truce had visited St Kitts a year earlier, by coincidence while *Shark* was there, and another had come on 16 May, six weeks before. This is an obvious sign that diplomatic contacts were being maintained. Puerto Rico had been one of the centres of Spanish maritime harassment, above all by privateers, in the 1730s, one of the main causes of the late war; no doubt the British did not want such activity to be resumed now that peace had returned.

Falkingham spent some time while at San Juan inspecting his ship, and found that the sheathing put on at Sheerness only two years before had been extensively penetrated by the *teredo* worm; the main timbers would be next. *Shark* sailed on 30 July, and visited the British islands of Tortola and Norman's, which lay east of Puerto Rico. At Norman's Island the governor came on board, perhaps glad of some company, but the sequence of gubernatorial visits surely means that Falkingham was being used as a compliant diplomatist.

At Antigua in English Harbour on 22 August Falkingham began work on the ship, but he did not get much done before disaster struck. On 8 September the ship was caught in a hurricane, which was regarded by the inhabitants as the most powerful they had experienced. Damage to the naval base was extensive; store houses, even those of stone, were blown down, guns on the wharf were blown into the sea, and the stores were blown away or scattered, to be looted by sailors and slaves afterwards. The accounts of events, above all that by the storekeeper at English Harbour, William Arthur, tend to ignore the actual storm in favour of its after-effects. Arthur lamented the destruction of his stores; Commodore Holburne worried about his ships. Casual mentions by both note that the houses in the rest of the island were almost entirely destroyed, and that the plantations – the actual sugar plants – had also been destroyed. Falkingham's log, needless to say, concentrated on the effects on his own ship. *Shark* was driven on shore (as was *Glasgow*, which was also in the harbour) and in the fight with the wind it had been necessary to cut down the masts. The ship nevertheless was refloated.[89]

The guns, the shot, and part of the stores in the ship had been moved on shore before the storm as part of Falkingham's preparations for maintenance. The chaos on shore meant that little could be done in the way of repairing the ship until some new supplies could be brought in. *Shark*'s crew was turned out to assist the storekeeper in recovering stores which could be salvaged, and in such tasks as soaking sails in fresh water to get the salt out. Falkingham went in a merchant ship to report to Holburne. Work was hampered in addition by the destruction of every boat on the island, both at English Harbour and at St John's on the other side of the island.

It took three months to repair *Shark*. The masts had to be replaced, sails had to be reinstalled, rigging had been torn apart and its replacement was not possible until supplies came in. And so on, an endless list of problems. It was not until 10 December that the ship was able to leave Antigua, and still more work had to be done at Carlisle Bay to make it properly seaworthy. Then *Shark* was sent back to patrol around the Leewards – Antigua, Nevis, Norman's, Crab Island, and as far as Puerto Rico again – a cruise lasting ten weeks, returning to Carlisle Bay more or less along the same route in reverse. In the next months it sailed repeatedly between Barbados and Antigua.

Finally, at the beginning of July 1752, *Shark* was ordered back to Britain. It sailed from Antigua on 20 July in company with Holburne's ship the *Tavistock* (50), but the two separated in a storm; Holburne in reporting this described *Shark* as 'a strong vessel', but this seems to have been wishful thinking; nevertheless, it arrived at Spithead on 5 September. A final voyage took it to Deptford, and there it was paid off on 2 October.[90]

The final pay list covers the whole of Falkingham's captaincy, 1749 to 1752.[91] The usual appalling loss by desertion was increased by a considerable death rate. Five men died at Antigua, at least some probably as a result of the hurricane, and six at Barbados in the hospital, of disease. Five more died at sea, and others at St Vincent – a total of sixteen deaths in three years.

The 'run' rate was begun at Sheerness before the initial voyage when twelve men deserted. Barbados (twenty-seven men) and Antigua (thirty-five) were the most popular destinations – presumably the opportunity of the hurricane chaos assisted those who went at Antigua. However, almost every other island the ship called at received some new inhabitants – Dominica (eight), St Vincent (two), Grenada (six) (even though it was a French island), Montserrat (two), St Kitts (twelve), Dutch Curacoa (six), Danish St Thomas (one), Tortola (two), and even Portuguese Madeira (one). One man, the ship's doctor, deserted at Puerto Rico. And four were left behind at Barbados in the hospital, and so had to be counted as 'run'. This was a total of 115 deserters. Falkingham had stayed at Barbados when the ship sailed for Britain, but he was not counted as a deserter, perhaps being covered by an order from Holburne. The ship returned under the command of Lieutenant John Brookes.[92]

This version of *Shark* had operated therefore for twenty years. After the time spent in West Indian waters it was probably in a poor state – worm had already eaten at the sheathing by a year before – and the damage from the hurricane may well never have been fully rectified. It was surveyed at Deptford on 6 December 1752 and found to need a major refit – though after ten refits in ten years, and then three years in the West Indies it is doubtful if a survey was really needed to reach that conclusion. A repair was proposed, and the Admiralty agreed to this. But the ship was not used again, and another survey on 29 October 1755 found it to be 'entirely decayed'. This time there was to be no refit or repair. It was proposed to take the ship to pieces, and sell those parts worth reusing; to this the Admiralty agreed on 4 November; the parts brought £211.[93] Twenty years (1732–1752) was a good age for a small ship which had been operated more or less continuously during that time.

During its career the fourth *Shark* had begun as a fast sailer, though its foremast was never satisfactory. It had been used repeatedly as a policing vessel, in the North Sea, North America, the West Indies; in the war of 1739–1748 it had clearly played a part commensurate with its size in Scottish, Dutch, and Spanish waters. It had been an active and worthwhile vessel.

The Patrols of Shark IV 1733 - 1739

Mainland (South Carolina)   (Florida)   Bahamas

1733
                                                                               Providence 29/11 – 6/12
11/12 Cooper R.

1734
27/2 Cooper R.   Providence 5-10/3
                                                                               Exuma 18/3-5/5
                                                                               Providence 10-28/5
3/6 Cooper R.

20/9 Cooper R.
                                                                               Providence 27/9-4/11
11/11 Cooper R.
1735
16/2 Cooper R.   Providence 23/2 – 8/3
                                                                               Exuma 16/3 – 5/5
                                                                               Providence 11/3 – 12/6
19/6 Cooper R.

18/9 Cooper R.   Providence 2/10 – 13/11

19/11 Cooper R.
1736
15/2 Cooper R.   Providence 21/2 – 16/3
                                                                               Catt I. 21 – 24/3
                                                                               Stocking I. 24/3 – 3/5
                                                                               Providence 10/5 – 9/6
16/6 Cooper R.

13/9 Cooper R.   Providence 26/9 – 10/11
22/11 Cooper R.
1737
17/2 Cooper R.   San Agustin 17/2- 26/2
26/2 Charleston
                            San Agustin 14 – 17/4
17/4 Cooper R.

11/9 Cooper R.   Providence 24/9 – 17/11
24/11 Cooper R.
1738
15/1 Cooper R.   Providence 21/1 – 12/3
                                                                               Stocking I. 15/3 – 9/5
                                                                               Providence 12/5 – 10/t
16/6 Cooper R.

15/9 Cooper R.   Providence 23/9 – 10/11

24/11 Cooper R.
1739
13/2 Cooper R.   Providence 21/2 – 29/5

5 – 18/5 Cooper R.
                                        20/7 Britain

Chapter 5

Shark V: a Sloop, 1775–1778, and a Fireship, 1778–1783

A certain degree of confusion exists over the *Sharks* in the 1770s and 1780s. *Shark* V existed from 1776 to 1778 and then had a second life as the *Salamander* fireship until 1783 (and is the subject of this chapter). *Shark* VI lasted for only a few months in 1780 before being sunk in a storm, and there is little information about it. Meanwhile *Shark* VII had been built as a replacement for the converted *Shark* V. There were therefore for a time in 1780 three *Sharks* existing simultaneously, even if one of them had had its name changed. This is odd, to say the least, and probably results from the fact that these ships were all built by private shipbuilders – and the fact that the Admiralty clearly had lost track of the situation, with one in North America, one largely in the West Indies, and the third in British waters. The one of the three which lasted longest, *Shark* VII – almost four decades – was, however, built under closer Admiralty supervision.

But that is not the end of it. Another *Shark* existed in 1794–1795 – *Shark* VIII – a small Dutch hoy, employed in the Channel until the crew mutinied and fled to France for refuge. And this time there can have been no forgetfulness, for *Shark* VII was active and busy, and had been noteable for its speed. More Admiralty confusion, perhaps.

I

After a pause of twenty years after the end of *Shark* IV, another *Shark* was commissioned; the approach of a new war – the War of the American Rebellion – therefore resurrected the name. This ship was purchased on the stocks in November 1775 by the Admiralty, having been built by the builders Randall, Gray and Bent at Rotherhithe, along with two other vessels. These three were evidently subject to periodic Admiralty inspections at stated stages of their construction. By February all three had their decks fitted; the builders reported this to the Navy Board, and on 28 February they asked for approval for *Shark* and the others to be launched, *Shark* on 9 March, and the 20-gun sixth-rates *Perseus* on 20 March and *Unicorn* on the 23rd.[1]

The captain appointed to the new *Shark*, John Chapman, was present at the ship by April and was writing to ask for such things as surgeon's necessities, and asking that the wooden stock of the anchors be replaced with iron versions.[2] His first monthly musters were sent up on 29 April, implying a reasonably full crew list by then.[3] Fitting out had taken place at Deptford, close to Rotherhithe, and Chapman's log lists the many items the ship needed – beer, water, iron ballast, beef, coals, barrels, pork, vinegar, flour, fat, suet, pease, oatmeal, butter, cheese, cables, and so on, just as every newly built or recommissioned ship did. Work had to be done on the rigging, receiving and installing the masts and the guns (it was to have sixteen guns, two more than *Shark* IV), and storing the ammunition. Men, experienced seamen, were transferred into the ship to form a disciplined nucleus for the crew.[4] Nevertheless, the ship was able to sail on its first extended voyage on 17 May, only three months after its launch.[5]

The ship's first destination was the West Indies. It sailed by way of brief calls at Plymouth and Falmouth, and at the Azores' island of Fayal (a change from Funchal); it reached Antigua on 14 July, a slow voyage. Several days were then spent caulking the ship, a task performed by black slaves owned by the Antigua dockyard, and on the 20th Vice Admiral James Young arrived on the 50-gun fourth-rate HMS *Portland* to take command on the Leeward Islands' station. *Shark*, despite a fire on board on the 21st, possibly accidental, though in view of later events not necessarily so, sailed that day.

Shark was therefore in the Leeward Islands as the rebellion of the American colonists became increasingly open and violent during 1776. One of the early American exploits was to raid the Bahamas for weaponry and gunpowder, a raid assisted by some of the islanders; another development was to commission American ships as privateers to prey on British trade. On 27 June (just as the rebellion was being made official by the writing of the Declaration of Independence), *Shark* encountered one of these American privateering ships off Martinique.

Captain Chapman had been sent to Martinique by Vice Admiral Young to deliver a letter to the governor at Fort St Pierre, perhaps no more than a polite note to inform him of his arrival and appointment, though even so innocuous a note would be a subtle warning. As *Shark* came out of the bay Chapman saw a ship wearing colours he did not recognize. As was the wont of all British warships, especially in the dangerous waters of the West Indies, he closed with the stranger and hailed it, first in French, then in English, fired a shot ahead of it, and hailed it again – three times, he said. To all this the stranger made no answer, which made Chapman instantly suspicious.

Chapman took *Shark* towards the unknown ship, which was evidently the intention of the stranger, for *Shark* received a broadside when close enough; Chapman appears to have been prepared for this – no legitimate ship would have failed to answer to so many hails and implicit threats – and returned the broadside with one of his own. The two ships then fired at each other for three-quarters of an hour, probably from a safe distance, since casualties were minimal on both sides.

This futile fight was stopped when a battery on shore fired two shots towards them, though Chapman decided that they had been fired at *Shark*. He turned away, and the two ships separated, with the stranger heading into the harbour of St Pierre. Chapman later returned and found that the ship was at anchor close to the shore, under the protection of the batteries. He also discovered that it was an American vessel, the privateer *Reprisal*, Captain Lancelot Weekes, carrying, as he well knew by then, eighteen six-pounder guns (more than *Shark*), and as he could appreciate, 120 men, quite enough to provide prize crews for any ships it captured.

Chapman 'remonstrated' with the 'governor' of the battery, who sent the protests on to the colonial governor at St Pierre and the commander of the battery. The reply was that it was judged that the firing was taking place within gunshot of the shore, and therefore within the limits of what was then generally recognized as territorial waters. Chapman, needless to say, denied this, and asserted that it was only the firing from the shore which denied him the chance of capturing the American ship, though the lack of casualties on either side seems to argue a certain hesitancy by both captains. Chapman does not seem to have appreciated that the fact that when he turned away when the shots were fired from the shore, he was implicitly admitting the French claim that the fighting was taking place inside their territorial waters (defined at the time as the distance of a gunshot from the shore, generally reckoned to be three miles); if he did understand this, he did not admit it.

Chapman made his report to Admiral Young, and sent on copies of the correspondence with the Martinique governor and the commander of the battery. Young also received a report from St Vincent that another American ship, described bluntly as a privateer, was at Soufriere Bay on St Lucia, a French island since 1763. The Admiral's correspondent in the island,

Valentine Moon, suggested that this was a consort of the ship which had collided with *Shark*.

Young forthwith reported to the Admiralty. The original fight took place on 27 July, and he wrote to London on 10 August.[6] This was seen at Antigua as an urgent matter because the French attitude locally appeared to be hostile to Britain, as evidenced by Chapman's account and Moon's reports. Given the history of the two countries over the previous century, this was hardly surprising, but an overt intervention in a civil war might be less usual, particularly in a colonial context. It might indicate a French decision to directly assist the American rebels, though this was to disregard the French case in the incident at Martinique. Young claimed that the Martinique governor's letter claimed that 'all kinds of protection ... is given to the American rebels'. The item from St Lucia seemed to confirm it and the American ship was now reported (this must have come from Chapman) to be refitting at Port Royal (Martinique); it had, he claimed, taken three prizes already. Young finished by stating that further correspondence with the governor was useless; he awaited instructions.

In London the First Lord of the Admiralty, the Earl of Sandwich, sent copies of all this to Viscount Weymouth, the Secretary of State of the Southern Department, the responsible minister in relations with France. It was now understood that the assistance given by the French at Martinique to the American privateer would also be provided most likely by the Danish and Dutch islands, and as a result 'the seas will swarm with' American privateers, which would be fatal to British trade. This 'assistance' was not illegal, in so far as there was any international law, but it was clearly unfriendly.

The Admiralty attitude was clearly bellicose, perhaps because the prospect of a French war was more agreeable, and familiar, than one against American rebels, perhaps alternatively in the hope that a French war might stop the rebellion, by the concept of both fighting a common enemy – the rebels and the British had done so only a little more than a decade earlier, and such a war might bring the Americans back to loyalty. But the matter fizzled out. The prospect of a French war as well as an American rebellion was hardly welcome in the less hot-headed parts of the British government. Lord Weymouth was notoriously lazy and inefficient, but perhaps he was also careful and deliberate; he would hardly be roused to action by such a report, which was hardly sufficient to justify a war; it had taken much more than this to force a war with Spain in the 1730s.

Shark meanwhile had continued its patrol. It was at Grenada in the first days of August, and brought a convoy of nine ships to St Kitts; clearly convoys were now more than usually necessary, with American privateers about. For the next two months, it sailed to various islands, to the Dutch island of St Eustatius, where American ships were also being welcomed,[7] to Dominica, and to Antigua to replenish stores, all in much the same way as its predecessor in these waters a quarter of a century before.

On 18 September *Shark* sailed to Montserrat, and on the way captured a Virginia schooner laden with tobacco and corn for Martinique; any American ship was now seen as an enemy vessel. A second visit to Dominica followed and then another replenishing visit to Antigua. At St Kitts in early November the crew were paid their prize money for the captured ship – an unusually speedy decision – and *Shark* sailed at once with a convoy of sixteen ships for Britain.

By this time Chapman had presumably realized that his ship was not a very good sailer, something indicated in its first transatlantic voyage, which had taken two months, where its predecessor several times took only five weeks. This was not particularly serious when sailing between the islands, none of which were more than a day's sail apart, even for a slow ship, but in an Atlantic convoy the matter became awkward. Normally the convoy's speed was determined by the slowest merchant vessel, and such small ships as *Shark* had to be employed in chivvying forward the last and slowest ships, as well as corralling those which wandered off the set course. Each night the numbers were counted, and it was most unusual to see all the ships which the convoy began with still in sight.

But now it was *Shark* which was the slowest, a humiliating situation for the navy. The writer of the log – no doubt Chapman's lieutenant – several times comments that the leading ships of the convoy had to slow down to allow *Shark* to catch up. It did not help that one of the merchant captains had to appeal for help against two men he accused of mutiny; Chapman took them off, sending two of his own men in their place, but this caused still more delay. After a month, when the convoy had travelled perhaps only halfway on their journey towards Britain, Chapman allowed four ships, the fastest sailers, to go ahead of the rest on their own, with a comment in the log that all the convoy sailed much better than *Shark*. (This official release would cover the merchantmen for insurance purposes, if they were captured.) Soon Chapman released the rest of the convoy and turned away for Barbados, arriving there in mid-December.

The other officers on the ship had been curiously vulnerable to accident and illness. The quartermaster was lost overboard on 9 November, and the gunner died on the 12th – neither event will have helped with the convoying – and it was not until returning to English Harbour in Antigua late in January 1777 that a new gunner was appointed by Admiral Young. Then on 11 February Chapman's second-in-command, Lieutenant Christian, was promoted to commander and given command of a transport going to New York.[8] His replacement was Lieutenant James Gambier, who had been made lieutenant only the day before his appointment to *Shark*.[9] Clearly this was a favour by Admiral Young to Gambier's father, who was the commissioner at Portsmouth dockyard, and was reputed to have the ear of the First Lord, Lord Sandwich; Admiral Gambier was soon employed as a senior commander in America, but proved to be ineffectual. Lieutenant Gambier only stayed with *Shark* for a month, being promoted to the sixth-rate *Mermaid* on 14 March. He was replaced by Lieutenant George Edwards a few days later.[10] This rapid change of officers and warrant officers cannot have been other than demoralizing for the crew and difficult for the captain, and was probably one of the causes of the trouble which developed in the ship later.

In May *Shark* went towards Britain as an escort for another convoy, along with three other warships. This time the ship stayed with the merchantmen for most of the way, but, no doubt impatient at their confinement and slow progress, the convoy effectively dissolved when it was about 100 leagues (350 miles) from Britain. It was still not yet clear, as it would be when the career of John Paul Jones gained publicity, that there was a privateer threat in the eastern Atlantic; hence the merchant captains' competitiveness in aiming to reach their home ports first won out over their prudence. This passage, however, had not been particularly slow, taking five weeks from St Kitts to the point of the convoy's dissolution. Some ships had been impatient to separate even earlier, especially those heading for such ports as Liverpool, since they had no wish to go into the English Channel. *Shark* arrived at Spithead on 23 June.

It had been a fairly expensive year for *Shark's* crew. Eight men had died, four of them 'at sea' (which might mean by accident or by going overboard); the rest died in several of the islands; two of the ship's marines had also died. Far worse, as usual, was the cost in desertions. Seven men had run at Deptford before the ship had even sailed, and one had not returned from leave; twenty-seven had deserted in the islands, mainly in Antigua, but also in other places. This was a total loss of forty-two men, half the ship's complement.[11]

Shark, being cleaned and tallowed, refitting and replenishing stores, and recruiting its crew up to strength, was at Portsmouth throughout July. There were concerns at the lack of specialists and officers – no surgeon (as usual), no mate, no master, about which Chapman wrote to the Navy Board, and was echoed by Admiral Sir Thomas Pye, the commissioner at Spithead. A temporary master was found, but the surgeon – a recurring problem for *Sharks*, of course – arrived at Portsmouth only after the ship had sailed.[12] It left Portsmouth on 27 July, but made only slow progress westwards, and called at Torbay and Plymouth before reaching Cork on 21 August.[13] There, a convoy of twenty-three ships was collected, but they did not sail until 3 September, and were then driven back into Cork harbour on the 5th; the delay increased the convoy by another ten ships which arrived at the port and chose to join. Madeira was ignored on this voyage once again, perhaps to make up time, perhaps because it was a known haunt of American privateers, but Barbados was, even so, only reached on 6 November, and English Harbour on Antigua on the 11th – a voyage from Portsmouth of fourteen weeks.[14] (In the process one man ran at Plymouth and six at Cork, three men having deserted at Portsmouth; as well, three men died at Plymouth.)[15]

The ship then stayed at Antigua for nearly four months, until April 1778. This long delay was caused by serious personnel trouble which developed during this time in both the local squadron and in *Shark* itself. To begin with, the rate of desertion from *Shark* was even worse than before – twenty men fled the ship at Antigua, and two had already left at Barbados. In January a series of courts martial revealed that unrest had spread through several ships. *Shark*'s carpenter, John Hiele, and the boatswain from another ship – both warrant officers – were accused of neglect of duty, disobedience to orders, and – probably the real reason for the court – secreting and circulating a paper signed by a great number of 'ships', which was intended to stir up a general mutiny. Three other men were also tried at the same time, two for involvement in getting the paper signed, and one for desertion.[16]

All were found guilty, but the punishments varied. Hiele, a warrant officer, was sentenced to be dismissed from the service and to be incapable of serving again for the next seven years; two of the others were sentenced to 500 lashes, to be inflicted in stages round the fleet, one to 300 and one – the deserter – to 100. This was not the end of the matter, of course, since it took time to administer the physical punishments; it was not until 13 March that the last flogging was administered, on which day *Shark* also received its new carpenter. And in the meantime it had been necessary for Chapman to send the master across the island to St John's to press men and to search for deserters, so short-handed had his ship become.

This is an episode which interestingly prefigures many of the elements of the great mutinies at Portsmouth and the Nore twenty years later. It seems clear that *Shark* was one of the centres of disaffection. It was obviously an unhappy ship, judging by the exceptionally heavy rate of desertion, but it is also clear that this was not the only origin of the incipient mutiny. The rapid turnover of officers and warrant officers in the previous year cannot have helped, but one would suppose that the ideas – equality, freedom – emanating from the American rebellion were also involved. It is also worth noting that the punishments varied between the warrant officer Hiele, who was, in effect, only dismissed, but who seems to have been one of the leaders, and those for the lower deck men involved, who were punished by lashes by the hundred. The British class system was clearly at work even in punishments for incipient mutiny.

At last, on 6 April, *Shark* sailed from Antigua, moving to St Kitts for three weeks, then to Tortola. On 3 May it sailed east once more, escorting a convoy, and later joining with another convoy, making a joint flock of 120 ships. The voyage lasted two months, no more speedy than *Shark*'s earlier convoys, but the sheer number of ships was clearly in part to blame for the slowness. *Shark* arrived at Cork on 3 July, and Plymouth on the 10th. Chapman was promoted to captain on 17 July.[17] On 1 August the ship was paid off, no doubt to the relief of both the captain and his crew.

It is probable that no one was pleased at *Shark*'s performance over the past two years. Apart from the unhappy crew and the close brush with mutiny, the ship's sailing qualities were in question – there was nothing good about a slow sloop, which was intended, above all, to be speedy and handy. At the Navy Board a sketch was made of the ship's sheer 'as taken for the set of water', clearly with the idea of discussing what was wrong.[18] This was dated 22 July 1778, while the ship lay at Plymouth, between arriving and paying off – the three-week delay in paying off was evidently therefore due to the Board's discussions about the ship's future. (It cannot have helped that the high rate of desertions and the involvement of the ship in a mutinous conspiracy had also tarnished the ship's reputation.) Five days earlier the Board wrote to Philip Stephens, the Admiralty Secretary, pointing out that they had been tasked with finding more fireships, but had been unable to do so. However, two sloops, *Shark* and *Porpoise* (16), both recently returned from the West Indies, 'were purchased from merchants and being full built are not well calculated for sailing' – which presumably means that they had been built more as merchantmen than as warships. (*Porpoise* had, in fact, been bought only the year before, and had been the merchantman *Annapolis*, probably American built, or owned.) The Board therefore proposed that one of them – or both – should be converted to fireships.[19] (The Board was being a little economical with the historical truth in this, since the builder had remarked that the *Shark*, and its two sister ships, was being built 'by us for the service', and the ship had been regularly inspected while under construction.)

A second letter described the complements required for fireships – fifty for *Porpoise*, forty-five for *Shark*, forty-five for *Fisher* (which was apparently added briefly to the list, but then dropped),[20] and that they would be armed with eight four-pounders and eight swivel-guns.[21] Since the complement of *Shark* as a sloop was twice that of a fireship it was clearly possible to man two new fireships at the expense of a single sloop. The paying off of *Shark* on 1 August was therefore the signal that the decision had been made to convert the ship. (*Porpoise* was also converted.)

This marked the end, technically, of *Shark* V, but it was really still *Shark* if under a new name – *Salamander*, a traditional name for a fireship (*Porpoise* became *Firedrake*) – and it is worth following the new/old ship's career in brief to the end. The ship had to be altered, in effect something like an extreme refitting, if not so drastic as a rebuild, just as *Shark* III had gained a second life after its rebuild in 1722.

The conversion from sloop to fireship was done at Plymouth, perhaps fairly slowly, for it was only in October that it was reported to the Board that the ship's sheathing had not after all protected it from the *teredo* worm; even in its relatively short time in the West Indies it had suffered serious damage, and authority was requested for the ship to be resheathed. Once that permission arrived, the ship could be ready by the end of the month; in fact it was undocked on the 23rd, and recommissioned as *Salamander* on 19 November.[22]

Having refitted the ship, however, it did not go far in its first year. It was sailed to Spithead in May 1779, having apparently stayed at Plymouth since it was commissioned. In June and July it sailed with the Channel Fleet as far as the Lizard, a voyage which included the decisive halt of the fleet in Torbay. By early September *Salamander* (and the fleet) was back at Spithead. The captain's log does not make the point, but the ship had in fact been participating in the greatest maritime crisis in the Channel since the English defeat at the Battle of Beachy Head in 1692. The Combined Spanish-French Fleet had hovered briefly off Plymouth in August, while *Salamander* was with the fleet in Torbay. Not knowing what the British intended, or indeed where their fleet was, the Combined Fleet dithered. The French ships were suffering badly from sickness and lack of supplies; after a few days the Combined Fleet broke up and retreated, rather to Spanish disgust.

The first captain of *Salamander*, since November 1778, had been James Kinnall. He was replaced by the Hon. Seymour Finch, who took command late in September.[23] By this time the immediate scare of an invasion from France covered by the Combined Fleet had passed, but it was not clear if they might try again. The Channel Fleet sailed from Spithead again late in October and spent most of November at Torbay or in the western parts of the Channel. *Salamander* took part in these movements, and on 24 November the ship was back at Spithead, where it remained, part of the time docked at Portsmouth, until April 1780.

It is curious that the Admiralty had been asking for fireships, since there never seemed to arrive an occasion for their use. They were not worth expending against a moving target, since it took only a minor manoeuvre to evade a fireship attack. They were therefore only worth expending against a moored fleet or ship, principally in a confined space such as an estuary or a harbour. The Spaniards used one in the siege of Gibraltar during this war, but with no success. *Salamander* was nevertheless attached to a series of fleets just in case; like so many unlikely and rarely used weapons, it was always necessary to have one or more available in case an opportunity arose when it could be employed. Otherwise *Salamander* was generally employed as a dispatch vessel, a scout, a convoy escort, and so on – just as it had been as a sloop. (Fireships might also be dangerous to one's own side: *Porpoise/Firedrake* caught fire and blew up in Falmouth harbour in 1781.)

After the winter *Salamander* was sent to the West Indies, though it moved almost as slowly as it had as a sloop. It was at Torbay on 19 April, but only got away on the 30 May, probably as part of the reinforcement sent to join Admiral Sir George Rodney.[24] The ship was at Barbados on 10 July – a slow passage (seven weeks from Torbay) – and then, after calls at St Lucia and St Kitts, it stayed at Antigua until January 1781. On 25 January, on the news of the declaration of war by the Netherlands, Rodney seized the opportunity to pillage the rich Dutch entrepôt island of St Eustatius, where there was a great quantity of accumulated goods gathered there as a result of the island's previously neutral (and so protected) condition. It had been used by American vessels as a trading centre where they could acquire European goods (often British), and sell their own produce. By this they could evade the British blockade, an annoyance which the British had repeatedly complained about. Once the Dutch entered the war, however – in fact as a result of a British declaration of war – their possessions became, to the British, and above all to the avaricious Rodney, fair game. This was what the Admiralty had predicted back in 1776 at the time they received the news of the confrontation of *Shark* at Martinique. Now Rodney greedily seized this chance to disembarrass the Dutch of their island and its wealth. From Antigua *Salamander* visited St Kitts and St Lucia, and arrived at St Eustatius the day after Rodney's pillaging campaign began, 4 February.[25]

At that point *Salamander* acquired another new captain. Finch was promoted to captain in February (and was in command of a frigate by December) and was replaced in *Salamander* by Edward Bowater, who eventually rose to be an Admiral, but was only promoted to commander after he took over command of the ship.[26] *Salamander* stayed at St Eustatius for another month, then from 20 March it visited St Kitts, Nevis, and Antigua for three months, while Rodney looted St Eustatius and organized the convoy for moving the loot to Britain (the convoy was largely captured by the French as it approached Europe). Meanwhile, Vice Admiral Sir Samuel Hood, with the main fleet, cannily fended off the French fleet under Admiral de Grasse near Martinique. *Salamander* was brought south to Barbados in May, and was part of the united fleet under Rodney there and at Tobago (which was captured by the French while Rodney was distracted) in June.[27]

The ship remained with the fleet thereafter. It was at Antigua in early August and left with the fleet, now commanded by Hood while Rodney went to Britain on home leave. On 10 August Hood took the fleet north to Virginia and then to New York. In North America the main American rebel forces were now marching south from New York towards Virginia, accompanied by the French army under General Comte de Rochambeau from Rhode Island, to attack General Lord Cornwallis, who had taken up a vulnerable position at Yorktown on the York River, but one from which he could be resupplied and reinforced by sea – if the British fleet could reach him. The British naval squadron at New York was taken on a cruise to the east by Admiral Graves, hoping to intercept a French convoy heading for Boston or Newport, Rhode Island. All except the American land army under Washington and his French ally Rochambeau were operating with inadequate or misleading intelligence, and it is something of a surprise that a naval battle eventually happened. *Salamander* was with Hood when he reached New York on 29 August, and it sailed with the fleet, which then included most of the squadron from New York, returned from its futile cruise to the east. The joint fleet sailed from Sandy Hook on the 31st.

Admiral de Grasse had delayed his own voyage north to deal with several matters in the French islands, with the result that the French delay and the British delay at New York cancelled each other out, and so the two fleets met off the Capes of the Chesapeake early in December despite Hood's speed and urgency and despite Grasse's relative slowness. But the French seized the crucial position, the entrance to Chesapeake Bay, and the British fleet, outnumbered and outmanoeuvred, and commanded hesitantly and barely competently by Graves (who was senior to the more competent Hood), was quite unable to dislodge it; nor could moving the fleet into the inland sea of Chesapeake Bay have succoured the British army at Yorktown. In the end Grasse blocked the attack of the British fleet in a battle in which the outnumbered British suffered a defeat, and then hoodwinked the British by a silent about-turn at night, leaving the British sailing south while the French returned north to block the entrance to the Bay; they were thus able to deliver the French siege guns to Washington's army, with which he and Rochambeau would soon destroy Cornwallis' position.[28]

Salamander, amidst the great line of battleships on both sides, cannot have contributed anything to the battle, its eight four-pounders being of little account, and no opportunity existed for its use as a fireship. (However, there might have been one had the two fleets conducted the fight inside the Bay: another reason for the French to block the entrance.) Indeed, the British fleet returned to Sandy Hook, the entrance to New York harbour, on the 19th, but *Salamander* had been there since the 16th, perhaps sent in advance to carry the news of the British defeat to General Sir Henry Clinton, the army commander. The ship was used later to reconnoitre the French position at the Capes, and it was back in New York by 3 November, perhaps carrying the news not only that the French were still off the Capes, but that on 19 October the British army under Cornwallis had surrendered and gone into captivity.

(There are no complaints about the ship's lackadaisical sailing, and it kept up with the rest of the fleet well enough. It was also readily used independently, and to deliver messages – as to New York after the battle. It would seem that the reconstruction it had undergone at Plymouth, and the lightening achieved by removing several guns, and half the crew, had much improved *Salamander*'s sailing qualities over those of its existence as *Shark*.)

Once Cornwallis' army was in captivity neither Hood nor Grasse felt the need to stay off the North American coast. On 11 November the British fleet under Hood left New York, and *Salamander* went along. A week earlier Grasse had ordered the French fleet south again. The next stage in the maritime war took place in the West Indies, where the French aimed to enlarge their conquests. North America had become a sideshow (though United States historians can never be convinced of this).

Before *Salamander* sailed, it had another change of captain. Bowater was replaced by Richard Lucas, a lieutenant promoted next year to commander.[29] The ship returned to Barbados by 17 December; next day it was sent off to St Lucia with dispatches; the French fleet had appeared off the island the day before, but had failed to make a landing due to the adverse weather. Returning to Barbados, *Salamander* intercepted and captured, after a fight, a boat crewed by a group of deserters, who were trying to escape both the navy and the island. A month later it was with Hood's fleet once more at Barbados, but it avoided Hood's fight at St Kitts. Instead it escorted a convoy to Gros Islet Bay on St Lucia – the island was clearly menaced by the French and it required supplies. But by 13 February *Salamander* was once more under Hood's orders and enjoyed the dismay of the French when Hood's fleet stole away from St Kitts by night, thereby doing to the French what the French had done to the British at the Capes.[30]

Rodney returned from leave in Britain on 18 February 1782 and was again in command of the fleet (including *Salamander*) on the 25th. *Salamander* stayed with the fleet in the manoeuvres which followed and which resulted in the battle of the Saintes on 12 April, in which Rodney's fleet broke through the French line; the victory prevented a planned French expedition against Jamaica. The small ships, including *Salamander*, did not, again, take part in the battle, in which the action was confined to the greater vessels. The ship had been damaged in mid-March, and was in and out of harbours and islands until January 1783.

In that time it also received yet another captain, the fifth since the ship was converted to a fireship. This was Commander James Deacon, who had been promoted to that rank in May 1782. The ship was at Port Royal, Jamaica, on 12 May when Deacon took over. Deacon's predecessor Lucas had been promoted to captain in April, and so was of too high a rank for such a small ship; Deacon's promotion to commander came at about the same time.[31]

Deacon remained in command of the ship for the rest of its life. It was based at Jamaica over the winter of 1782/1783 and sailed on a cruise through the Windward Passage on 12 March. The familiar landmarks from earlier *Shark*s' voyages in these waters appear in the captain's log – Cape Tiburon, Cape St Nicolas, Cape Francois – and the ship went into the southern Bahama islands as well – Great Inagua, Long Key, Rum Key, Watling Island. The Spaniards had sent an expedition which had seized control of Nassau and New Providence Island in the previous year, the latest in a long list of minor British possessions from the Mississippi eastwards taken by the Spaniards. (Florida had been a British colony since 1763, transferred at the end of the Seven Years' War.) Nassau in fact was quickly retaken by the local militia, the islanders thereby again demonstrating their essential independence of British imperial authority, as they had throughout the war – they had actively traded with the American colonies in revolt, while refusing inducements to join the rebellion. *Salamander*, a small ship weakly armed, could do little about any of this, but it could investigate the other Bahama Islands to see if the Spaniards – or any pirates as well – were in control of any of them. Finally on 1 May *Salamander* sailed east across the Atlantic, probably in charge of, or as part of, a convoy, though this is not noted in the log. The ship arrived at Spithead on 8 June. It was paid off at Deptford on the 28th.

The curious thing about this *Shark's* career is that the almost-unarmed *Salamander* took part in, or was near to, several of the great battles of this war – the Capes of the Chesapeake, St Kitts, the Saintes – and was close to the great maritime Channel crisis of 1779 – whereas its better-armed previous version, as *Shark* V, never came near such an action; neither, of course, had any of *Shark* V's own predecessors since *Shark* I at La Hougue in 1692, even when *Shark* IV had served throughout the War of Austrian Succession. But apart from some damage it incurred in some unknown way in 1782 near Barbados *Salamander* came through unscathed.

The ship was paid off quickly, even before the various parts of the Treaty of Paris were agreed in late 1783 and early 1784 – there were several treaties, but the war was effectively over by early 1783. The ship was then sold in mid-August, which further confirms the dissatisfaction of the Admiralty with the ship.[32] It was probably a slightly better sailer as *Salamander* than it had been as *Shark*. Being lighter – sixteen small guns as opposed to sixteen large ones, and with half the crew and so fewer stores – it should have been nippier and handier. Of course, after the peace was agreed, the government, as always, went on a campaign of cost-cutting, which inevitably meant a reduction in the fleet, at least for a time, and therefore the removal of any unsatisfactory small ships. Yet at the same time there was still another *Shark* – *Shark* VII – in the Royal Navy, and there had been yet another while *Salamander* sailed – *Shark* VI.

Chapter 6

Shark VI: a Sixth Rate, 1780

The sixth *Shark* was both the largest of the early set of eight ships of the sailing-ship variety, and the one with the briefest life. It is also in a sense the orphan of the pack, in that little is known about it – which is, of course, a function of its brevity. It was acquired in the midst of the War of the American Rebellion, probably in 1779, by purchase.[1] That is, it was probably fully built as a private ship, and had to be adapted for warship service, which was in part the essential problem with its contemporary and predecessor *Shark* V / *Salamander*. This adaptation would probably include installing its guns, of which the ship carried twenty-eight or thereabouts. This made it a sixth-rate warship, a small frigate, or a very large sloop, and gave it a definite rating, whereas its earlier sisters had been all too frequently included in 'small vessels' when lists were made. It may be presumed that the alterations necessitated by its conversion from a private ship to a warship were part of the reason for the ship's eventual loss. The installation of the guns will certainly have altered its sailing qualities, above all by changing its centre of gravity to a much higher level.

There are in effect no records of the ship's activities. Its captain in the end was Howell Lloyd, who had been commissioned as a lieutenant in 1772, and was rated as a captain in May 1780, at which time he was captain of the sixth-rate *Fowey*.[2] *Shark*'s first captain before Lloyd is not known. Again, the larger ship required a higher rank – earlier and later *Sharks* all had men of the rank of lieutenant or commander as their captains. There are, so far as can be seen, no surviving muster lists, though one must have been organized when the ship was first manned; probably it was not sent in to the Admiralty and went down when the ship sank. It is not even clear if the building and commissioning took place in Britain or in North America, though the former is by far the more likely; yet the only record of the ship is that it was active in North American waters, so its purchase may have been made there. And without a muster, there is no pay list. Similarly no captain's or master's log survives. Nor is the ship recorded in the lists of ships maintained at the Admiralty; it appears that Rodney never reported his appropriation of it into his fleet.

On past form, Lloyd's assumption of command in May 1780 will have been followed by at least two months of hard work; recruiting the crew, gathering stores and equipment, and taking the ship on a preliminary cruise to detect faults and problems. Also on past experience, various adjustments to the ship, the masts, the rigging and so on will have been needed, and all the time the crew was simultaneously being recruited and the ship was suffering the usual desertions. This is only assumption, of course, in this case. If these things happened with this ship, in Britain it had a British crew, or if in America, it had an American crew, presumably of loyalists; in either case the crewing took place late in 1779 or in the early part of 1780.

This preliminary period may well have taken a couple of months, and was followed by orders to sail to North America, probably by the usual route by way of Madeira, a voyage which might take up to two months, so that the ship is unlikely to have arrived in North America before September. Where in North America the ship was to be based is not known, but New York is likely to have been the first choice by far. Charleston is also possible, since it had been taken by the British earlier in 1780; Halifax is also a possibility; but both of these are perhaps unlikely; some ships were also stationed in the York River; they fell into French hands after the battle of Yorktown.

Lists of various ships can provide clues as to *Shark*'s posting. It was not part of Admiral Rodney's fleet at St Kitts (or indeed anywhere in the West Indies) at the end of July, of which we possess a full list by Rodney himself;[3] and this indeed is probably too early for its arrival in the west (if it was coming from Britain). Not long after this Rodney sailed for New York, arriving there with line of battleships and frigates in the middle of October, but *Shark* was not among the fleet then.[4] When he sailed on 16 November, back to the West Indies, however, *Shark* was one of the ships in his fleet, and Howell Lloyd had been transferred to it from *Fowey*.[5] *Shark*, therefore, was probably already in New York when the fleet arrived, or it reached the port soon after, and was taken into Rodney's fleet, as were some other ships already at New York. (The *Salamander* fireship, *Shark* VI's predecessor, was also part of Rodney's fleet.)

As Rodney sailed from New York his fleet was caught in a storm and scattered. Several of his ships were damaged or sunk and *Shark* was one of the casualties. He reported this in a letter to the Admiralty on 30 November, but it is clear from his account that *Shark* had been sunk on the 17th or 18th – though no one was an eyewitness so far as is known; it was the ship's absence ten days after the storm which convinced Rodney that it had been sunk.

It had been a bad hurricane year in the West Indies, with two very powerful storms causing enormous damage in both the Leeward Islands, notably St Lucia, and in Jamaica, with much loss of life and great damage to the warships which were caught in their paths. But November is too late for hurricanes, and it seems probable that it was a lesser storm, though one which was clearly fierce enough, which the fleet encountered somewhere north of the Bahamas, and which caused *Shark* to sink. The ship had been at sea from New York for only fourteen days, and it is unlikely to have reached the West Indies in that time.[6]

There were no survivors from *Shark* VI.

Chapter 7

Shark VII: a Sloop, 1779–1818, Part One: 1779–1794

I

The decision to have another sloop called *Shark* was taken in October 1778, and by 20 November it was ordered from Thomas Walton, a shipbuilder of Hull, shortly after the decision was made to convert *Shark* V to a fireship. The Admiralty Agent at Hull, Thomas Nicholson, reported on progress in July 1779, and said that the builder was offering to provide blocks and deadeyes; the offer was accepted.[1] It took a year to build the ship, which was launched on 26 November 1779, a much slower building process than earlier privately-built versions. The new ship was fitted out during the winter, partly at Hull using materials sent from Chatham in the *Jeremiah and Mary* transport, which needed convoying, now that war with France (and Spain) had begun, and that American rebel privateers were active in British waters.[2] Some of the materials had been intended for the frigate *Serapis* (44), but that ship had been captured by the American privateer *Bonhomme Richard* (40), captained by John Paul Jones, in a fight off Flamborough Head in September (not far from where the new *Shark* was being built).[3] *Serapis* had put up a powerful fight against *Bonhomme Richard* and its fellow frigate *Alliance*, and had sunk its enemy, though it surrendered in the process; in this fight *Serapis* had successfully defended the ships of the Baltic convoy it was escorting, a fact generally ignored. *Serapis* had therefore accomplished its assigned task.[4] It clearly had no need of further supplies from Chatham.

The first captain of the new *Shark* was Isaac Vaillant, who took command on 15 February 1780. He had been a lieutenant since 1761, and a commander since 1777.[5] This was scarcely a stellar career, but all promotion had been slow in the time of peace between 1763 and 1776. He spent three weeks after taking command at Hull collecting stores and fitting out, and by early March the ship was sailing south along the east coast to the Nore, then back again as far as Leith. This was convoy escort work, as usual.[6]

But the fitting and equipping of the ship was not yet complete. On 6 April it went into the dockyard at Chatham, principally to have copper sheathing fastened. Other matters had also concerned Vaillant even while he was sailing: he asked for supplies of both surgeon's necessities and boatswain's stores in March, and asked again in April for surgeon's items, specifying that they should be for three months and for 125 men – and then, of course, he had to ask again in July.[7] It took some time for the copper sheathing to be requisitioned and then delivered; the ship went into dock eventually on 6 May.[8] Copper sheathing had only recently become the normal equipment for ships of the Royal Navy, and the bigger ships had been given priority. For a small ship to be so equipped was fairly unusual so far, but would give it extra speed and endurance. The particular usefulness of copper-bottoming was that the West Indian *teredo* worm's ravages were, if not wholly defeated, then slowed, and in colder waters weed was not able to secure a serious grip, and this also permitted coppered ships to sail better and faster, as well as having a longer life.

While at Chatham Vaillant asked that the guns installed at Hull should be replaced by carronades, and he also wanted a supply of timber so that barricades could be fitted on the quarterdeck, perhaps temporarily, at need.[9] He clearly expected, reasonably enough in the North Sea in wartime, to have to fight. While at Chatham also the work of the shipbuilder at Hull was inspected, and the rather patronizing verdict was rendered that the ship was well built.[10]

Shark came out of Chatham early in June, spent a week at the Nore, then sailed, perhaps on a new shakedown cruise, as far as Bridlington Bay and returned to the Nore on 6 July; Bridlington, near Flamborough, was the target for Baltic convoys, where those going east gathered, and those coming from the Baltic dispersed; *Shark* may well have been escorting convoys in both directions along the east English coast. The ship then spent much of the time from 23 July to 25 November patrolling off the Sussex coast, or lying at the Downs, and escorting convoys. This was the period when a possible invasion threat existed; the south coast needed to be attended to, smugglers caught (and information extracted from them), privateers deterred; while at the Downs *Shark* was thus kept busy boarding and inspecting ships. On 23 October the captain reported the loss of his cutter in boarding a ship off Dunkirk; he asked for the replacement to be a 6-oared cutter instead of the lost 4-oared version.[11] Finally Vaillant took the ship into Spithead on 25 November, and, having been promoted to captain, he was there replaced as *Shark's* commander by Lieutenant Robert McDouall (or possibly McDougall).[12]

The pay list compiled for the period October 1779 to April 1780 – Vaillant's period in command – counted two men dead, one at Sheerness and one at sea; of desertions only one ran at Spithead, but twenty-six went at Chatham and two at Sheerness, while others had gone at other ports where the ship had called: ten went at Hull, where the ship had been originally manned, and others at Yarmouth Roads, Leith, and Eastbourne.[13]

II

McDouall's lieutenancy had lasted even longer than Vaillant's. He had reached that rank in 1759, and was made commander in 1780, over a month after taking command of *Shark*. But then he rose to captain in July 1781 – wartime was a helpful period for promotion. (He eventually rose to be an admiral in 1813.) His captaincy of *Shark* was slow to get going, but when it did he took the ship farther afield than any previous holder of a *Shark* captaincy.

Shark stayed at Spithead throughout the winter of 1780/1781. McDouall had a problem with his surgeon, as did every captain of *Shark*, complaining in February that he had not yet appeared, nor had his 'necessities' – another repeated complaint by *Shark* captains. He had already asked to return unserviceable slops (working clothing) to the dockyard store. In February he told the Navy Board that his master had 'absconded himself without leave', and asked for a replacement to be appointed. He sent the muster list up on 8 March.[14]

The pay list compiled for 1780–1781 counted two men dead, one at Sheerness and one at sea; of deserters only one ran at Spithead, which was where the ship had been since McDouall took command, so the rest had deserted under Vaillant.[15] The ship sailed on 13 March as part of the guard of a convoy of transports.[16] The transports were initially intended to reinforce Gibraltar, which was under siege, but there was also a force included which was intended to attack the Dutch colony at the Cape of Good Hope (and to go on to attack Java and the Spice Islands afterwards), a set of East India Company ships, and another small convoy for the West Indies. *Shark* was part of the Cape group, commanded by Commodore George Johnstone, a loud, scatterbrained politician-sailor with extremely good political connections.

The joint force sailed south towards Spain. The Gibraltar contingent turned away to the east, and the Cape force went on southwards with the Indiamen. Johnstone had a relatively small naval force of two ships of the line, three fifty-gunships and several smaller vessels, and the transports carried four battalions of troops commanded by Major General William Medows. Johnstone detached part of his naval force to Madeira for replenishment, and the West India convoy left at the same time. The rest of the ships went on to Porto Praya in the Cape Verde Islands for their own replenishment.

The orders for Johnstone's expedition were complex. They attempted to take account of a great variety of possible alternative situations, and this in the event left considerable leeway for the commanders if they chose to exercise their initiative. The main point was that if Johnstone failed at the Cape, most of the soldiers were to go on to India; if he succeeded in taking the Cape, part was to go on, leaving a garrison at the Cape. The warships were to return to St Helena to help escort the returning East India Company convoy to Britain, which gathered at that island. But there were plenty of ifs and buts so that nothing was really clear. And in all this *Shark* had its own special mission.[17]

One of the informal agreements between the national belligerents was that Catholic priests who were captured by the British were to be returned to their homes. One such priest, Don Francisco Gorman, apparently had his home in Brazil. He was a passenger on *Shark* and the ship was therefore detached at Porto Praya to take Father Gorman on to Rio de Janeiro, or at least to the 'coast of Brazil'. It may be assumed that the gathering of intelligence was also part of McDouall's aims. *Shark* was also to escort the East India Company packet *Rodney* part of the way, until both were clear of any likely enemy forces. The two ships separated on 30 April, out of sight of the Brazilian coast, and *Shark* reached Rio de Janeiro on 4 May. There the priest was landed and the ship was supplied with food, water, and wood.

The Portuguese Brazilian authorities insisted that the ship must anchor well clear of other ships in the harbour. They put guards on the supply boats and on the gangplanks, both to prevent the escape of slaves onto the ship, and to prevent the desertion of any British sailors onto the land – there are several kinds of slavery. This was all rather to the bemusement of the British, and the captain, unusually, commented on it in his journal – but this was also useful intelligence, implying a vigilant if suspicious government system in a country allied with Britain. On 6 May the Brazilian Adjutant General, as the log terms him, came on board, perhaps to express thanks for the return of the priest, but also no doubt to check that his guards were doing their jobs. The ship sailed again on 7 May. There had been precious little opportunity of gathering much information, though the strict precautions of the port authorities were worth noting, and an alert captain could see a great deal from his anchored ship.[18]

Commodore Johnstone meanwhile was facing a series of troubles and taking several bad decisions. He had a tendency to detach ships for odd purposes, so when he anchored at Porto Praya he had several ships fewer than when he started, though the East India ships were still with him. He was also unprofessional (he had not held an active naval command at sea for fifteen years), and in the harbour his squadron, which arrived in disarray and in several sections over several days, was anchored in a disorderly fashion. Also he did not realize, though he should have assumed it, that the French had caught wind of the expedition; indeed, they knew a great deal about the composition and intentions of the force, and they had sent out a force twice as strong as Johnstone's to intercept it. They had also sent a ship to warn the Dutch at the Cape that they were now at war with Britain, if they did not yet know, and that there was a British expedition heading their way. Like the British, the French ships were carrying troops who were to go on to India when they had attended to matters at the Cape. The French squadron was commanded by the greatest French fighting admiral of the age, Admiral the Bailli de Suffren.

Suffren caught up with Johnstone at Porto Praya, having missed the ships Johnstone had sent into Funchal. Taking both the British and his own captains by surprise he attacked immediately, pell-mell and headlong. The fight was confused and, more because of the French captains' incomprehension of Suffren's intentions than their own abilities, the British fought off the attack – the Indiamen, of course, were relatively well-armed, so the French fight was not just with the warships. Suffren pulled his ships out, and Johnstone, with a final attack of sense, gave up the chase he had begun and returned to guard the transports and the Indiamen which he had left in the harbour. He then waited there for another two weeks before sailing on, thus allowing Suffren two weeks' start on him in their voyages to the Cape, which now had become something of a race; Johnstone does not seem to have realized this, though once again he should have. So Suffren had landed his troops and guns at Cape Town to assist the Dutch defence long before Johnstone was anywhere near, and the Dutch governor had already been alerted by the arrival of the French privateer frigate *Serapis*, which had arrived earlier.

Shark meanwhile had sailed on from Rio alone, with the intention of joining Johnstone once more at the Cape. Johnstone had not yet arrived when *Shark* reached the vicinity, however, and the French squadron was spotted in Table Bay. McDouall did not at first identify the ships as French warships, but as a Dutch convoy. (Just to add confusion, there really was a Dutch convoy, but it was moored to the north at Saldanha Bay.) Captain McDouall went in towards Table Bay, perhaps believing that the governor still thought that the Netherlands were neutral. Meanwhile Suffren reasonably assumed that *Shark* was a frigate sent by Johnstone to gather preliminary information, though Johnstone had not apparently thought of this elementary precaution; Suffren was evidently crediting him with more initiative and naval intelligence than he possessed. *Shark* was approached by *Serapis*, which was sent out by Suffren to investigate, but which McDouall at first thought was a Dutch ship. McDouall hoisted Portuguese colours and answered the frigate's hail in a version of Portuguese, but the answer from the frigate was disbelieving – it cannot have been difficult to distinguish a British warship from a Portuguese vessel, at least from close to, though everyone had been busy confusing themselves and everyone else.

McDouall finally realized that the approaching ship was French, and that it was the *Serapis*, and that therefore the squadron in Table Bay was French. This *Serapis* was the ship captured in a ruinous condition by John Paul Jones a year before. It had been sold by him to the French and was then acquired and rebuilt by the French navy. Once *Shark's* captain understood the situation, he immediately turned to get away, for he was considerably outmatched in power. The two ships exchanged broadsides, then *Serapis* chased *Shark* for the next four hours. It was catching up and was about to resume firing when McDouall saw a distant sail on his lee bow, and desperately pretended to make a signal to it, though he had no idea what it was. *Serapis* assumed that any ship at sea must be British, and anyway had pushed *Shark* well away from the Cape. It veered off.

This was another of those curious meetings and coincidences. A British ship masquerading as a Portuguese vessel fought a French ship which was formerly British, in a Dutch port in Africa – and *Shark* had had incorporated into its construction some of the repair materials which had been originally intended for its enemy. Also *Shark* had summoned to its aid an unknown ship, so that the stronger *Serapis* broke off the attack, even though it was almost within firing range, and the unknown ship (if it actually existed) could not have possibly arrived for a considerable time. (It is also worth noting the constant misidentifications made by all sides, providing many of the elements of confusion in the encounter.)

Shark was in fact fortunate to escape. *Serapis* was a much more powerful ship, with three times *Shark's* guns (44 to 14), and was apparently also the better sailer, for it had caught up with *Shark* at the end. (*Serapis*, however, did not survive for long. Only a month later it was anchored at a port in Madagascar, and an officer was preparing brandy for issuing to the sailors by watering it – the French form of the British grog, which was carried in a very concentrated form – when a sailor dropped a lighted candle into the brandy barrel; the subsequent explosion and fire destroyed the ship.[19]) *Shark* went on to St Helena, arriving on 4 July (just as *Serapis* was heading for Madagascar).

Johnstone's force arrived at the Cape after *Shark's* escape, and after Suffren had left for Mauritius and India, but there were French troops reinforcing the garrison, and Johnstone, after some argument, accepted the determination of General Medows that an attack at the Cape was no longer feasible. Johnstone hung around at the Cape, consulting and arguing with Medows and his ships' captains for some time. Then he discovered the Dutch convoy in Saldanha Bay and captured most of it with the assistance of Medows' troops. This cooperation annoyed some of the sailors, particularly the captains, who feared that they would have to share the prize money with them; in the event the prize court decided, on some arcane grounds, that the Dutch ships were not prizes, and neither sailors nor soldiers were awarded anything.

Medows was then allowed to go on to India, taking all the troops with him, though his orders had envisaged sending the putative Cape garrison back to Britain if it was not needed in Cape Town. But his arrival with his troops in India was decisive in the war against Hyder Ali, a good example of a creative disobedience to out-of-date orders. The French ships and troops under Suffren went on to Mauritius, setting up the extraordinary contest between his forces and those of Admiral Hughes in the Bay of Bengal over the next year. Medows' main reason for taking all his forces on to India was that he understood that Suffren had taken extra forces there. Johnstone, on the other hand, stuck rigidly to his instructions, and took his remaining ships back to St Helena, whereas they would have been much more useful helping Hughes in Indian waters.

Johnstone eventually arrived at St Helena after *Shark* and its convoy had sailed – so failing in yet another of his missions. When *Shark* arrived at the island there were several ships already there, including eighteen East India Company ships. Once they had all watered and resupplied, *Shark* sailed for Britain as one of the escort. The convoy finally left St Helena on 30 July, and reached the Downs on 22 October, a slow passage which must have left McDouall grinding his teeth in annoyed frustration; escorting a slow and already well-armed East India convoy, which had a well-armed escort already, was not the best use of a coppered sloop.

III

McDouall had been promoted to captain while he was away (actually while he was at St Helena), and was therefore replaced as captain of *Shark* by John Maitland, who took over the ship at the Downs on 3 November.[20] The day before he was replaced McDouall sent a list of the ship's defects up to the Navy Board, and Maitland did the same once he had been in command for a month.[21] The ship had been at sea continuously for the past seven months, so some defects were inevitable. In 11 December the ship was ordered to be fitted for 'Channel service'.[22] A pay list compiled to January 1782 listed desertions at Deal and Sheerness (and twelve more unlocated); but it also lists two men who died at Deal and the Downs, five others who died at places not stated, and eight who died 'at sea'.[23] This was no doubt one of the products of McDouall's long voyage. The navy could not win in the manpower stakes – a long voyage prevented desertions, but more men died. There were, not surprisingly when the Portuguese precautions are remembered, no desertions at Rio.

The ship's work under Maitland for the next year was in the North Sea. On 8 November it sailed north to escort the Baltic convoy home; in the process Maitland rescued the crew of a brig out of Peterhead which was in danger of sinking. *Shark* was back at Sheerness at the beginning of December, and sailed again in January with a convoy to Hull. This was now the ship's base for a time, at White Booth Roads.[24]

In the Humber late in March a storm drove the ship over the 'New Sands'. 'She kept stricking (*sic*) and striving over the sands', commented the author of the captain's journal; the rudder came unhung, and leaks started (all very reminiscent of the experience of *Shark* IV at Cork forty years before). Despite firing guns as a signal of distress, no help came, which suggests that the power of the storm prevented any helpers from setting off. In the end, at about 9.00 pm, the ship got off the sands, or was driven right over them. The night was thus survived, but the ship was seriously damaged and leaking. In the morning the ship's boats were sent off to an armed ship nearby for help, but the cutter was seen to be overwhelmed by the waves. The six men on board were killed.

It was, apparently, not possible to effect proper repairs in the Humber, though ironwork for the rudder was obtained and the rudder repaired. The lack of a dock at Hull or Grimsby was the problem. So the ship was patched up enough to sail back to Sheerness, where full repairs were made. Altogether the ship was out of action for two months.

Shark resumed its work on 16 May, escorting a convoy to Ostend, and bringing another back, then over to Dunkirk and back, and then to the Downs and return. The Austrian Netherlands were then the only non–hostile coast between Gibraltar and the German Bight, though not particularly friendly even so, and convoys were clearly required if any trade at all was to be accomplished. (Dunkirk was part of France, of course, but a convoy could be released there if the escorts waited to see that no Dunkirkers came out to molest the ships.) The ship's routine was varied in June and July by a voyage to Beachy Head, then back and forth between Ostend or Dunkirk and the Downs from the middle of July 1782 through to May of 1783, with visits to Beachy Head or Dungeness for a certain limited variety. Maitland was then superseded as captain.

The pay list for Maitland's captaincy showed a crew only too anxious to leave.[25] Eight men died in the fifteen months of the accounting period, including the six men in the storm-driven cutter in the Humber. But the rate of desertion was tremendous. The complement of the ship was 125 men. In that fifteen month period, four left in the Humber, fifteen at Sheerness, and four at Yarmouth; but at Deal, where the ships in the Downs often called for supplies, and men had therefore to go on shore, thirty men ran. This was a total of fifty-three desertions; with the dead, the ship had lost just about half of its complement in only a little over a year.

IV

A new captain, Valentine Edwards, took over on 24 May 1783 (and he had to sign that last pay list).[26] The ship stayed at Sheerness, repairing and refitting, until August, and in September a new series of repetitive patrols began, this time off the east coast of Scotland, the ship being based at Leith.[27] This was the same area as *Shark* IV had operated in under Middleton's command in the 1740s.

By this time the American war was over; Britain ceased effective military operations in North America in February 1783, the victory of Rodney at the Battle of the Saintes had brought an end to French enterprises in the Caribbean, and the usual peace treaties with Britain's enemies were agreed between September 1783 and early 1784, in a series of agreements collectively called the Treaty of Paris.

For the next four years *Shark*'s work was to patrol the east coast of Scotland, always under the captaincy of Commander Edwards. The first months give the routine. The ship stayed at Leith until 21 September, then sailed to Inverkeithing, and back to Leith, in effect a patrol of the Firth of Forth. Then followed a voyage as far as Buchan Ness, and a return to Leith, where the ship stayed for three weeks. Brief voyages in the Firth of Forth in the winter were interspersed with long stays at Leith. Buchan Ness was visited again in March. Then in April a longer cruise brought the ship further north, first to Cromarty and then to Orkney, in company with the frigate *Daedalus* (32), and a return to Leith once more early in May.

This was a smugglers' patrol, searching for illegal importers of the usual smugglers' goods – wine, brandy, tobacco – in the same way that *Shark* III had done here and in Cornwall fifty years before. It is not clear if the ship intercepted many smugglers, or that the encounters with boats, smugglers' or otherwise, were all recorded in the log. Some of these certainly are recorded, but it seems likely that a fruitless interception or investigation was usually not mentioned. As usual the log is informative only about the weather, anchorages, and supplies.

The first interception noted in any detail occurred in July 1784, when the brig *Lively* of Peterhead was stopped and found to be loaded with wine. It had no papers, and two small boats had apparently taken off some of the cargo a short time before. These were also intercepted: one had thrown overboard whatever it had been carrying; the other had brandy and wine. The case was then handed over to the customs.

The Peterhead/Buchan Ness area was evidently seen as a major centre of smuggling activity, probably because, like the English south coast, there were lots of coastal villages and small ports, where small boats were based and where they could be quickly unloaded – the whole population was probably involved, or at least in the know. Late in July *Shark* sent a party onshore in the large cutter to search for smugglers; there is no sign that they found any. Other landings were made in search of intelligence on smuggling, and at times boats were encountered or chased, off Aberdeen and off 'Stone-hive' (Stonehaven). More often than not those which were intercepted turned out to be customs cutters, who had no need to fear capture; others no doubt escaped, or evaded interception, implying to the pursuers at least some guilt, though not being willing to be subjected to a naval search would be as good a reason as any to get away.

Captain Edwards remained in command of *Shark* all this time. Most of the work of the ship was done in the Firth of Forth – lots of small ports again – and along the coast as far as Peterhead, but with occasional cruises to Orkney or Cromarty in the summer, and one visit to Lerwick in Shetland. In October 1787 *Shark* at last left Scottish waters for a short visit to the Nore, possibly to report wear and tear, but was sent north again at once. Presumably it was by this time somewhat worn, for after another month at Leith and in the Firth of Forth, the ship returned to the Nore, and this time, on 14 November, it went into Sheerness, where it was paid off; it remained there, inactive, but no doubt refitting, for the next two and a half years. Edwards was promoted to captain later in 1787.

The work of catching smugglers in eastern Scotland had not been very productive, at least as far as *Shark's* log records, but one of the reasons for withdrawing the ship, apart from its worn condition, was probably that smuggling had become less profitable than it had been. The government of William Pitt from 1784 onwards had embarked on a series of reforms to the old, encrusted, and outdated customs' duties regime, which involved reducing their complexity, disentangling the system, adjusting the relevance of the charges, and generally making it less expensive to import goods legally, and so in many cases it had become not worth the risk of being caught evading the law by smuggling. It also increased the government's tax-take from such duties, and therefore reduced the need for such patrols as *Shark* had been carrying out, and so had reduced government costs.[28]

Captain Edwards was more successful than most captains of *Sharks* in holding on to his crew. There is no record of any man deserting during his first two years (1783–1784) in command, though in the next year ten men ran at Leith on various occasions. Leith in fact was the destination of choice for deserters, probably because it was almost the only place the ship stayed at for any length of time in these years. When it returned to Sheerness, four men ran. But over the four and more years of Edwards' captaincy he only lost one man killed and twenty-eight to desertion, which was an unusually good record. No doubt the fact that it was peacetime and so none of the men had been impressed into the service, and so were all volunteers, had a strong effect on their willingness to remain.

One curiosity is that ten of the deserters went in the last year, when it must have been clear that the ship was soon to be taken out of service. One must suppose that the prospect of being discharged into another ship was repugnant, and the deserters were willing to sacrifice their pay for their freedom. It may also be a backhanded tribute to Edwards, if the prospect of another ship after his captaincy was one the men did not wish to endure.[29]

V

Shark, refitted, was brought back into service in July 1790. After a period of peace and recovery for all concerned, the international situation was again developing towards new crises in several areas, and the various naval powers in Europe had been building up their strength since the end of the American war. This included Britain, which flexed its naval muscles in that very year, 1790, in a crisis with Spain, the Nootka Sound crisis. In France, which had also revived its naval arm, just as had Spain, the crisis was internal, as the Revolution developed in several different and unexpected and dangerous directions. The Prime Minister William Pitt also got himself involved in a new crisis in 1791, the Ochakov crisis, in which he seemed intent on fighting Russia, another developing naval power. In the end he was dissuaded when the Empress Catherine simply ignored his threats, while the Admiralty insisted that it could not afford to fight the Russians, especially since, if Britain became involved in fighting in the Baltic and the Black Seas, this would very likely entice other naval powers to join in. France and Spain together had more line-of-battle ships than the Royal Navy; with Russian ships added the Royal Navy would be heavily outnumbered, as well as being divided and sent into the most distant and unknown seas.

It was thus at a time of increasing naval tension that *Shark* was brought back into service. The new captain was John Dilkes, a lieutenant since 1762, and a commander since 1782 (and so of the same vintage as the last four captains); he was promoted to captain not long after taking command and was thus replaced by George Brisac on 16 October, having commanded the ship for only three months.[30] Under Dilkes, who had taken command on 16 July, the ship was almost as comatose as it had been when laid up; it spent some time fitting out at Sheerness, then waited at the Nore for a week before going to Spithead, where it waited again for over a month, apart from a two-day visit to Weymouth. Captain Brisac, however, on 18 October, only the second day of his command, intercepted a Norway smack filled with contraband – geneva (i.e., gin), rum, brandy – and took it into Portsmouth to the Customs House.[31] It seems that some smugglers were not yet wholly deterred by lower profits.[32]

In November the ship was dispatched once again to the West Indies, leaving Spithead on 5 November and reaching Funchal in Madeira on the 20th. It sailed again on the 22nd and arrived at Barbados on 10 December. This was clearly a very fast ship, taking only five weeks from Portsmouth to Barbados.

It visited Grenada and then returned directly to Spithead. The purpose of this voyage is not stated, but it presumably concerned the end of the Spanish crisis, which was resolved in October when Spain backed down; had war broken out the Caribbean would have been a major theatre.

(On 30 December there occurs one of those curious entries in the log which emphasize the strange ironies and contradictions of navy life: three men were 'punished' – i.e., flogged – for 'drunkenness and riot'; the very next entry is that grog was then served to the crew.)

On its return to Spithead, *Shark* was given yet another new captain, the Hon. Arthur Kaye Legge. High family connections – he was of the family of the earls of Dartmouth – had presumably assisted a swift rise from lieutenant in 1789, and he was to be promoted to captain by February 1793;[33] it is also quite probable that such connections assisted him in gaining this new command, for active commands were fairly scarce in peacetime. Brisac had been *Shark's* captain for only nine months, and had seniority as a commander over Legge (twelve years seniority as a lieutenant and two months as a commander), though Legge gained his captaincy first (by two months).

Legge's term in *Shark* lasted until January 1793, twenty-two months, and then he was succeeded by Scory Barker, who commanded for much of the rest of 1793.[34] The ship was used throughout Legge's term, and well into Barker's, to patrol in the Channel;[35] it was in many ways a reprise of its work on the east coast of Scotland under Edwards, and that of *Shark* III in the western Channel, calling repeatedly at a series of ports, presumably on policing and anti-smuggling duties. The ship was based at Spithead at first, and patrolled along the coasts of Dorset, Devon, and Cornwall. Then its bases became Plymouth and Fowey, clearly concentrating on the Cornish smuggling problem, just as *Shark* III had – though the log does not record any interceptions or arrests, if there were any.

The Cornish coast patrol was varied by occasional visits outside the area, to Guernsey and Scilly, presumably on policing duties, but it called in at Plymouth six times and at Fowey four times between September 1791 and March 1792, and therefore it was working constantly through the winter. In April 1792 it also visited Milford Haven and Guernsey again. Patrolling the western part of the Channel continued until July, when the ship joined the fleet under Vice Admiral Sir Richard King at Spithead for a larger and more intimidatory patrol through *Shark's* area. After this display of naval power, directed no doubt at the French, who had become very belligerent, *Shark* stood guard at Weymouth through much of September as the royal family took a seaside holiday there, then it resumed its patrolling until January 1793 when Barker took over command. He then spent the first three months doing much the same as Legge.

VI

War broke out again between Britain and France in February 1793, just a few days after Barker took command. This may well not have been a coincidence, since it seems likely that he was a better seaman than Legge; certainly he had more experience since he had been a lieutenant since 1777, and a commander since 1787. On 17 February *Shark* captured a French brig, and Barker sent a lieutenant and five seamen on board to take the prize into Portsmouth; he also took at least some of the French crew on board *Shark* as prisoners. This provided a new experience, and a reminder that the Channel patrols were now much more dangerous; it was no longer a matter of intercepting smugglers, though they were the ship's prey as well as the French. And, of course, when the war began, the practice of gathering merchantmen into convoys, escorted by naval warships, was at once resumed. *Shark*, not surprisingly, was soon employed on such work.

The destination of the first convoy the ship escorted was Newfoundland, and this was to be the main station for *Shark* for much of the next five years. The convoy was gathered at Spithead, and after calling at Plymouth on 21 April, arrived at St John's, Newfoundland, on 27 May. *Shark* remained there until 11 June. The governor was Vice Admiral Sir Richard King, the former commander of the Channel Fleet. He had recently used the small sea power which was based at Newfoundland to seize control of St Pierre and Miquelon, two small French islands just south of Newfoundland, which could have provided a serious threat if they were to be used as a base by French privateers; this also prevented the French from fishing these rich seas.[36]

Shark was retained by Admiral King at Newfoundland for the summer. It patrolled along part of the south coast, no doubt searching for any French ships, warships or fishing craft, which may have arrived without realizing that the islands had been taken over. Nothing seems to have been found. The ship returned to St John's on 19 August and left next day for Britain. It arrived at Spithead on 3 September, having made the Atlantic crossing in just 14 days. This was taken note of in the Admiralty as something of a record.[37]

The casualty and desertion rates in this new period of *Shark's* career were substantially less than earlier, though no obvious explanation for this exists. Between 1790 and 1791, only one man died, at the hospital at Haslar, though thirty-five deserted, mostly at Portsmouth (twenty-two), but also at Madeira (three) and Barbados (seven), which is pretty smart work, by those who ran, considering the very short stays of the ship at both these ports.[38] In the last year and a half before the war began, when the ship was in the western Channel most of the time, no men died, and the deserters were few, ten in all only. This was the captaincy of Legge, who seems to have been able to hold his crew better than most, even though he called frequently at a whole series of small ports.[39]

A new captain was appointed on the ship's return, Commander John O'Bryen.[40] The ship was in and about Portsmouth and the Solent during October, and on 5 November was at Spithead collecting stores. It sailed on the 10th with a convoy across the Channel to Guernsey, and then on to Jersey, staying there until 21 December, returning by way of Torbay to Spithead early in January, where it stayed for the next four months. Another convoy was gathered for Newfoundland, but there was no point in sailing there until the summer, since ice would prevent ships reaching any part of the island. The convoy was at first under the command of Rear Admiral Sir James Wallace, but as it came to Southern Ireland it was scattered by a storm. The main part of the shipping went into Cork, but *Shark* and the ships with it took refuge in Waterford. It seems that then the two parts of the convoy remained separated. Finally on 19 June they got away once more, with *Shark's* ships reaching St John's on the 14 July – not a bad speed for a westward crossing by a group of merchant ships.[41] The winds in the North Atlantic are consistently westerly, and it was normal for ships to take the long route, south to Madeira and then west and north along the American coast. To Newfoundland from England, however, it was worth trying the direct route, and a voyage of four weeks was remarkably fast; this was the second of *Shark's* convoys to go quickly – the last had taken five weeks.[42] This time *Shark* was to remain at Newfoundland as a part of the regular naval squadron attached to the island.

Chapter 8

Shark VIII: a Gunvessel, 1794–1795

The absence of *Shark* VII in Newfoundland for several years in the 1790s was perhaps the reason the Admiralty used its name for another vessel, though in the event the new *Shark* (VIII) did not last long, though its brief history fits into the history of the 1790s all too well.

In the emergency of a new French war, which already by 1794 was becoming increasingly difficult, when the French revolutionary example was potent for badly paid, badly fed sailors, virtually enslaved in the ships, and commanded by captains and officers all too often disdainful of them, the great mutinies at Spithead and the Nore in 1797 were hardly a surprise – except to the Admiralty. There had been warnings enough. The unrest experienced in the Leeward Islands in *Shark* and other ships in the 1770s reappeared in home waters; Bligh's *Bounty* became notorious, and *Shark* VIII was one of the vessels where a successful mutiny took place, without any repercussions for any of the mutineers, so far as can be discerned.

Shark VIII was a 'Dutch hoy' bought by the Admiralty; it was an actual Dutch vessel, but this was also the term used to describe the English version of such a ship, used for various activities in the English Channel. It had a crew of thirty, was armed with three 32-pounder and one 24-pounder guns, and was commissioned in April 1794.[1] The first captain was Lieutenant Charles Burlton; from 30 March next year, it was commanded by another lieutenant, Titus Allardyce, whose experience of command began with this ship – he had been promoted to lieutenant in that month.[2]

The ship had been purchased in February 1794, and had been fitted out as a warship at Woolwich during April and May – it sailed on 25 May; it was 65ft long and 14ft wide, with its four guns.[3] It was classed as a gunvessel, though it was in fact about the size as the first three *Sharks*, which had all been better armed and manned. It was assigned in 1795 to the squadron of Captain Sir Sydney Smith, who was operating offensively in the Channel with a collection of frigates and small ships. In that year Smith decided to establish batteries on the St Marcouf Islands, not far from the mouth of the River Seine.[4] (This was the area where the first *Shark* had operated after the Battle of La Hougue almost exactly a century before.)

Smith's enterprise was part of the British naval blockade of the coasts of Normandy and Brittany. The planting of the batteries on the Marcouf Islands was presumably part of that work, though their position is unlikely to have done more than marginally restrict the seagoing activities of any French ships, rather than preventing it entirely; the impression one gets is that Smith ordered the process because he could do it, not because it was particularly useful for the war effort. The islands were in the Bay of La Hougue, more or less halfway between the estuary of the Vire and St Vaast la Hougue. Smith had put the crews of two or three small ships, including *Shark*, on the islands to build the batteries, and left the supervision of the work to a group of young lieutenants, including Allardyce. The sailors did not like the work, some of them seeing it inevitably as a holiday, and they lazed. One of the officers, Lieutenant Henry Hicks, was in command, being the senior lieutenant, assisted by Lieutenant John Elliot of the gunvessel *Piercer*. Both of these men had held that rank for many years, since 1780 and 1782 respectively; they were not the sort to get good work from the men.[5] Smith does not seem to have believed that a man of higher rank and more enterprise was needed. If so, he was clearly wrong. Smith himself seems to have stayed away, busy with other schemes more directly designed to enhance his reputation.

On the island Lieutenant Hicks reprimanded the boatswain of the *Piercer* for shirking his work, and for letting the men under him similarly laze. The boatswain, Shepherd, refused to obey Hicks' orders, on the ground that he was subject to Elliot's authority as a member of the crew of the *Piercer*. The argument developed into a confrontation between Shepherd and his men on one side, and three of the lieutenants on the other. In the end Shepherd was punished by twelve lashes, and another man with six, for defiance and insubordination. The relative lightness of the punishments implies that the lieutenants were seen to be largely at fault. Smith turned up to support the officers, as he was bound to do, but it seems that he was less than enthusiastic in the matter. It was, of course, in part his fault for not making the chain of command clear.

The only account we have which is close to the events comes from the pen of Lieutenant James Gomm, commander of the *Tickler*, who was one of the three officers who confronted Shepherd.[6] It is self-evidently partisan, as one would expect, effectively a complaint at his treatment in the aftermath of the later mutiny, and makes a clear suggestion of senior officers' protecting their own kind. A more distant account (in time, at least) by Sir John Barrow is also partisan, not surprisingly since he was writing a biography of Smith. It is noticeable that the whole episode is ignored in Smith's latest biography, even though the episode reveals a good deal about the man.[7] Smith is one of the heroes of the French Revolutionary War, and biographies of him are invariably laudatory; events not reflecting well on him are ignored, downplayed, or, in this case, omitted.

For the episode was not over. Shepherd complained about his treatment, and in such a convincing way that a court of enquiry was set up. Gomm complained that he and his fellow officers were given no opportunity to testify, nor to call witnesses, and it seems that the senior officers, Smith included, having been pushed into an enquiry, were keen to bury the whole affair. This implies that Shepherd had a good deal of popular support among the sailors, and perhaps among the officers. The lieutenants were sent to Britain and the men they hoped to call as witnesses were dispatched to distant stations and ships, or so Gomm complained. All the officers were superseded in their commands, and none of them seem ever to have served again, at least not in command. This included Allardyce of the *Shark*, whom Gomm comments had been wounded, though how is not stated – it cannot have been in the dispute with the men, since this would have called for a much more serious court martial. His command passed to another young lieutenant, John Watson.[8]

This episode is relevant to *Shark* because of what happened next. It is not clear how involved the men of *Shark* were in these events, though Allardyce certainly was, and no doubt the men got a more or less accurate account of them fairly quickly. It is obvious that discipline on the Marcouf battery site was poor, for whatever reasons. Smith himself must bear a good part of the blame (which must have coloured his recollections of everything), because he was the man who selected the officers to see to the work, and they were not competent. Dispersing the rebellious group of sailors into other ships and removing the incompetent officers would do little to improve matters, especially as the French revolutionaries were apparently succeeding in their war against the rest of Europe.

Shark's crew mutinied in December 1795, several months after the events which centred on Shepherd. It seems unlikely that the precise reasons for the mutiny were known at the time, for Gomm, who devotes a paragraph to it in his pamphlet, clearly did not know any details, and he was as likely as anyone to be in touch with the officers involved in it, and who were in the know. The crew overpowered the officers, Lieutenant Watson in particular, but this must also mean the boatswain, the gunner and the midshipman, if there was one on board. Gomm suggests as possible reasons either too lenient or too rigid discipline, demonstrating that he did not know anything about its precise causes. (He was no longer on the island at the time of the mutiny, but he did understand the problems in a general way – he was also writing after the great mutinies of 1797, which will have coloured his recollections.) But he also remarked that Marcouf was a place where a plot had been formed earlier to seize the boats at the island and presumably go to France. This is in fact what *Shark*'s mutineers did, having overthrown the officers; they sailed the ship to St Vaast la Hougue (ironically in view of the fighting there a century before, and *Shark* I's involvement in it). There they handed the ship and themselves over to the French authorities.

The single pay list of *Shark* VIII which survives records the services of the crew until late in August 1795. This is four months before the mutiny, of course, but the details may provide some insight into the crew's attitudes. Between the constitution of the crew in June 1794 and the compilation of the pay list over a year later, one man had died, and sixteen deserted – out of a complement of only thirty men. They had been leaving regularly since June, but the rate of desertion had certainly increased since Allardyce became commander on 30 March 1795. Before then eight men had run in the period June 1794 to March 1795 when the ship was at Sheerness; in April to July 1795, seven more left. The ship was at Portsmouth in October and November; no pay list survives for these months, but one would expect that more men will have run during that visit.[9]

This was clearly not a contented, willing crew. On the other hand, the desertion rate was scarcely worse than that experienced by any other *Shark* since the 1730s. It would be easy to blame Allardyce, who must certainly share some of the blame, but futile. It is in fact a reflection of the widespread discontent of the ordinary sailors in the Royal Navy by the 1790s, which only two years later blazed into the great strike at Spithead and the revolutionary mutiny at the Nore. The mutiny of *Shark* in 1795 was one more of several powerful indications of that discontent which the Admiralty and the government ignored.

None of the mutineers were ever discovered or punished. Their officer, John Watson, was not prosecuted, though he had lost his ship. He was back in Plymouth by April 1796, obviously speedily released by the French. He was employed again, but only rose above lieutenant when the war was over.[10]

Chapter 9

Shark VII: a Sloop, 1779–1818, Part Two: 1794–1818

I

The French navy became more active once a more or less settled government existed in France from 1794, and an active vessel such as *Shark* would be valued; Newfoundland and its fishery was always a French target. Almost at once after the ship reached Newfoundland on 1 July 1794, Captain O'Bryen was sent along the coast to the north of St John's, to Fogo and Temple Bay. Several 'islands of ice' were seen even at this late date – the term 'iceberg' was not yet current. The ship was back at St John's early in September, and remained in the harbour until November. It then spent the early winter of 1795/1796 patrolling the southern Newfoundland coast, then remained over the winter at Ferryland, south of St John's.[1] It sailed into St John's harbour on 15 April, and a week later to Halifax, Nova Scotia, where its copper sheathing was repaired. This had been damaged by the ice during the winter, and part of it had become detached.

The ship was back at St John's in the middle of June, when the harbour was clear of ice, and then spent the next month along the southern coast once more, calling at Trepassy, Capelin Bay, and Aquafort. This was the area where foreign fishermen were liable to operate, and it was both French (enemies) and Americans (illegally present) who were being watched for. A rumour was heard of five French frigates off the coast, and after a call at St John's to report this, the ship was sent off to Halifax on 26 July (taking no less than eighteen days for the journey) and then on to report to Admiral George Murray, who commanded a squadron of ships off the Virginian Capes. *Shark* stayed with him only one day, so it was presumably delivering the message about the French frigates. By way of Halifax it was back at St John's on 21 September.

It turned out that the rumour of the French frigates had been true, though there were actually seven ships in the squadron, and while *Shark* had been away delivering the messages at Halifax and to Admiral Murray, that French squadron, under Admiral Richery, had menaced St John's. A good deal of preparation for local defence had already been made since the war began, and, as the French hung about indecisively outside the Narrows which are the entrance into St John's harbour, the local militia were assembled and posted on Signal Hill above the Narrows, in full view of the French ships, furnaces were lit to heat the shot, the great chain across the Narrows was raised and fastened, and three schooners were prepared as fireships for use when the French ships hopefully collided with that chain.

All this preparation was clearly obvious to the French – and was intended to be – and Admiral Richery decided that St John's was far too dangerous a place to attack. The preparations were thus successful. Instead Richery took his ships south to Bay Bulls, where they landed and burnt the town, captured a couple of small merchant ships, and then destroyed what structures remained on St Pierre to deprive the British of the use of the island.[2] No doubt when *Shark* returned the crew heard excited accounts of the matter. Apart from the schooner-fireships, the ships in the harbour had not been used; there were only two present at the time, a 50-gun ship and a frigate. *Shark* could hardly have contributed much to the defence had it been present.

Another local cruise followed, and *Shark* was back at St John's again on 12 October. In December it was at Halifax once more, and wintered there until May of 1797. The damage caused by the ice the previous year had no doubt persuaded the Newfoundland governor to agree to this. (And all governors of Newfoundland themselves went back to Britain for the winter, spending little more than three or four months of the summer on the island; quite possibly Captain O'Bryen took the decision to over-winter at Halifax himself.)

O'Bryen had been promoted to captain during the summer, and was replaced later in 1797 by Frederick Warren,[3] himself newly promoted to commander, who took over on *Shark* on 1 September.[4] By that time the large frigate *Latona* (32) at St John's had suffered a mutiny in imitation of those at Spithead and the Nore earlier in the year. It was put down by the firm resistance of the officers, swords in hand, and the marines with fixed bayonets – and by the determination of the governor, Vice Admiral William Waldegrave, Lord Radstock, who promised to burn the ship, crew and officers and all, if the mutiny continued.[5]

Back at St John's by 11 August, *Shark* escorted a convoy to Sydney, on Cape Breton Island, and a month later, with Warren in command, it brought another convoy back – Newfoundland relied on imports of such necessities as flour, especially for the long winters. That the British were convoying ships between these two nearby colonies suggests that the French naval threat was still potent. One of the major annual maritime events at Newfoundland was the dispatch of a series of convoys in the late autumn, to Britain and to Portugal, carrying preserved fish for sale particularly in southern Europe. (*Shark* IV while at Gibraltar had captured some French ships on this trading run fifty years before.) By 1797 both France and Spain were hostile, and France controlled much of Italy, so the ships could not bring their fish, which was deemed a necessity in the Catholic lands, directly to those countries. But Lisbon was available as a trans-shipping port, so more than one convoy headed for Lisbon every autumn, whence the fish could be sold on to other destinations. *Shark* took one of these convoys south in October as far as the Portuguese island of Fayal in the Azores, though it then had to return north for the winter, which this year meant spending no less than seven months locked in the ice of St John's harbour, from 7 December 1797 to 1 June 1798.

Released at last on 1 June the ship set off on a voyage circumnavigating the island, calling at a series of outposts on the south coast – Trepassey, St Mary's, Placentia. The main problem of illegal fishing, however, was in the western ports, which such ships as *Shark* rarely reached. There was evidence of illicit American fishing in these seas, and of illegal trading by the Newfoundlanders with the American ships. When caught the Americans were to be removed or deterred. At St George's the American schooner *Deborah of Chatham* was seized for 'illicit trading', and sent to St John's. *Shark* then sailed on through the Strait of Belleisle and then east northabout, calling at Trinity and then St John's. The voyage took almost two months, and afterwards the ship stayed in St John's for another month.

Shark sailed again on 1 September, and a week later it joined with *Latona*, no longer mutinous, in chasing an American ship suspected of illegal trading. *Latona* fired on the chase, but it was *Shark's* carpenter who went across to make good the damage. (The ship does not seem to have been detained.) This cruise lasted a month and then the ship returned to St John's on 21 October. On the 23rd it was sent back to Britain, where it arrived at Plymouth on 20 November. It then staged slowly up the Channel, staying for two weeks at Plymouth, two at Spithead, and on 24 December it finally reached Sheerness; there it was paid off, and remained to refit and repair the ravages of several years in the harsh northern waters and winters.

The years in and about Newfoundland had been less expensive in manpower than those in the West Indies, but still plenty of men had escaped. Eight had died, four of them drowned, one at Halifax and three at St John's. Halifax and St John's had also been the main places where men had deserted, not surprisingly, for these were the only sizeable places where the ship had called. Four ran at Halifax, but St John's received twenty-one men; one ran at Ferryland, and one at Burin. Otherwise Portsmouth, Torbay and Yarmouth were the usual destinations in Britain (fifteen men) and two at Lymington.[6]

St John's was a small community, largely of fishermen and men associated with that trade, most of whom knew each other, so the deserters must have been sheltered locally – they could also get civilian jobs if they could escape being caught by the navy. When the captains or the governor began a periodic search for deserters they generally found one or two men who were careless, but it was always difficult to persuade the locals to surrender them. After all, apart from a natural sympathy for pressed men, skilled sailors were a prime necessity in Newfoundland.

II

Shark returned to service in August 1799, with a new captain, Philip Broke, who was to become one of the star frigate captains of the age. He had risen quickly, lieutenant in 1797, commander in January 1799 (and captain in 1801), this time mainly through ability, though good connections certainly helped.[7] His obsession was gunnery, and this shows in the log of *Shark*, as in other ships where he had authority. (It was the superb gunnery training he had given his men in *Shannon* which brought the defeat of *Chesapeake* in a quarter of an hour in 1812.)[8]

He had little opportunity to shine, except for practice and drill, in *Shark*. Broke and his ship waited for three months in and around the Thames Estuary before being sent on a clear mission. Broke took command on 21 August 1799, but then there was the usual fitting out, storing and checking which was always necessary with a new crew or a revived ship. It was not until 9 December that the ship left Sheerness, and then it was in Yarmouth Roads or the Swin, for over a month, and in the Downs until 6 February 1800. Finally on that day the ship began to escort a convoy west along the Channel. Off the Isle of Wight Broke stopped a cartel ship carrying French colours, and took out seven English prisoners, who clearly should not have been held there.[9]

Shark returned to Yarmouth Roads by 17 February, then went north to Flamborough and the Humber. In all this time Broke had exercised his crew at the 'great guns' in the ship at least seven times, which is six times more than other captains had done, and he went on with such exercises as long as he was in command. *Shark's* task off the Yorkshire coast was to receive the Baltic convoys which set off from British waters from that area, and to protect them across the North Sea; the returnees arrived there from the Baltic and Hamburg, and divided into those going south to London and the south coast, and north to Newcastle and Leith; escorts were therefore needed for these coastal voyages; similarly those heading east for Germany and the Baltic arrived from several ports of origin along the east coast, and gathered off Flamborough Head for the North Sea crossing; these were vulnerable on their way while in small groups. At times, as on 7 May, *Shark* might escort the southward convoy. These convoys were sometimes enormous, several hundred ships. The Baltic trade in naval stores was vital to the navy, and to shipbuilding generally, and food supplies from Germany and Poland were important when British harvests were poor. In the summer, when the Baltic was open, the outgoing convoys were escorted across the North Sea; the returning group came out of the Baltic in the autumn, so long as the sea was open; convoys for Germany were more frequent.

On 16 May *Shark* was off the Dutch coast, and stayed in the area of Goree at the mouth of the Scheldt for a fortnight. This was, as in the time of *Shark* IV in the 1740s, a danger point, since the whole of the continental North Sea coast was under French control or influence, and might be a source of invasion forces, or of privateers or raiding squadrons. The opposite, of course, had also happened, with the unsuccessful British-Russian invasion of the Netherlands during 1799.

Shark was back at the White Booth Roads in the Humber by 30 May and a fortnight later it escorted a convoy outwards. It sailed east again on 20 June from the British coast, and was off Heligoland on the 22nd, and collected a return convoy on 7 July. This was escorted as far as Yarmouth, and on to the Nore. A return convoy was gathered at Yarmouth in August and *Shark*, with *Lynx*, another sloop, sailed for the Baltic on the 16th. That a convoy of forty-eight ships could be protected by just two sloops on a voyage across the North Sea is a signal of the overwhelming power of British navy at the time.[10]

No captain's log exists for the latter part of Broke's captaincy, but from the master's log the career of the ship can be equally well followed. The voyage to the entrance of the Baltic in the late summer of 1800 was slow. It was not until 3 September that the Skaw, the northern tip of Denmark, was seen, and it then took another week to reached Elsinore (where one man drowned and another deserted). The return voyage went to the Firth of Forth, and took as long as the outward journey, finally arriving at Yarmouth on 1 October, having sailed slowly south from the Isle of May in the firth over several days.[11]

There followed another series of voyages between Yarmouth and the Dutch coast, where *Shark* was part of the naval blockade of enemy coasts. Only one notable incident merited recording in the log, the interception of a ship sailing from the Russian White Sea port of Archangel to Portugal with a cargo of wood; it was sent in for examination and adjudication; it may have broken Britain's blockade rules, but at the time Britain was annoyed with Russia because of the revival of the idea of an Armed Neutrality among the northern powers, and the harassment of Russian shipping was a way of conducting the dispute.

A later voyage illustrated another aspect of Britain's war effort. *Shark* took on board twenty casks of specie at Yarmouth and carried them to Cuxhaven, where they were unloaded on to a cutter, *Swinger*.[12] This was to be a subsidy for an ally in the greater war, but the cutter failed to deliver it. In the time covered by the voyage from Britain to Cuxhaven, Prussia had turned hostile and had moved troops in to occupy the electorate of Hanover, of which King George III was elector. The subsidy was probably for the Hanoverian government, to enable it to continue resistance. The cutter therefore kept hold of the casks of specie and with *Shark* it collected a convoy and aimed to return to Britain. It took some time to get out of the estuary, due to a build-up of ice, but when the convoy sailed it reached Orfordness within three days. The contrast with the Baltic convoy's slow crossing the year before is very marked.

At Yarmouth, Broke, who had been promoted to captain on 14 February, was superseded in *Shark* by Commander James Carthew.[13] By 4 March the ship was crossing as before to the Dutch coast.[14] On 30 March it was sent to Cuxhaven again, perhaps delivering a convoy to that port, or to the Danish ports of Wusum or Tonning on the Schleswig coast, but its main task was to collect Prince Adolphus and a party of fourteen men or more, who were leaving Hanover in the wake of the Prussian invasion.[15] Carthew dutifully carried the men back to Britain, but later complained of being considerably out of pocket as a result of having to feed so many men. The prince and his party were landed at Yarmouth on 15 April.[16] The ship then sailed south to the Nore. Another crisis was brewing in the north, between Britain and Denmark, and the waters around Denmark were not safe for small ships; the crisis led in the end to the destruction of the Danish fleet at Copenhagen in 1801.

III

Shark now sailed west along the Channel, collecting a new convoy on 19 June at Falmouth, having replenished at Spithead. The destination of this convoy was the West Indies, but this time it was Jamaica, not the Windward or Leeward Islands. The voyage was relatively slow, at least by *Shark's* standards, but Jamaica was reached by early August by way of stops at Madeira and (British occupied) Martinique. It stayed at Port Royal (Jamaica) for only a week before escorting another convoy back towards Britain, beginning on 27 August.

The route, for a change, avoided the Windward Passage, and went westabout round Cuba, passing the Isle of Pines and Cape San Antonio (Cuba's western point) and so taking advantage of the strong eastward current. The log mentions the Loggerhead Keys, in the Dry Tortugas, so the convoy was kept well away from Spanish temptation out of Cuba. The ship had apparently been ordered to return to Port Royal by 16 September, but it went on through the Bahamas, passing Bimini – and so using the strong northward Bahama current – and then cutting east through the islands as far as Harbour Island, at which point it released the convoy, and turned back for Jamaica, arriving at Port Royal on 15 October.

In December (1801) the ship acquired another new captain, Carthew having been promoted to captain in June (he received command of the *Crescent* frigate). He was succeeded by James Johnstone, still only a lieutenant, who was eventually promoted to commander in August 1802.[17] He read himself in as the new captain of *Shark* on 29 December.[18]

There is a gap of three months (October to December) between the end of Carthew's log and Johnstone's assumption of command, but the ship was at Port Royal on both dates, and it may be assumed that it remained there under the command of a lieutenant or the ship's master until a new captain was found. That Johnstone was only a lieutenant when he was appointed suggests a possible shortage of suitable candidates in Jamaica – and Johnstone turned out to be only moderately successful as a commander.

By this time peace had been agreed between Britain and France, which was now under the dictatorship of Napoleon Bonaparte; neither party expected the peace to last, and both manoeuvred to secure useful positions, political, military, and naval, in preparation for the next war. In Britain a new First Lord of the Admiralty, Lord St Vincent, came into office with the fixed notion that the administration, and in particular the dockyard administration, was corrupt to the core. He was not entirely wrong, but his remedy was disastrous, and it brought the Royal Navy to a disorganized and much weakened condition. This, however, was not very dangerous in Jamaica, though the dockyard there was scarcely efficient – it used slaves, of course, just as did the English Harbour dockyard in Antigua, and such labour was never efficient, though relatively cheap. And cheapness was St Vincent's overriding goal.

Shark under Johnstone sailed from Port Royal on 2 January 1802. He complained in the log that the purser was absent without leave, and he had to sail without him. Johnstone had been given a diplomatic task, concerning the Mosquito Indians of Honduras, who were allied with the British. Their King George II had been assassinated in November or thereabouts, and their weaponry had been plundered. They wanted new supplies, which the British were willing to supply, but this might annoy the Spaniards, who had been behind the killing and the theft. So a flag of truce was sent to the Spanish governor of Panama, and he came on board *Shark* on 9 February for discussions. The ship was then at 'St Andrews' – San Andres Island in the Gulf of Panama. (Three men deserted there.)

Shark then sailed past Porto Bello, and on north along the Central American coast. It was back in Port Royal on 12 February, and the Jamaican governor, George Nugent, received a new letter from the Mosquitos with a detailed appeal, dated 2 February, which had presumably been collected by Johnstone.[19]

There was some indiscipline on the ships at Port Royal, and ten men were accused of mutiny on the *Syren* frigate.[20] On 27–28 February five of these men were hanged on *Syren*; early in March one of the men from *Syren* was pardoned, but another was flogged round the fleet. (Three men were perhaps acquitted.) On 11 March *Shark* sailed on a coastal voyage along the north coast of Jamaica – Port Antonio, St Anne's, and on to Lucea and Montego Bay, stopping at each small port in turn, sometimes more than once. This turned out to be too tempting for many in the crew.

Johnstone had already had three men desert at San Andres Island on 15 February, during the voyage to Central America. Now on this cruise he lost men at almost every port: eight at St Anne's on three different occasions during an eight-day visit, two at Falmouth, two at Lucea, one more at St Anne's on a second visit, two at Montego Bay. These desertions more or less ceased when the ship returned to Port Royal, or at least they were no longer recorded in the log. But the dockyard and port at Port Royal were well-guarded and much more difficult to escape from, which is no doubt why the deserters chose to leave the ship elsewhere.

A second voyage to the north coast occupied June, and then another week was spent at Port Royal, replenishing. The ship sailed again on 16 July, and ten days later was in the Windward Passage. It was still at sea on 15 August when it was caught in a hurricane. The ship was 'closed all in a violent storm and very heavy sea, the ship sending very deep and shipping a great quantity of water, under bare poles and hatches battened down'. The log supplies a strange position, suggesting that the ship had been driven into the mid-Atlantic; this was perhaps calculated by dead reckoning at the end of the storm, and it certainly took the ship ten more days to reach Barbados, where it took in fresh water, no doubt needed after such an ordeal. The ship was in a good enough condition, however, to sail next day, by way of Curacao, reaching Port Royal on 5 September. Johnstone may have been particularly bad at man-management – witness all those desertions, but he had succeeded in preserving his ship through a terrific storm. The hurricane had stuck somewhere north of Hispaniola, so far as can be seen, so ending at Barbados implies that the ship was driven a long way out of its course, and certainly into the Atlantic.

Johnstone was replaced next day by another captain, Samuel Herring, who had been promoted to commander in May.[21] (Johnstone had reached that rank in August.) On 17 September the ship sailed again, through the Windward Passage once more, to the Bahamas, reaching New Providence Island on the 30th. It stayed there for ten weeks.[22]

The Bahamas had changed since previous *Sharks* had visited the islands and patrolled in the archipelago. The islands' record in the American war had been ambiguous, to say the least, but, except for the brief Spanish occupation in 1782, and an American raid for arms in 1776, they had remained under British control, though busy with clandestine trade with the rebels, as they had done in previous years. As a result they provided a refuge for American loyalists who had no wish to be subject to the new republican regime (operated by their political enemies, who were vengeful), and it had been a loyalist expedition from Florida which had helped recapture Nassau from the Spaniards in 1782. To the population of about 3,000 which had lived there in 1775, 8,000 loyalists were added after 1783, mainly from the southern states, and they brought their slaves with them. They spread out from Nassau, establishing plantations and finally planting permanent settlements in the out islands.[23]

The larger population and the plantation system both encouraged more trade, still mainly with North America (to the annoyance of the loyalists), and rendered the islands at last definitively British. With a new substantial population they had become important enough to be worth defending, but at the same time the islands now also required more policing. This was no doubt one of the reasons for the presence of *Shark*, and while it was there a detachment of the 7th Regiment of Foot arrived in transports from Halifax. (The peace with France had permitted French forces to be sent to reconquer St Domingue from the ex-slaves; should they succeed the French presence would pose a standing threat to the British islands; reinforcing the region was a sensible precaution.) The new United States was equally concerned, and President Jefferson had a diplomatic delegation at Paris hoping to acquire Louisiana (which was now French again).[24] There also arrived at Nassau American ships with goods – one from Africa with slaves, and two from the United States, both claiming to be in distress, though this may have been a ruse to get into the harbour to conduct some illicit trade. (This was the same problem that *Shark* had been combatting in Newfoundland.)

Another contact with the continent was the arrival of blacks, apparently from Florida, who were escaping slavery. This was the beginning of a large movement which became more important when Florida was seized by the United States from Spain later. Probably the refugees were originally from the southern states, and had escaped into Florida (returned to Spain in 1783) where slavery was illegal. So the Bahamas were receiving British loyalists and their slaves, plus escaped slaves, all from the land which had rebelled from Britain in the name of liberty.

On 12 December *Shark* sailed from Nassau (having buried two sailors and left three deserters there), and went on a cruise through the out islands – Catt, Watling, Crooked, Inagua – and stayed briefly at Crooked Island to repair a sail. At Grand Caicos provisions were sent onshore for the inhabitants. The Turks and Caicos were another set of islands where American loyalists had settled, but their annexation to the Bahamian government in 1799 was unpopular. This was exactly the sort of imperial situation where the presence of a Royal Navy ship like *Shark* might help to reduce local tensions. A visit to the Turks Islands followed.

The ship returned to Jamaica on 5 January 1803. After receiving supplies it embarked a detachment of the 60th Foot at Port Royal and transported the men to Port Antonio on the north coast. Jamaican society was a curious mixture of a small number of whites, large numbers of black slaves, some free blacks, and a resistant group of escaped slaves and their descendants who had successfully defended their freedom several times against colonial militias and imperial forces over the past three quarters of a century. These Maroons, as they were called, were scattered in village communities through the mountainous centre of the island, and some of these were not far from Port Antonio. Governor Nugent visited one of these communities in 1803; the visit ended with a display of their war exercise: 'their military manoeuvres seemed to consist entirely of ambuscades.'[25] The Maroons were clearly able to make a politico-military point to the governor. (It had been ancestors of this people who had raided the Port Antonio area back in the 1730s, in the time of *Shark* III, incidents which were the beginning of the First Maroon War.)

In 1802/1803 the island was at peace, if briefly, but not far off there was the great French expedition aimed at reconquering the French sugar colony of St Domingue (modern Haiti). The slaves in that colony had freed themselves during the confusion of the Revolution, and vigorously resisted re-enslavement. The French army Bonaparte had sent was busy dying of yellow fever, and many of the healthy soldiers presented easy targets for the rebels. This hideous war, which left the colony in complete ruin, since both sides practised scorched earth tactics and massacres, could not avoid having repercussions in the British slave colonies elsewhere in the West Indies.[26] The Jamaicans feared the result whatever happened. If the French conquered, there would be a great and victorious French army menacingly close, which would be available for conducting conquests when (not if) a new Anglo-French war began. If the blacks won, there would be a grand black army of former slaves close by to act as an inspiration for the Jamaican Maroons and their still enslaved fellows on the plantations.

Shark went on from its task on the north coast of Jamaica to a cruise through the Windward Passage, close to St Domingue, no doubt collecting information about the French intentions and fortunes, and the black successes. Its destination was again Grand Caicos, Crooked Island, and Turks Island, all of which might be considered vulnerable to a French attack or a campaign of black liberation. In the middle of February 1803 it came back the same way, passing close to Cape St Nicolas Mole, arriving at Port Royal on the 20th. A week later *Shark* was cruising round the west of Jamaica, then along the north coast once more. It was at Montego Bay on 3 March, and at Port Antonio on the 7th – the governor was visiting Port Antonio at the time – and eventually it returned to Port Royal early in May.

The next voyage was to Belize to collect a convoy. This was another colony over which some central control was now being exerted for the first time. It had been formally constituted as a British colony only in 1798, and was under intermittent pressure from the Spaniards in much the same way as the Mosquito Indians in the same region. But it was a major producer of mahogany, which was presumably the main part of the cargo of *Shark*'s convoy. The ship stayed in local waters for five weeks, no doubt waiting for the ships to be loaded and the convoy to be assembled. During *Shark's* time at Belize Captain Herring died, on 9 June. The command was taken over by 'T M' who brought the convoy out through the Yucatan Passage and then east past Cuba.[27]

The ship was there caught yet again in a 'great storm', on 27 August, in much the same position as the year before. There was enough warning to get the hatches battened down and the crew called up on deck, but when the storm struck, the three topmasts had to be cut away, the sails were taken in or were blown out, and the ship 'strained' a great deal. The guns, and even the quarterdeck, were thrown over the side, while the ship laboured and shipped great quantities of water, and began leaking badly.

Nevertheless, *Shark* survived this storm as it had the one the year before. It was not until 30 August that repairs could be got under way, mainly by pumping the ship out and repairing the destroyed rigging. What had happened to the convoy is not noted, but the ships were either sunk or scattered. *Shark* turned south through the Windward Passage, heading for refuge and repair at Jamaica. It was fired at by a schooner on the way, no doubt sensing an easy prey as an obviously damaged ship, but the attack was not followed through. The ship reached Port Royal on 9 September, and went into the dockyard for repairs to be made.

In this last year in the West Indies three men of the crew had died (including the two at Nassau and the captain at Belize); forty-four men had deserted, at just about every port the ship had visited: three had run at Belize (good timing, in view of the hurricane), three at Nassau, and in Jamaica men had left the ship at St Anne's, Morant Bay, Montego Bay, Falmouth, Port Antonio, Lucea, and Port Royal, just as in Johnstone's captaincy. One had even left at Madeira on the way across the Atlantic. Most of these men had escaped the hurricane, but their absence must have made the task of the remaining crew much more difficult.[28]

Shark may have returned to port, and been repaired, but it seems very much as though this second storm-battering within a year had imposed too much strain on the ship's condition. So far as can be seen the ship never again left Port Royal harbour, once its essential repairs had been made in 1803–1804. It remained moored in Port Royal harbour for the next fourteen years. It was used successively and sometimes concurrently as an office, as a prisoner hulk, and as a convalescent ship for men sent across from the Port Royal hospital, sailors who had recovered from injury or illness, and whom the navy did not want to get away. Only once in that time, right at the end of its life, did it move with any purpose, and this move brought its death.

This was not the ship's intended future, of course. When it arrived back in Port Royal from its latest fight with a hurricane, it had to be repaired first of all. This took several months. The log of Captain Herring was continued by his temporary replacement, but it ends in August or September 1803, and the next captain's log, that of John Ayscough, begins on 1 February 1804, when he took command.[29] By that time the repairs had been accomplished, but it had clearly been decided that the ship could not be risked at sea any more. The unfortunate crew were then set to oakum-picking, perhaps the least welcome of all the navy's many unpleasant tasks.[30]

One of the main reasons for avoiding sending the ship to sea was no doubt the outbreak of a new French war. The news arrived at Jamaica by way of the *Hunter* brig-sloop in June 1803.[31] The current commander-in-chief, Vice Admiral Sir John Duckworth, used *Shark* as a headquarters vessel, so enabling him to put his more seaworthy ships to sea.

The long agony of St Domingue was coming to an end, assisted by the inability of the French to send any more troops, thanks to the renewed British command of much of the sea. The victory of the blacks and the dying of the French continued throughout 1803 and into the next year, and a new war meant that the French in the island whose struggle had been viewed with such mixed feelings in Jamaica, were now clearly an enemy. The British sugar planters were pleased to see the destruction of their most productive competitor, as well as the elimination of a great military threat, but at the same time they were horrified by the victory of the former slaves. It was obviously necessary for as many of Duckworth's ships to be at sea as possible. In 1805 the French finally evacuated their lost colony, leaving it almost completely devastated. The British received the refugee soldiers – the few who still lived – as prisoners of war. Some of the soldiers were interned on *Shark* when they came to Jamaica.

Almost the final blow to French power in the Caribbean for the next decade came in February 1806 when Duckworth, then commanding a squadron off

Spain, pursued a French squadron across the Atlantic (against orders) and destroyed it off the coast of San Domingo (the Spanish half of the island). He brought his ships and his captures to Jamaica for repairs; the colonial assembly gave him £3,000 in recognition of the relief they felt.

IV

There can, in the circumstances, be little more to say about *Shark* VII. Ships are meant to sail, and if one is moored in a harbour permanently, it has in effect ceased to be a ship. *Shark* received a new captain on average every five months during its last years, from 1804 to 1818.[32] It was evidently being used to assist some men one stage up the promotion ladder, and in others to employ aged lieutenants at a loose end. Some of these men held the office for less than a month; on the other hand, two men were its captain twice[33] and two men three times.[34] Many of the captains had been lieutenants for ten years or more, and rose to commander on being appointed to *Shark* – perhaps their gratitude for their promotion outweighed the boredom of the job, at least for a time.

The sheer tedium of a job in command of a stationary ship in what had become a backwater post is evident in the captains' logs, all of which, without exception, consist of scarcely more than two lines for each day, with the briefest of notations of weather, and the occasional notice of another ship's arrival in the harbour. Nevertheless, even with no action to allow an officer to distinguish himself or to catch the eye of a senior officer, four of these men eventually rose to become admirals, though hardly as a consequence of their captaincy of this ship;[35] at the same time, one got himself murdered,[36] and another was killed in action later.[37]

The complement of the ship had been reduced to seventy men, though what they had to do is something of a mystery, and the crew was rarely at full strength. Desertion was a constant problem, no doubt partly because of boredom and partly because it was relatively easy to run with the ship so static, and probably with officers who were less than officious or attentive. Death was also a constant presence, both from the unhealthy Jamaican climate and from the fact that the ship was populated in large part by convalescent sailors. In a pay list dated 1813 ten men are noted to have died, and eight had been sent to the naval hospital – almost certainly a virtual sentence of death in itself; nineteen men deserted 'from duty' – that is, directly from the ship – and ten more from other opportunities. In the last two years of the ship's existence, under the last captain, fifteen men deserted from a variety of opportunities. This smaller number is perhaps because the complement had been allowed to run down – it was peacetime by this time and so there were fewer men to fall ill and have accidents. In February 1818, at the end, only sixteen men were left to be discharged.[38]

In that 1813 pay list a particularly assiduous clerk made a point of recording the origins of all the supernumeraries on the ship – that is, the patients. They were convalescent, or had been discharged from other ships whose captains found them annoying or insolent or inefficient or stupid – some appeared three or four times in *Shark*'s list; the list provides a small window into the composition of the British navy at the end of the Napoleonic War.

Their origins were tremendously varied. The largest number were from the British Isles, of course, as one would expect, but they amounted to only half of the eighty men listed. The rest came from Africa (six men), various West Indian islands (Dutch, French and British – fifteen), several European countries (Germany, France, Sweden, Denmark, Holland – eleven), and from North America (five); one was from India. (It is worth noting that in 1813, all the European states mentioned, except Sweden, the Dutch and French islands, and the United States, were active British enemies.) The sea and the navy was, as is shown in every similar list of this period, an international place and institution, and the Royal Navy accepted recruits from anywhere, though this particular list does seem to emphasize this aspect more than usually.

There were only two events which stirred the somnolence of *Shark* in that last decade and a half. In 1815 the crew of the ship helped put out a fire – along with the crews of two other ships – which threatened to destroy the whole dockyard, or so it was said afterwards.[39] (True to their kind until the end, in the last two years of its life, fifteen of *Shark*'s men had deserted, four of the patients had died, and even three of the patients had 'run'.)

The end came in 1818, as, of course, it had to. The deterioration of the ship's condition will have been obvious to any captain with any knowledge of ships. The captain at the time was Lieutenant Charles Newham Hunter, who had been at that rank for twelve years, but, more to the point, he had been captain of *Shark* on and off three times over the past two years. He therefore knew the ship well enough. It had suffered from leaks, probably constantly, since the damage caused by the hurricane on 1804, and on 11 June 1818, it was realized that the inflow of water through a leak, or leaks, had suddenly greatly increased – or perhaps the increase had just been noticed. The pumps were operated but the water could not be cleared, though the rise seems to have been contained. Nor could the leak itself be located; there were in fact probably several.

Next day the water was again rising, despite the pumping, and Hunter asked the port admiral for help. He was ordered to sail the ship into shallow water – though 'sailing' was something the ship could no longer do. In effect, the ship was dragged into the shallow water by cables anchored on land, and brought to anchor in water two fathoms deep, its keel resting on the muddy bottom; this was the last 'voyage' of the old ship. The pumps made no progress, indeed the reverse, and the ship slowly settled into the mud. Next day, 13 June, the weight of the ship on the cables attaching it to the shore pulled the cables out and the shore down, and the ship canted off to starboard. It finally fell over onto its side, filled with water, and sank. The remains were fished up in pieces, and those worth selling were sold.[40]

Interlude, 1818–1894

With the sinking of *Shark* VII at Port Royal in 1818, the sequence which had begun in 1691 was broken, apparently decisively. There had been times, fairly lengthy in some cases – over twenty years between IV and V – when there had been no ship called *Shark* in the Royal Navy (and two occasions when there had been more than one simultaneously), but after 1818, there were no *Sharks* for nearly eighty years. At the end of that interlude, the new *Sharks* were of a different type, and had very different fates.

It is therefore worth halting at this point, just as the Navy did in its production of *Sharks*, to consider what these ships had done, what use they were, and whether they had fulfilled their purposes. They were all, after all, small vessels, the sort, as I suggested in the introduction, which are generally disregarded in naval histories, unless they get in the way of the greater ships, or arrive inadvertently in the midst of greater events. And yet the navy concentrated a large fraction of its resources in building and using these ships. It seems unlikely that the practitioners of sea power were wrong in this, even if the historians do not appreciate the sea dogs' priorities. It was Nelson, after all, who was insistent that he needed frigates and more frigates, and in that he would undoubtedly have included sloops and even smaller vessels if he could have been given them. He did not want them as fighting vessels, though frigates could be tough; he needed these smaller ships for their speed, and as reconnaissance ships, and this is how the first *Sharks* were often used, though this was not their only use, for they were very versatile.

The eight *Sharks* so far considered were generally classified as sloops or thereabouts; the only one of them which was bigger than a sloop sank almost at once, and the one smaller than a sloop was carried by its deserting crew to the enemy. The use to which these vessels were put was more or less constant from 1691 to 1803: primarily they were convoy escorts in wartime, but this varied with episodes of intelligence gathering, and carrying messages. In peacetime, when they were not simply sold off at the end of their useful lives, they were as often as not used to combat smuggling. Their small size was an advantage here: they were perhaps less threatening than a larger ship, and certainly less obvious, and so they might be forgotten by the smugglers (though this seems unlikely), but they were also nimble in competent hands, their shallow draught meant they could follow smugglers' ships and boats close to the shore, and at the very least they could be a deterrent. Their employment as coastal patrollers in the two Jacobite rebellions was a very similar activity to the anti-smuggling patrols; the work of *Shark* VII at Newfoundland was of much the same type. Other uses included repetitive patrolling, particularly in the West Indian islands, but this might be classified as the same work as their anti-smuggling activities in Britain, with the added spice of menacing a peacetime enemy, particularly Spain.

Their employment alongside of, or as a part of, greater fleets is one which is conspicuous by its absence in these ships. The first *Shark* was certainly used by a series of admirals in command of larger forces, but it was because the ship was nimble and was a relatively small target for the enemy that Benbow and Shovell used it. *Shark* V's reconfiguration as *Salamander*, and *Shark* VI briefly, were with Rodney and Graves in the American fighting, but neither was seriously involved in any fighting. Standing in the line of battle was not their function.

A further, and less regarded purpose of these small ships may also be noted: they were repeatedly commanded by men who very quickly ascended the promotion ladder to captain. Especially in wartime it was very unusual for a man to command any *Shark* for much more than a year. In peacetime, however, it was normal for a man to command for several years at a stretch – Symonds in IV in the 1730s and Edwards in VII in the 1780s are examples. Thus the ships were being used in many cases as practice-commands, to weed out men who were destined for later and higher commands (and discard those not considered competent) – and several of the ships' captains did in fact rise to admiral rank, if they survived, though many of these did so simply by having reached post-rank and then lived on.

It may therefore be said that ships such as the successive *Sharks* were generally valued for the variety of the tasks they could perform – unlike a line-of-battle ship, for instance, which had really only one function – and for which their design, speed and relative cheapness fitted them. They were armed, to be sure, but only very rarely indulged in any fighting. The reaction of Captain McDouall in *Shark* VII in the face of the menacing French frigate *Serapis* was typical, and exactly correct – he turned away and fled the scene, and then escaped by a trick. When new *Sharks* were commissioned, in the new navy of steel and steam, they were built to face a new and even greater threat, and were designed and built to be aggressive, as well as speedy and nimble, and this would have horrified the captains and Admiralty officials who contemplated the uses of the wooden-walled sloops in the eighteenth-century navies. But then the new ships rather more accurately reflected the reputations of the fish they were named for.

Chapter 10

Shark IX: a Destroyer, 1894–1911

For over three quarters of a century *Shark* was a name not used in the Royal Navy. No doubt the sad decline and end of *Shark* VII, and the disgraceful end of *Shark* VIII, were discouraging precedents, but the main reason was probably the decreased size of the Royal Navy in the years after the end of the war against Napoleonic France. When new ships were built they generally replaced expiring ships, and were often named in continuation. *Shark* was not a name which resonated with victory and enterprise, but in addition, fish names have not been all that popular with the Admiralty; only the fiercer fish – shark, pike, sturgeon – have given their names to their floating human-built rivals, at least until there was a desperate search for names with the enormous expansion of the navy in the emergencies of the two world wars.

During that period of about eighty years the Royal Navy went through a whole series of changes, above all in its ships. In 1818 the Navy had only sailing ships; by 1896 they were almost entirely mechanical. In this basic change were included the brief use of paddle steamers replaced by screw steamers, wood replaced by iron replaced by steel in ship construction, the growth in size and weight and firepower of the ships, the change from smooth bore, relatively short range guns to guns with a much longer range and firing shells. And the new *Shark* came at the start of another series of great changes.

When a new type of ship was developed which was intended to be an attacker, however, the *Shark* name was revived. This was originally the torpedo-boat or torpedo-boat destroyer, designed to launch a Whitehead torpedo at an enemy ship. (Curiously, the weapon was devised first, and the means of delivering it only later.) This was clearly a serious threat to the larger ships, and a counter was soon developed, which was the torpedo-boat destroyer. But this in turn was soon armed with torpedoes, so that it became the thing it was intended to counter. (In Britain these became simply destroyers; in Germany, for example, they were still torpedo-boats.)[1]

The type was a ship very likely to be called *Shark*, quick, and with a serious bite. *Shark* IX was built in 1895–1896 as one of a large number of these smaller vessels. The originals were *Havock*, *Daring*, and *Ferret*, built respectively by

Yarrow, Thorneycroft, and Laird in 1893, 275 or 325 tons and 185–190ft long, but their small size rendered them not very seaworthy, and the next set, including *Shark*, were of a slightly larger type – *Shark*, built by Thomson on Clydebank, was 325 tons and 205ft. The contemplated use of destroyers was usually in groups or flotillas, for they were light in build and very vulnerable, for in an attack most torpedoes missed their target; by launching a spread of these weapons from a number of destroyers it was more likely that one would hit; also almost any other warship they met was likely to be bigger and better armed, so there might be safety for some, in numbers and in speed.

So the destroyers became protectors of the larger ships (where they had been intended to be their menace), designed to keep enemies at a distance, so that the big ships could concentrate on fighting their peers. The idea of a battle fleet, therefore, which was made up of capital ships (one or more battleships before the Great War, or an aircraft carrier later) which was attended and screened by a flock of smaller ships, cruisers and destroyers, was developed. The rationale was that the destroyers would intercept an enemy and give warning of its approach, and get in a preliminary disruptive attack. It was not really acknowledged that the destroyers, besides being vulnerable, were intended to be sacrificed on behalf of the bigger ships.

The development of the destroyer as a ship type occurred at the time when these new tactics were being worked out, and the destroyers themselves evolved along with these tactics, essentially by becoming bigger and faster and better armed. In other words, they became the replacement for the smaller ships of the old wooden navy, available for a whole variety of tasks, but this time these included defending the big ships, a task sloops and similar craft had not been suited for in earlier eras. The changes were directly the result of the development of the torpedo, which not only became a weapon launched from torpedo-boats, and destroyers, but, of course, this also became the main weapon of the new submarines; indeed, without torpedoes, submarines would hardly have been worth developing. In 1889–1892, for example, the small vessels tended to be counted altogether as 'flotilla' ships, at that time consisting of sloops, gunboats, and torpedo-boats, all of these in effect being vessels whose design led on to torpedo-boat destroyers in the next years.[2] It was Captain AJ Fisher – 'Jacky' Fisher – who was appointed Controller and Third Sea Lord at the Admiralty in 1892 who initiated discussions with shipbuilders for the new type, so beginning a career of innovation and naval disruption.[3]

Before considering the career of *Shark* IX, therefore, it will be worth looking at the ways in which the destroyer-type developed. The earliest destroyers, starting with *Havock* and *Havant*, launched in August 1893 and January 1894 by Yarrow shipbuilders on the Thames, were, in comparison with later ships small, around 300 tons, and with 3, 4, or 6 guns, and two or three torpedo tubes. Also *Havock* was powered by a 'locomotive' engine, *Havant* by a 'water-tube' engine, as a deliberate comparison – the latter soon became the standard engine for all destroyers. Two other boats had been ordered from Thorneycroft on the Thames. Both ships, *Daring* and *Decoy*, were in fact ordered before those from Yarrow, but they took longer to build. Yarrow completed their two in 1894, Thorneycroft theirs in February and June 1895. Clearly this variety indicates that the Admiralty saw the early ships as to a degree experimental, and indeed it had been carrying out experiments during 1893 to find a suitable design.

The size of these early versions grew slowly over the next two years, but only one of the ships built between 1893 and 1898 was over 400 tons. All were armed with one 12-pounder gun and five 6-pounders, and most had two torpedo tubes; two had three tubes and only three 6-pounders – an indication of continuing experimentation, as was the one ship, *Express* of 1897, which was much larger than the rest at 499 tons. By the second half of 1894, however, Thomson and Naval Construction and Armaments (of Barrow, later taken over by Vickers) were in the game, and in 1895 no less than eleven yards were building destroyers of the Thorneycroft type – fifteen had been built in 1894 (including *Shark*); twenty-seven in 1895. This diversification was a deliberate move by the Admiralty in order to spread the expertise; it also helped to innovate improvements.

These were all of the initial small type, but their size did constantly creep upwards. Three ships from Laird's were almost 400 tons in 1895, and next year the average was 350 tons or so. By 1898 it was over 370 and in 1899 three of the ships built that year were 400 tons or more, almost double the size of the first ships only six years before. In the next year most of the ships built were of 400 tons or thereabouts. These were built, at first, almost entirely by the Thorneycroft and Laird firms, with none by Yarrow for several years – there was a disagreement when the Admiralty insisted it could send the designs for the ships to other yards. It was evidently the original types from the two yards which were approved by the Admiralty. The same was the result of a version produced by White's yard, a little larger than most, but that yard was commissioned to build the 'normal' type next year.

Various extra items were added to the ships as time went on – searchlights, for example, or extra torpedo tubes; the funnels had, in some cases, such as *Shark*, to be heightened, since at high speed flames blew out of the funnel, thereby betraying the ship's position at night. They only very rarely, however, achieved their designed speeds, despite an almost desperate search by shipbuilders to increase it. The original boats (such as *Shark*) had been intended to maintain twenty-seven knots for up to three hours, but none of them was able to do so; later designs were intended for thirty or thirty-two knots, and tended to achieve this only in carefully designed preliminary trials, where extra stokers and even hand-picked coal was used. The Admiralty had to be content with a slightly lesser standard in speed than they had hoped for.

Launching of new ships ceased after March 1901 for twenty months. The gap was perhaps as much the result of government financial constraints, thanks to the unexpectedly high expenditure on the Boer War, as to the obvious need to reconsider destroyer design after the slow growth in size, and with the experience of these early boats' performance. So that hiatus was in fact used to produce a design for a bigger destroyer type, powered by rotary engines, as developed by Charles Parsons with the experimental *Turbinia*. These were less likely to break down during their highest speeds, produced much less vibration, and achieved marginally greater speeds. Orders were placed during 1902 and the first of the new ships, of 550 tons, was launched in January 1903 at the Palmer shipyards. This was a clearly very standardized design, enforced on all the builders – Laird, Palmer, Hawthorn, Yarrow (back in the game), and Thorneycroft, were the only builders employed during 1903, 1904, and 1905. Only half a dozen ships in those years deviated from the norm of 550 tons and 225ft by 23.5ft by more than five tons and 6in. And all the deviants were larger and all of them came from the Yarrow yard. There may have been some discomfort, however, in the fact that these larger ships were armed in exactly the same way as their earlier versions, with one 12-pounder gun, five 6-pounders, and two torpedo tubes.

In December 1904 a further improvement was tested. Two destroyers, *Peterel*, using the normal fuel of coal, was tested against *Spiteful*, fuelled by oil. The ships ran a series of trials around the Isle of Wight. In speed over a measured mile, *Spiteful* was marginally faster, but *Peterel* consumed slightly less fuel (by weight); so in actual performance there was in effect virtually no difference. The real advantage of oil was in the number of stokers required – three for oil, six for coal – cleanliness on board, the time taken in preparing to sail – ten minutes with the oil, an hour and a half with coal – and the complete absence of waste material to be dumped over the side when oil was used. The results were clear, and oil became the preferred fuel for the Navy.[4]

By 1905, therefore, another redesign was under way, possibly assisted by the observed use of destroyers in the Russo–Japanese War of 1904–1905. A group of 'coastal destroyers' was built in 1906 (and one in 1907), more or less of the size of the original first destroyers; in fact they were a little smaller, and were armed with only two guns, but with three torpedo tubes. No doubt they were intended to be able to get closer to the enemy and to his ports. Indeed, they were quickly reclassified as torpedo-boats soon after entering service, and no more seem to have been built.

Once again, the new destroyer type took a major leap in size. After the absence of any new ships (apart from the coastal destroyers) in 1906, the next design was for ships of about 870 tons. During this construction gap the builders Palmer had tried their hands at a smaller design. They built a ship of 440 tons, armed with three 12-pounders and two torpedo tubes, and launched it in September 1906; a second version was produced a little later. Laird also built two different ships, of the old 550 ton size, but armed with four 12-pounders and two tubes. Both of these speculative designs were overtaken by the new Admiralty version, which was bigger and better armed, though they were all eventually purchased by the Admiralty.

Five of the larger, 870 ton type were built, each by a different shipbuilder, and each armed slightly differently, but at the same time the earlier smaller ships were evidently seen to be under-gunned, and all those built between 1903 and 1905 – the 550 ton ships – were rearmed with four 12-pounders, the 6-pounders being taken off. And yet those bigger ships were only armed with three of the bigger guns, though two of these were later given two more 12-pounders in 1911.

In 1908 and 1909 the newer, bigger, 'River'-class destroyers became the norm. The armament changed, some having two 4-inch guns and two torpedo tubes, others having one 4-inch and two or three 12-pounders plus two tubes. These ships had a weight of almost a thousand tons, and indeed two were over that size, which made them more than three times the size of the original destroyers of fifteen years before. This type continued to be built through 1910, but most of the destroyers of that year were somewhat smaller, 20ft shorter, 1ft narrower, and 200 tons lighter, and armed with two 4 inch and two 12-pounder guns. Ten of the larger vessels were built (to add to the ten of the previous year), and fifteen of the 750 ton version.

By the end of 1910, therefore, there was a great variety of destroyers in service, ranging from the earliest ships of less than 300 tons to the newest of over 1,000. Over 180 destroyers had been built in seventeen years, though ten had fallen victim to a variety of accidents. The decision to switch to oil as the propulsive fuel, made by 1905 for ships to be built next year, also triggered a decision to decommission the oldest and smallest of the destroyers. (Oil propulsion was not, of course, wholly new, since vessels such as submarines had necessarily been powered by oil from the beginning.) Two of the earliest destroyers had already been disposed of: *Ferret* and *Hornet*, built in 1893, were respectively dismantled and sold. Now in 1911 and 1912 all but three of those built in 1894 were sold, as were eleven of those built in 1895. Some were still being sold off in 1914 – *Zebra* was sold on 30 July of that year, a fact very suggestive of the unexpectedness of the Great War – but the disposals were presumably at least in part replaced by the arrival of new ships from the builders' yards, and the approach of war both accelerated the building of new ships and stopped the selling of the older ones. The replacements were often literally that, being named for retired destroyers, so the names continued.[5]

In all this *Shark* takes its place as typifying the whole process. *Shark* IX was one of the earliest types, built in 1894 by Thomson on a pattern a little larger than the very first destroyers, at 325 tons. Coal-fired, it was mothballed in 1896, by which time the newly built destroyers were already often somewhat larger again. When *Shark* was revived in 1899 the typical destroyer being built was a quarter larger, 10ft longer, nearly 2ft wider and 70 tons heavier. When it was revived from retirement a second time in 1903, the new ships were twice its weight. On the other hand all those new ships were armed in much the same way, and next year the Admiralty built those coastal destroyers, which were even smaller than *Shark* and its contemporaries, so the smaller ships were clearly seen as still useful.

But in 1907 the ships of 1903–1906 were re-gunned, making them more powerful, and the new ships in that year were often over 800 tons. The 1910 ships at either 750 or nearly 1,000 tons were far above the power, speed, and size of the oldest destroyers, which by this time were no doubt subject to increasing wear and tear – they had proved to be very vulnerable to storm and heavy seas, many receiving serious hull damage, which was reported in the China seas, in the Mediterranean, and the waters around Britain.[6]

So in 1912 *Shark* IX was replaced by another *Shark* – X – which was one of the new type, 935 tons, 267ft long, 27ft wide, and armed with three 4-inch guns and two torpedo tubes. It was one of eight such ships built that year on this pattern. During that year also the last of the slightly smaller 750 ton set was built – and the older ships were progressively removed as these new ships came into service. So *Shark* IX was sold in 1911 and *Shark* X arrived in 1912.

The life of *Shark* IX had in fact spanned the time in which the purpose of a destroyer had changed radically. The original name of the type, torpedo-boat destroyer, was precisely descriptive, in that they were intended to destroy enemy torpedo boats. The menace in the 1890s had been seen as coming from France, where the naval doctrine of the *jeune ecole*, which emphasized commerce raiding as a viable strategic option for a state with lesser resources and fewer ships, had held sway. The Admiralty's nightmare was the appearance of large numbers of nippy torpedo boats suddenly attacking and sinking its great battleships and cruisers with little or no warning – and capturing and/or sinking British merchantmen in the Channel. Hence the aim of destroying these little craft. By 1910 or thereabouts, however, this was no longer the issue, and the protection of the battleships against other battleships – German, now – was the problem, so the new destroyers were intended to act as protectors of the great ships.

Having considered the context of *Shark* IX's fifteen-year career, it is now possible to look at the work the ship did. The ship was commissioned in 1894 but not put into any form of service for over a year. The log for 1896 records what seems to be the early trials of the ship, first in the English Channel between Plymouth and Spithead in January, and then across to Berehaven in south-western Ireland, shuttling back and forth between that port and Queenstown, in February and March. On 21 April it took part in peacetime manoeuvring with a squadron of ships, and on the 30th it went up the Kenmare River for target practice. In May it went farther west, to Glengariff and Valentia, then back to Berehaven. Torpedo loading and launching was practised, then the ship returned to Devonport. On 28 May at Devonport it was paid off and assigned to the B Division of the Reserve Fleet – in effect it was laid aside for later use.[7]

This period of retirement ended in May 1899. The arrival of a new war, albeit far off in South Africa, but in which the continental powers and their navies seemed to line up against Britain, necessitated a display of naval power as a reminder of the difficulty those powers would have in intervening in Britain's Imperial War. *Shark* re-emerged at Devonport and was recommissioned, manned and supplied. Its captain – in effect the ship's first captain – was Lieutenant Commander Francis E. Walters, who took command on 17 May 1899, when the South African crisis was building up. (The war actually began in October.)

The ship roamed back and forth along the Channel for three months, then sailed north to the North of Ireland and the Clyde Estuary for exercises in 'steam tactics' and firing and torpedo practices. These were perhaps taken rather more seriously now in the more dangerous international circumstances than in the ship's first cruise. Then the ship returned to the Channel, to Plymouth, Penzance, Falmouth, Devonport, Portland, and Portsmouth. This routine continued through 1900 and into 1901, when *Shark* took part in fleet manoeuvres, its captain then being Lieutenant Commander Douglas Hamilton-Gordon. Then in August of the latter year the ship's company was paid off once more. The crisis, which was never much of a crisis in naval terms, had ended.[8]

Shark returned to service in 1903, after over a year's break, but only for another half-year. The record of its activities is much the same as in its earlier appearances, operating in the English Channel and the Irish Sea above all, with exercises in Southern Ireland in August; then the ship went on an extended cruise through the Irish Sea and north through the Western Isles of Scotland. From the several destinations it called at, this would seem to have been almost a holiday cruise, though the sailors will not have accepted that description, no doubt.

A preliminary visit to the Firth of Clyde involved calls at Lamlash, Gareloch, and Campbeltown, but then there followed a leisurely progress north through the Inner Hebrides. Three days were spent at Oban and then a visit was paid to Ballachulish. A call at Loch Hourne implies a route through the Sound of Mull and the Sound of Skye; further north there were calls at Loch Torridon, Aultbea (in Loch Ewe, where the Grand Fleet took shelter a dozen years later) and Ullapool. The northward progress ended at Loch Glen Dhu and Loch Eriboll on the north coast of Scotland, and was followed by a visit to Stornoway and then a return southwards, calling again at Oban and Gareloch in the Firth of Clyde. One its way back to the Channel the ship called in at Dublin, Wexford, Milford Haven, and Pembroke, thereby completing a cruise in which it had visited all four of the United Kingdom countries. In August the ship returned from Queenstown in Southern Ireland to the Channel, calling at Penzance and then Portsmouth, but then it returned to the Bristol Channel and sailed north again to Bangor in north Wales.

This was clearly not really a holiday, of course, though the pleasure of a visit to the autumn Highlands was surely appreciated. But the ship deliberately called at a whole series of deep-water sea lochs, and this cannot have been accidental. It would seem that the purpose was a reconnaissance of some sort. The prospect of a European war was looming steadily closer, and the Admiralty was conscious of the menace of both torpedoes and submarines. Its traditional British method of warfare was to clear the international seas of enemy ships as far as possible, both warships and merchant ships, and then confine the remainder to their home ports by a close blockade. However, this was increasingly unrealistic in the face of the new weapons, particularly torpedo-armed submarines and destroyers, which were personified by such ships as *Shark* and its successors. The fleet bases in Britain were well known to all possible enemies, and they mainly existed to face an enemy to the south – that is, France or Spain – but the strength and enmity of both Russia and Germany was growing, which meant the threat now came from the east across the North Sea (as it had in the seventeenth century with the Dutch). It seems that the Admiralty was taking the precaution of searching out the possibility of using the lochs of western Scotland as bases. No doubt the officers in *Shark* took measurements of water depth, the possibilities of establishing bases, and of ways of closing off the lochs against enemy raiders.[9]

This cruise was followed by another year of unmanned inactivity at Portsmouth, but in December 1904, the ship was recommissioned and manned again, and it stayed in service for the next seven years. On the other hand, it did not do very much, except take part in occasional cruises or manoeuvres, with occasional torpedo practice and firing practice. For months at a time it stayed, virtually immobile, at Portsmouth, and even when it moved it often went no further than Spithead or Southampton. It went on one exercise across the Channel to the Channel Islands, and it took part in fleet exercises in the North Sea, being based at Burntisland in the Firth of Forth for the occasion. Firing and torpedo practice usually took place off south-west Ireland, but increasingly this happened in Torbay. At no time in its life did the ship move away from the waters around the British Isles. This concentration, of course, reflected the new naval priority after 1900 of a possible war with Germany, but at the same time, by that date the ship seems to have been largely disregarded as a useful weapon of war. It was, that is to say, already by the early twentieth century almost obsolete.

It cannot be said that *Shark* had been hard-worked, but by 1910 it was clearly close to the end of its life. The new destroyers were bigger, faster, oil-powered, more reliable mechanically and better able to face the heavier seas, and more manoeuvrable. *Shark* IX was now out of date, and therefore both vulnerable and a drag on the rest of the fleet.

Conditions on board this ship were, however, strikingly different from those which the logs of earlier *Sharks* had revealed, and suggest the overall humanizing of service in the Royal Navy which had taken place during the nineteenth century – another of the great changes in the service – and this reflected also the general change in wider attitudes during that time. The ending of slavery in the British Empire and the cessation of any idea of pressing men into service went hand in hand, of course, at least until war demanded so much human material that conscription was enacted – but conscription was a much less brutal and random process than the press gang. Punishments were minor – flogging was abolished – and so were the transgressions by the sailors – the humanizing went both ways. The logs of *Shark* ships in the twentieth century record no examples of desertion; there were only the occasional cases of absenteeism, usually lateness in returning from leave, and never involving more than one man at a time.

Under normal circumstances – that is, in peacetime – the ship operated a five-day week, just as did many civilians. Leave was relatively generous, and, of course, periods of excitement were extremely limited, and in the case of *Shark* IX, non-existent; the ship never once fired its guns at an enemy. Opportunities for education for the sailors were available; indeed, any such opportunity would have amazed the men of the Napoleonic wars, but it was realized that the human material in the navy was as valuable as the ships, if not more so. By now it was increasingly necessary that new techniques were taught as new equipment was acquired and the better the basic education of the sailors the easier it was for those techniques to be inculcated. The ship had its own football team, and leave was quickly granted wholesale whenever there was a match – always on Saturday afternoon, of course.

Work on board, however, was generally as tedious as that in earlier *Sharks*, and not in fact all that different from many of the civilian jobs which were the alternative employment for the ordinary sailors. The worst task was coaling, from which only the captain was excused – a major incentive to seeking promotion, one would have thought – and the advent of oil-driven ships was clearly a boon to all sailors. Otherwise cleaning and polishing the ship – or painting it – was the normal daily activity, though these were probably much less unpleasant tasks than on a wooden warship. But so engrained was the issue of cleanliness and 'smartness' that even the last of the ship's logs reveals that, even as the ship was being dismantled around them, with the guns removed, stores taken out, and the ship being moved on its last minuscule supply of coal to its final resting place, cleaning still went on. When the disarmed ship was sold in July 1911, presumably for breaking up, the buyers bought a semi-dismantled, disarmed, sparkling ship.[10]

The history of this *Shark* is therefore somewhat depressing. Within a few years of being commissioned the ship was clearly barely capable of performing its original function, having been overtaken by its successors in size, speed, and probably armament, and by 1903 it was too small and not speedy enough. By the time it was scrapped and sold it could not keep up with the big ships destroyers were supposed to screen. Its contemporaries were also being gradually scrapped as the new oil-fired destroyers, bigger and faster, were built. And yet some of its fellows from the 1890s remained in service throughout the Great War, though hardly in the roles expected of them when they were built. *Shark* IX paid the penalty of early obsolescence for being one of the earliest destroyers – in that it was a true successor of earlier *Sharks*. But it had been part of the navy which controlled the world's oceans, and the fact that it never fired its guns or its torpedoes in anger is actually a mark of the success of the navy in enforcing a worldwide oceanic peace.

Chapter 11

Shark X: a Destroyer, 1912–1916

I

The advent of oil as a propellant fuel for warships and the menace of submarines armed with more or less accurate torpedoes had brought the great development of destroyers from destroyers of torpedo-boats to protectors of fleets. The new version of these ships, typified here by the second *Shark* destroyer, was three or four times the size of the early vessels of the 1890s, better armed and faster. As well, a clear role – or rather, a series of roles – had been worked out for them in war, above all as fleet scouts and escorts. Originally intended to fight torpedo-boats, they had become much more versatile, combining the roles of torpedo-boats, defenders against torpedo-boats, submarine hunters, escorts to the big ships, and were soon to become minelayers and convoy escorts. They turned out, that is, to be adaptable to many tasks, just as their wooden predecessors, sloops and brigs, had been. Many of these tasks, however, were liable to put destroyers in the post of most danger, notably that of fleet scout and escort, where they were intended to be the ships which first contacted the enemy fleet.[1]

The tenth *Shark* was one of the new ships of the *Acasta* class, 935 tons, armed with quick-firing guns and torpedoes, and capable of thirty knots or more. It was built at the Swan Hunter shipyard at Wallsend on the Tyne, launched in July 1912, and was commissioned on 3 April 1913 when Commander Anselm JB Stirling took command of it at the builders' yard. It was almost two years since its *Shark* IX predecessor had been decommissioned. In a curious repeat of the first cruise of *Shark* VII a century and a third before, the first voyage of the ship was south along the east English coast to Sheerness. On 7 April at Chatham the Lords of the Admiralty arrived for an inspection. Five days later the ship received its ammunition and completed with oil, topping up with 130 tons. To any sailor transferred from an older ship to a new one, the sight of oil being piped on board through a pipeline was one no doubt much appreciated after the rigours and effort and dirt of coaling. (One of the purposes of the large-scale decommissioning of the older destroyers was to make available their men for the crews of the new ships.)[2]

Again, in what seems to be an almost deliberate reminiscence of its predecessor *Shark* IX, the new ship sailed west along the Channel to Devonport, then took part in exercises before going on to Queenstown in Southern Ireland. This time, however, it then went quickly to the north, for its firing practice was conducted in the Firth of Clyde, with Brodick in the Isle of Arran as its temporary base for the occasion.[3] More exercises followed in the firth, including visits to Troon and Ayr, then the ship sailed north to the seas west of the islands of Tiree and Jura for fleet exercises as part of the First Battle Squadron. This was clearly a much more purposeful process than anything done by its predecessor.

These fleet exercises lasted only a day or so, and the ship returned to Brodick on 8 May for refuelling. It was based there for most of the rest of May during which it carried out torpedo exercises, and took part in a torpedo competition. Then it sailed still farther north to Orkney, arriving at Longhope at the southern entrance to Scapa Flow on the 30th. More exercises with the battle cruisers followed in the first week in June. It sailed west to Stornoway in Harris with the Fourth Destroyer Flotilla and then returned south to visit south Wales (Milford Haven, Pembroke, Swansea) in mid-June. A voyage south to the Channel, to Portland and Spithead, in the third week of the month was followed by a return by 14 July to Scapa Flow, this time sailing by way of the North Sea route. More manoeuvres followed, and at the end of them the ship was at Queensferry in the Firth of Forth.

There followed a cruise with the battle fleet in the North Sea. The ship went into Chatham and Sheerness for much of August, but then sailed north to Fortrose in the Moray Firth, arriving on the 24th. It had a firing practice on the 25th and 26th off Nairn, night battle practice on 28th with the destroyer flotilla, and a preliminary battle practice on 3rd, and then the real thing on 4th September off Invergordon in the Cromarty Firth. Then the ship sailed north to Orkney for more firing practice. On 17 September it was back at Queensferry in the Firth of Forth, and it stayed there for a week.

There was a substantial workout for the new ship. It had in effect circumnavigated Britain in that time, had visited several ports in the four countries, but more to the point from the navy's point of view, its captain and crew had learned their role in various formations from a destroyer flotilla up to a full fleet. This rigorous learning process was a much more purposeful process than anything undergone by *Shark* IX, and is an indication that the navy was now much more in earnest in contemplating and preparing for a war than it had been a few years before. There had been little in the time of the previous *Shark* to compare with all these exercises and manoeuvres – four such occasions in the first three months of the ship's existence.

Northern Scottish waters were the ship's operating territory in the next months, just the region in which it would be expected to fight if – when – the German war came. It was realized that the traditional blockade of enemy ports was no longer possible because of the menace of submarines and torpedoes, and new naval bases at Cromarty, in the Firth of Forth, and at Scapa Flow, were being developed; the new blockade was a distant one, confining the enemy to the waters of the North Sea and the Baltic. In October Stirling was replaced by the man who became the ship's captain for the rest of its (and his) life, Commander Loftus Jones. He took over at Queensferry, then brought the ship south to Chatham for the next three months. It was then based in the Channel until April 1914, in a tedious reminiscence of the non-work done by its immediate predecessor, visiting Portsmouth and Portland. It was often part of a small squadron of similar ships, at first the destroyers *Spitfire*, *Sparrowhawk*, and *Acasta*, of the same class; of these *Acasta* was to be a frequent partner.

II

In April 1914 *Shark* sailed north once again to Brodick in Arran, where more exercises followed for a few days, then, based at Campbeltown in the Mull of Kintyre, the ship spent a month patrolling in the area.

This was a time of heightened political tension in Ireland, where the Protestants, overwhelmingly concentrated in the north, were determined that the proposed parliamentary bill granting the whole island Home Rule, which would inevitably mean a Catholic-dominated Irish administration, should be resisted, if necessary in arms. The Protestants were organizing themselves, drilling in military formations, and arms were being acquired. This was the time also of the 'Curragh Mutiny', when senior army officers claimed the right to refuse to enforce the government's authority on the north even if ordered to do so.

The patrolling by *Shark* and its fellow destroyers was part of the government's response to the Irish situation, a variation of the old role of earlier *Sharks* in attempting to prevent smuggling or to intercept communications between Jacobites in Scotland and the continent. It was also, perhaps rather dishearteningly, a repetition of *Shark* II's patrolling around the north coast of Ireland two centuries before, at the time of King William III, when it had been Catholics who were in rebellion. Politics in Ireland had hardly moved on since his time.

From Campbeltown, from which the ship had been able to patrol the North Channel, between Scotland and Ireland, the ship moved in early June to Moville at the mouth of Lough Foyle. After a short visit to Portsmouth the ship was back at Campbeltown for a couple of days, and then began a close patrol of the nearby part of the coast of north Ireland. The ship's base was at Buncrana deep inside Lough Swilly, in Donegal. From there it patrolled the nearby coast, an intricate area of long sea-loughs, where arms landings could easily take place with little difficulty – though the fact that the local population was Catholic may have been a more inhibiting factor than the presence of *Shark*. For there is no indication that the ship intercepted any smugglers; and of course, whether it deterred any is also unknown.

All this was, of course, rather late in the day if prevention was intended. The Curragh Mutiny had been in March, and the most spectacular arms smuggling exploit, the landing of a consignment of German rifles by the steamer *River Clyde* at Larne had taken place at the beginning of April. *Shark* did not reach the region until the end of that month, and whatever ship had been on patrol had missed the arrival. But perhaps these patrols had some effect in deterring other attempts, or in emphasizing the government's intention of enforcing its authority. But Ulster was tense all through the summer.[4]

III

Shark was at Buncrana on 27 July 1914, but was then ordered north to Scapa Flow, where it arrived on the 29th. Its arrival here was part of the British government's response to the unfolding of the international crisis in late July which led to the beginning of the Great War on the 30th. The ship now patrolled in the Pentland Firth for a day, then on 4th August, the day the British government declared war (but not until 11.00 pm), it was at Cromarty, one of the anchorages for the Grand Fleet. Returning to Scapa on 9 August, *Shark* formed part of the submarine screen for the Grand Fleet, and for the next two months this was its role; based at Longhope at the southern entrance to Scapa it sailed with the fleet as Admiral Jellicoe kept it at sea as much as possible, in hopes of a great battle with the German High Seas fleet, which had no intention of obliging its enemy by indulging in a battle.

There followed a sequence of patrols both with and without the bigger ships. Each patrol lasted a day or two, then there were two or three days spent in port. At first based at Longhope, *Shark* and its fellows were soon based further south at Invergordon in the Cromarty Firth, closer to where any action was likely to be. It is surprising how quickly the ship settled into a patrolling routine, though it is clear that the vessels were being worked hard. The first half of December was this routine: at Invergordon until the 3rd, then on patrol with the destroyers *Acasta*, *Spitfire*, and *Hardy* from early on the 3rd to late on the 4th. Four days in port was then followed by another overnight patrol, then two days in port.

This routine was disrupted on 14 December when, instead of a patrol keeping fairly close to port, the destroyers went out past Kinnaird Head and south-east into the North Sea. The German fleet had come out, aiming to lay a trap for the Grand Fleet. An advance force would bombard towns on the Yorkshire coast, a process guaranteed, it was thought, to make the British see red. So it did, but not to the extent of being careless. *Shark* and its fellows – seven of them altogether – were ahead of the six super-dreadnoughts of Admiral Warrender, and the Battle Cruiser Squadron of Admiral Beatty was not far off. They knew a substantial German force was at sea, but did not know that the whole High Seas Fleet was following along behind to catch the British.

Detecting such traps was in fact one of the main functions of the destroyers which formed the screen ahead of the big ships. In the darkness of early December 16th the seven destroyers in line ahead were suddenly aware that there was a strange ship nearby, and when it was challenged it opened fire. It was the German destroyer *V-155*, and its first shots struck the leading British ship, the destroyer *Lynx*, and put it out of action; a second destroyer, *Ambuscade*, was holed, and also dropped out. The German ship then retreated to regain touch with its fellows, and meanwhile the light cruiser *Hamburg* had, correctly, rushed forward when firing was seen. It encountered the surviving British destroyers, and hit *Hardy*, but *Hardy's* reply shot destroyed the cruiser's searchlight, and when it also fired a torpedo, *Hamburg's* captain turned away. He reported this to the German fleet commander, Admiral Ingenohl, who was not pleased to hear about the torpedo.

Shark was now leading the remaining four destroyers, and they encountered a set of five German ships. Without hesitation Loftus Jones led the four in a charge at the enemy, which included at least one light cruiser. This action persuaded the Germans that there was something more than a few destroyers on the British side – shades of *Shark* VII's ruse to escape *Serapis* – and meanwhile the British had also begun to realize that the same situation existed on the German side. The Germans turned away. Both sides' destroyer screens had done their jobs in locating the enemy screens, and the subsequent battle would be up to the big ships.

However, no real battle resulted. Admiral Ingenohl was stretching his instructions to and beyond their limits, and the news of torpedoes being fired at *Hamburg* was unsettling. He ordered the whole High Seas Fleet to turn away and return to its bases. *Shark* and its three companions followed on, not knowing what was ahead of them, until about 7.00 am, when they spotted the light cruiser *Roon*. It was accompanied by several German destroyers, a squadron which was acting, in fact, as the rearguard of the German fleet. At first the British assumed that it was a detached force of destroyers only, similar to themselves. Again *Shark* charged, until Jones suddenly recognized one of the enemy as a cruiser, and then saw that there were two other cruisers in front of him as well.

Shark challenged the ships before it to identify themselves, then turned and ran with the other destroyers. They were chased by the three German cruisers, but outpaced them with some ease, though when the cruisers broke off the chase the British did not realize this and continued to flee as fast as possible towards the battle cruisers. At 8.50 am, by which time it was light, they sighted the light cruiser squadron screening the battle cruisers, and took shelter with them. At 3.30 in the afternoon, they were sent into port to refuel, for their hours of high-speed running had drastically depleted their supplies. They could claim, with a good deal of exaggeration, to have defeated the German High Seas Fleet – but only when they finally realized that they had been in contact with its outriders; at that point no doubt pride was mixed with thankfulness that they had not come any closer to it.[5]

IV

Patrolling followed for the next sixteen months, sometimes with the Grand Fleet, sometimes with elements of that fleet, sometimes with only one or more other destroyers. The ship was based at Cromarty or Invergordon until January, when it went to Newcastle for a docking and a clean, a scrape and a refit, and the crew got a more substantial leave than a day at a time they could have, very occasionally, in Orkney. The war had speeded things up: the docking lasted only a fortnight. Then it was back to Invergordon, and regular patrolling again.

Whenever it was believed that the High Seas Fleet or a portion of it was at sea, the Grand fleet, or a portion of it, went to sea, hoping to meet and sink the enemy. The destroyers did so as well, as part of the screen. The battlecruisers made such a sortie late in January, but with no result. Otherwise *Shark* and its fellow destroyers patrolled regularly in the waters before their base, searching for any change in the situation, the presence of a German vessel, a new minefield, the evidence of a submarine. And usually little or nothing was found.

At the end of April *Shark* moved back to the Orkneys, being based at Gutter Sound, an anchorage between the large island of Hoy, and the smaller island of Cava, where the hills of Hoy provided some protection from the west and the south-west winds. The regular patrol beat was the Hoxa Sound patrol, covering the southern entrance to Scapa Flow and the dangerous waters of the Pentland Firth, between there and the Scottish mainland, around the island of Swona and the Pentland Skerries, an area where the currents were strong and difficult, the storms fierce, and the rocks fearsome.

The ship patrolled this area repeatedly, usually in company with another destroyer, though sometimes it seems to have been alone. Occasionally it was sent off on a different patrol, but almost always in and around the Northern Isles, and at other times it was based for a while at Invergordon or Cromarty. So, for instance, it was based at these latter places from February to 1 March, after which it was based once more at Gutter Sound. The first patrol in March was in the eastern part of the Pentland Firth – the Skerries and Swona – but then it went to Lerwick in the Shetlands; after another survey of the Pentland Skerries, it went to Kirkwall, just across the low peninsula from Scapa, but mostly the ship was in the Pentland Firth.

There was clearly an understanding that the repetition of the same routine would dull attentiveness, but at the same time a variety of tasks and destinations would help keep men alert.[6] The more difficult waters like the Pentland Firth deserved to be watched by men familiar with them, being fundamentally dangerous – three destroyers were wrecked in the Pentland Firth during the war (and two more by mines). At times the ship intercepted merchant ships to examine their cargoes, and their manifests to see if they were breaching the British blockade policy – though this was the task mainly of the Northern

Patrol of requisitioned merchant ships based in the Shetlands. The battering of the ship in the northern seas also required the ship to be regularly refitted and repaired. (It seems unlikely that the lighter and more fragile destroyers of *Shark* IX's vintage could have operated for long in these waters.) When refitting times came, it was usually when a larger ship was going south and *Shark* could be used as its screen and at the same time go in to a dock for a clean and polish. It spent ten days in the dockyard at Govan on the Clyde in late June 1915, during which the crew was given a week's leave.

The patrols were a little more varied on its return to Scapa – the Flotta patrol, the Hoy patrol, the Swona patrol – but all of them took place close to Scapa, and all were designed to protect the big ships, just as *Shark's* task at sea was to be a screen for battleships and battlecruisers. In September it performed this latter task, when the battle fleet sailed south along the western Scottish coast; *Shark* spent a couple of days at Loch Eriboll, one of the sea lochs reconnoitred several years before by *Shark* IX on its romantic voyage through the Western Isles. The rest of September was spent patrolling in Orkney waters, then it was sent to Belfast as escort and then to the Mersey.

A return to the north involved a patrol around Skerryvore, and then, based once again at Gutter Sound, this was followed by a visit to Cromarty. It was time for another dockyard inspection by then, and in mid-October the ship provided part of the screen for the battleship *Russell* as far as the Clyde, and then went into dock again at Govan for a week.

The patrolling was interrupted at irregular intervals by exercises, one of which took place with the Second Battle Squadron in October, after *Shark* came out of the Govan dock. Then there was another patrol in the Pentland Firth, followed by more exercises, this time with the Fourth Battle Squadron. It is obvious that these small ships – all the destroyers with the Grand Fleet were operating in this way – were being worked very hard, even if the patrols lasted only thirty-six hours, and the intervals between them were of two or three days. The contrast with the generally leisurely, not to say lackadaisical, life of *Shark* IX is stark; the occasional shuffle round Portsmouth harbour which was interrupted by even more occasional firing practice off Southern Ireland had been no preparation for a serious war.

Occasional incidents interrupted the patrol-and-exercise routine. In December after one of the Hoxa patrols, the midshipman of *Shark*, Robert Foley Knight, was investigated for leaving the ship without permission, but also, more seriously, for failing to act to help Lieutenant Vigus of *Acasta*, who was adrift in a boat whose engine had failed. To be adrift in December in the Pentland Firth in an open boat was to be in great danger – exposure and drowning were perhaps the least of the dangers. Knight was reprimanded, and the incident, most unusually, was recorded in the log along with Knight's acknowledging signature.

Being at sea around the Orkneys in a well-built destroyer in the winter cannot have been much more enjoyable than Vigus' experience. Between Knight's reprimand on 8 December and the next docking on 13 March the ship went on patrol fourteen times, mainly in the Pentland Firth, but occasionally to Invergordon or other parts of the Orkneys; it also had two sessions of torpedo practice, and one of exercises with the fleet or part thereof. And on six occasions it formed part of the anti-submarine (and anti-mine) screen for a battleship which was moving from one port or anchorage to another. For variety, at the end of January the crew was taken on a route march while the ship was at Cromarty. A route march in northern Scotland in January would perhaps help persuade the sailors that life in the destroyer was not so bad after all.[7]

V

After the docking in March 1916, in the River Tyne once again, no more logs of *Shark* X survive to reveal the ship's activities. (Each log recorded the ship's actions for two months; a new one would have been started on 1 April.) The ship returned to Invergordon from the Tyne, and went on two more patrols from there until the end of the month, but the log for April-May is no longer extant, for at the end of May the ship was once again caught up in a battle – of Jutland – in which it was sunk. What is known of the ship's actions in the battle comes from post-battle enquiries, which were prolonged, if intermittent. With the sinking of battlecruisers and damage to many other ships, the loss of a single destroyer was at first seen as unimportant, but as details were revealed over the next months, the navy seized on the story as a way of boosting morale. It was, after all, not clear for some time whether Jutland was a serious defeat, a great victory, or yet another indeterminate fight, and a tale of apparent heroism was always useful.

Shark, along with its fellow destroyers *Acasta*, *Ophelia*, and *Christopher*, was part of the screen in front of the Third Battle Cruiser Squadron of Rear Admiral Horace Hood. Two light cruisers, *Chester* and *Canterbury*, also formed part of the screen. The squadron was detached by Admiral Jellicoe to join Beatty's force of battlecruisers, but finding any ships in the dark and then in the haze of the morning proved to be very difficult. About 5.30 am the screen encountered a group of four German light cruisers, but it was some time before they were recognized, either as cruisers or as German. *Chester* went close to identify them, and was hit by a barrage from all four. The battlecruisers turned towards the firing and drove the light cruisers away, damaging two of them and sinking *Wiesbaden*. Admiral Hipper, in whose squadron the cruisers were, replied with a great cloud of destroyers – thirty-one of them – led by the light cruiser *Regensburg*. They were met by the cruiser *Canterbury* and its four destroyers, which included *Shark*.

The five British ships charged the thirty-two German ships, who were sufficiently confused as to believe there were many more than five of them. In the fight *Shark* was the one British vessel which was lost – though *Acasta* suffered serious damage as well. A shell destroyed *Shark's* forward gun turret, another hit the engine room, and a third destroyed the bridge. The rear turret was also put out of action. Unable to move, the ship seemed to be a sitting duck, but it still had one gun, amidships, which could be fired.

Acasta came alongside, and its captain, Lieutenant Commander John Barron, offered help, which would have involved towing *Shark*, or evacuating it and then sinking the empty wreck. Loftus Jones refused, with the reply that *Acasta* should look after itself and said 'don't get sunk for us', which, given the surrounding crowd of German destroyers, made sense. A pair of German destroyers approached *Shark*, but Jones, acting as gunner's assistant on the midship's gun, fired at them and damaged *V-48*; both withdrew.[8] But he was wounded in the exchange, when a shell hit him and took off his leg, though the shell did not explode. He was amateurishly fixed up with a tourniquet by one of the men. This was *Shark's* last bite, though, and as two more German destroyers approached, Jones ordered the ship to be abandoned – he had already insisted that the ensign, which had been shot away, be hoisted again. About thirty men went over the side into some rafts. The German ships fired two torpedoes into *Shark* and sank it.[9]

VI

No one on the British side knew what had happened to the ship, and, of course, the Germans had no idea what ship they had sunk. The crew who survived were on rafts in the cold sea – the temperature of the water was 48°F (8°C)

– and most of those who had left the ship, including Jones, died in the next hours. A Danish merchant ship, the *Vidar*, happened upon the last survivors on a raft about 10.00 pm, and pulled them on board. There were seven at first, but one died before the ship reached Grimsby next morning. When the admiral commanding on the East Coast sent their names to the Admiralty and to Jellicoe on 3 June, this was the first anyone knew of the sinking of *Shark*, though, of course, it was known that it had been seriously damaged – Barron of *Acasta* could report that – and was missing.

But this was only the beginning of another little bureaucratic saga. Commander Jones' widow made it her business to find out what had happened to the ship. She located and interviewed the survivors and compiled a report which she sent to the Admiralty. There, clearly with some surprise, it was finally realized that the last fight of *Shark* had been just the sort of event the navy liked to celebrate, the defiance of a small ship against overwhelming odds – stories of Gilbert and the *Revenge* will have stirred.

The Admiralty, however, could not possibly accept the report of a grieving widow as the final explanation of the loss of one of its ships. A new investigation, two months after the *Shark's* loss, was set up properly under naval auspices, conducted the same interviews, and reached essentially the same conclusions as Mrs Jones – with a few carefully identified corrections to her account. In the process it was discovered that *Shark* had fired a torpedo at a 'battle cruiser', and a hit was claimed, but several other British ships were shooting at it at the same time – and the battlecruiser was not identified. It was also, of course, irrelevant to the loss of the ship.

Meanwhile Jones' body had been washed up on the coast of Sweden. Other bodies of men killed in the battle were found at sea or were washed up on the coasts of Denmark and Norway for weeks afterwards, all of which were carefully reported by the local authorities. The Germans published the names of those whom they had taken prisoner, reporting through the Red Cross in Geneva. None of the prisoners were men of the *Shark*, so no further information was going to be found. In the Admiralty the bureaucratic wheels ground on. As soon as he had read Mrs Jones' account Admiral Beatty had suggested that Jones' actions merited the award of the Victoria Cross. (The other such award from the battle was also made posthumously, to Jack Cornwell, the boy on *Chester* who stood by his gun until killed.) If Jones was to be awarded a medal, then the rest of the survivors also merited their own recognition. And what about the Danish captain and his crew? The original suggestion had widened to considering awards of various sorts to a dozen men.

The *Vidar* must have had a gruelling experience, peacefully crossing the North Sea only to find itself in the middle of the biggest sea battle ever fought. Its gesture in stopping to recover the British sailors was clearly not only a humanitarian act, but also a brave one, and it was suggested that the master be given a gold watch as a gesture of thanks. Captain Ole Hansen Christensen replied to this by pointing out that in fact it was his chief officer and four of his crew who had done the rescuing and providing for the rescued men. So the Admiralty had to think again, again. The offer of the gold watch could not be withdrawn, though this was certainly considered; in the end the chief officer was awarded an engraved silver cup, and the four seamen got £5 each.

By that time the *Vidar* had been located and arrested by a German patrol, and the master and his crew had been interrogated by the Germans for several days. (Denmark's hostility to Germany dated back fifty years to the brief Dano-Prussian war of 1864, when two large provinces were annexed to Germany; any Danish action which might seem to favour the British was regarded with deep suspicion by the Germans.) The sailors and the master were eventually released. It was the end of August by this time, and on 8 November the presentations were made at Hull, with a full column report in the Hull *Daily Mail* next day – clearly a propaganda move to show up the German conduct in persecuting honest sailors who had been left to die by their German assailants. But Captain Christensen had been so unnerved by the German detention and interrogation that he had vowed not to sail the North Sea again, a fact carefully publicized in Britain. His gold watch was accepted for him by the new master of *Vidar*.

The *Shark* survivors got their awards. Jones was given the posthumous Victoria Cross, no doubt accepted with due ceremony by his widow, without whose work it would never have been given; she had done as much as her late husband to gain it. Petty Officer William Griffin, the senior surviving sailor, was given the Distinguished Service Medal, and the other four survivors a lesser award. As usual the class system played its part.[10]

VII

Shark had performed its assigned function, just as had its wooden sloop predecessors. For almost two years it had repeatedly sailed on protective patrols. It had taken part in two of the major naval battles of the Great War, the Scarborough Raid and Jutland, and in both actions it had been aggressive and had shown its teeth. It seems that the ship was more aggressive than other destroyers, twice at least leading the charge of a small force against a larger German force, and fighting successfully even as it was sinking.[11] This must be ascribed to Loftus Jones' captaincy and leadership, as well as to the renewed Royal Navy spirit, which had clearly largely suffocated in the previous decades as the institution became more bureaucratic and self-conscious. If only by the example he showed of the attacking spirit, Jones had deserved his Victoria Cross.

Chapter 12

Shark XI: a Destroyer, 1918–1931

I

It was probably inevitable that, once the presumed heroic sinking of *Shark* X became known, another ship of that name would be built. A new 'class' of destroyers was constructed in 1918–1919, 'S' class, and the new *Shark* was one of these. Over forty of this class of ships were ordered. They were to be something over 1,000 tons, 260 to 270ft long and 27 or so ft wide – the variation being due to the differences between those built at the several yards. The first of the class was launched in January 1918 – so they had been in the planning for several months before that – and the last two were cancelled in mid-1919. The last to be launched was *Shikari* in July 1919. *Shark* came in the middle of the process, built at the Swan Hunter yards at Wallsend, like its *Shark* X predecessor, and launched in June 1918.

The first commander, Lieutenant Stuart Bonham-Carter, took over the ship on 8 June. The ship spent only a short time on some basic trials in June and July, before sailing from Wallsend to Sheerness for loading with ammunition and stores, and then going down-Channel to replenish with oil at Devonport. By 19 July it was replenishing further at Gibraltar. It sailed east through the Mediterranean as part of the escort to a convoy on the 24th, and was carrying an officer and five ratings to Malta on the same voyage. By the end of July the ship was at Brindisi in the heel of Italy.[1] This was the active centre of Allied sea action in the Adriatic, with ships of most Allied states stationed there.

II

This was a swift progress from the dockyard to a war footing, and there was no delay in the Adriatic. The day after *Shark* arrived at Brindisi the ship was part of a patrol exercise in local waters, an exercise which involved meeting an 'attack' by an 'enemy' force, firing practice and torpedo practice; and that night the ship was out at sea on 'night patrol' searching for enemy submarines. The patrol involved quartering an area of sea, and stopping every half hour, shutting down the engines, and then listening for five minutes. There is no evidence in the ship's log that anything was ever heard in any of these patrols, but it was the only way submarines could be detected, at least at night.

The speed with which the new destroyer had been sent into action, or at least near to it, is a measure of the urgency felt in all areas of the war to see the fighting finished during 1918. The war in Syria produced a great and decisive victory for the British Imperial force in a battle in September; the Salonika Front was broken open at much the same time; the Allies were advancing inexorably on the Western Front from August onwards. In the Adriatic, where the war was a mainly naval one, aggression had been tempered by the indecisiveness of the Italian naval command, but in October a grand joint naval action was finally organized, a bombardment of the Austrian-occupied Albanian city of Durazzo.

Shark was part of the operation, as a screen for the cruiser *Lowestoft*, which was carrying the senior British commander, Rear Admiral WA Kelly, and two other cruisers, *Weymouth* and *Dartmouth*, along with three other destroyers. The fleet which was assembled for the operation was large, menacing, international, and largely ineffective in the execution of the operation. There were British, Italian, Australian, Greek, and United States ships involved, and, as could be expected, cooperation was poor. The idea was to use the cruisers to bombard the shore batteries and defences, and to send in destroyers to sink the three Austrian warships in the harbour. In the event this last part was cancelled, and the bombardment was barely effective against the Austrian warships. They unsportingly dodged about in the harbour, successfully evading the shells sent against them, and suffered only minor damage.

On the other hand, the Austrian submarine *U-31* succeeded in torpedoing the cruiser *Weymouth*, damaging its stern, though not its rudder or propeller. This was one of the ships *Shark* was screening. *Shark's* log of the action is typically cryptic, noting the enemy opening fire, and *Shark's* own opening fire, and that *Shark* fired its own torpedoes, but not at what target. A second enemy submarine was driven off with depth charges, but *Shark* was not apparently involved in this fight. Judging by the restocking next day, the ship also fired a considerable number of shells, presumably at the land or the harbour.

The fleet was then returned to Brindisi, with *Shark* screening the larger ships as before, particularly the injured *Weymouth*. Despite much confusion when more than forty ships arrived more or less simultaneously at the entrance to the cleared channel leading into the harbour, in the dark, no collisions occurred. (*Shark* docked at last at 8.47 pm.) The success of this aspect seems to have impressed Admiral Kelly in *Lowestoft* more than any other part of the operation. It was claimed to be an overall success by those who commented on Kelly's report in the Admiralty, and the two enemy submarines were claimed as sunk and damaged, though this was not correct. But no one could claim that the Austrian ships in the harbour had even been damaged, and this had been the main purpose of the operation. The real answer to the operation came next day, when it was seen by reconnoitring aircraft that the Austrian army was evacuating the city – which must have been planned well before the Allied bombardment.[2]

III

Shark was rearmed next day, receiving two torpedoes and eighty-four shells. It was on patrol again later that day, staying out until 6 October. By that time it was clear that Durazzo was being evacuated by the Austrians, and naval operations had to move further north. *Shark* was directed, along with much of the British naval force in the Adriatic, into the Aegean, where it was clear that not only had Bulgaria collapsed, and requested an armistice at the end of September, but the Ottoman Empire was approaching the same condition – Allenby's army in Syria was well on the way to reaching Aleppo, and in Thrace a British force was preparing to cross the Maritza River and advance on Constantinople. The Salonika army headed north into Serbia aiming to invade Austria-Hungary's home territory.

Shark sailed from Brindisi on 10 October, and arrived next day at Piraeus, moving on to Mudros on the island of Lemnos, the Allied naval command centre in the Aegean, on the 12th. It patrolled to the north of the island during the next days. It visited Pyrgos Bay on the island of Samothrace, carried a general to Stavros (Katostavros) on the Greek mainland, and on 28 October it carried a group of soldiers to Dedeagatch on the Bulgarian Aegean coast, close to where the attack on Constantinople was being prepared. Then back to Mudros on the 29th, the day the Ottoman Empire asked for an armistice. That is, the ship was being used, as so often with *Sharks* in the past, as a combined taxi-service-cum-patroller.

By this time the Ottoman Empire as well as Bulgaria had agreed to an armistice, Austria–Hungary was visibly breaking up, and the German Army was in retreat everywhere in France and Belgium. But the war was not over, and on 4 November near Mudros, the British battleship *Agamemnon* and the Greek cruiser *Giorgios Averoff* indulged in some gunnery practice fully within earshot of the Turkish coast; *Shark* was part of the destroyer screen; two days later it was range-finding for *Superb*, the flagship of the new British commander-in-chief, Admiral Gough-Calthorpe.

The move of *Shark* and the other British ships from the Adriatic into the Aegean had been partly to exert pressure on Turkey, but it was just as much to pre-empt naval command in the Aegean from the French; the Royal Navy then outnumbered the French ships in the area, and Gough-Calthorpe was sent to Mudros, where he outranked the local French commander, Admiral Amet. The Turkish plenipotentiaries, as it happened, were accredited only to the British, quite reasonably since the British had done most of the fighting against the Turks, so it was British armistice terms which were presented and agreed in the negotiations at Mudros; Gough-Calthorpe was assiduous in excluding Amet from the discussions.

The armistice arrangements included an Allied occupation of the Straits, and on 10 November *Shark*, carrying some army officers, sailed through the Dardanelles to Constantinople. The Gallipoli peninsula had already been occupied by Allied forces, but the channel had not yet been fully swept for mines. The voyage must have been very tense and carefully conducted; *Shark* was, of course, being used as a possible sacrifice if the Turks chose to disregard the armistice and fight on. But now it was the turn of the capital of the empire to receive an Allied delegation of officers.

Shark's voyage to Constantinople was in fact for the purpose of delivering an advance party to make arrangements for the implementation of the full armistice terms. The formal installation of the Allied presence in the city and the arrival of Admiral Gough-Calthorpe took place on 12 November, with the Allies no doubt in high glee at the news of the German armistice the previous day. *Shark* had sailed back to Mudros on the 11th, no doubt to report the successful delivery of the advance party, and the relative safety of the passage through the Dardanelles. It was then also part of the official party which arrived on the 12th, having traversed the Dardanelles three times.

Constantinople had not been occupied, in the sense of a large Allied force taking over control. The Turks were told that the forces sent to the city would merely be a General Headquarters to command the forces in occupation of the coasts of the Dardanelles and the Bosporos, the latter of which were taken over in the next days. *Shark* meanwhile was sent into the Gulf of Ismid, east of the Bosporos, where the British ships later anchored. It was in that area that the 10,000 or so German and Austrian troops who had been in Constantinople were concentrated by Allied orders – by this time they were also no longer fighting. Clearly *Shark's* voyage was only a reconnaissance as far as Ismid city, and it returned to Constantinople on the 18th.[3]

IV

The ship now had a new job, again a reconnoitring voyage into unfamiliar waters, through the Bosporos (both banks now occupied by Allied troops) along with its fellow destroyer *Tribune*, which had been part of the screen at Durazzo. They were to sail as far as the Crimea in order to explore the conditions, humanitarian and above all political, in southern Russia.

The defeat of Tsarist Russia by Germany and its allies had involved the steady advance of German military power across the north coast of the Black Sea as far as the Crimea and beyond. The surviving Russian fleet in that sea had withdrawn eastwards from its main bases at Nicolaiev and Sebastopol to Novorossisk on the east coast, but it had then split into two parts: one group of ships had gone back to Sebastopol to be taken over by the Germans, and the other had stayed at Novorossisk and had been scuttled. The defeat of Germany in the west had now upset what had become for a time a local balance of forces, and southern Russia had meanwhile broken up: the Ukraine was proclaiming its independence, as were the 'Don Cossacks', and the Caucasus provinces. The various parties in Russia – Tsarists, Bolsheviks, and others – had begun to resolve their differences by violence, stimulated of course by the initial resort to force of the Bolsheviks in their *coup d'etat* in St Petersburg; meanwhile the people, in whose name most of this was theoretically going on, starved.

Shark and *Tribune* picked their ways carefully through the Black Sea, watching insistently for mines and submarines. They were off the Crimea by 20 November, conducting a zigzagging patrol, just in case an active submarine, German, possibly, or Russian of any party, should take a shot at them. They then returned to Constantinople on the 23rd, reported what they had found, and were sent out again on the 25th. This time they looked into Sebastopol in more detail, and then investigated the situation to the west at Odessa and Nikolaiev, where *Shark* landed an armed guard to make enquiries as to the local situation. The Allies had divided the responsibilities in the Black Sea geographically: the French took the west, and sent forces to Odessa and proposed to occupy Sebastopol when they had more troops. The British were particularly interested in controlling events in the eastern part of the sea and beyond in the Caucasus and Central Asia. They sent a force to Batum, whence they took measures to gain naval control of the Caspian Sea, which was imagined, if it fell into Bolshevik hands, to become the base for an anti-colonialist threat to India.

The visits of *Shark* and *Tribune* to Sebastopol and Odessa were part of a quick early survey of the whole of the Black Sea to which other destroyers contributed as well. The cruisers *Grafton* – an old ship but well-armed – and *Canterbury* – the same which had been with the previous *Shark* at Jutland – were the command centres. Patrols were put on shore and made contact with the German forces, with the local Volunteer Army, with the Bolsheviks, with the forces aiming to establish an independent Ukraine, and with any other group claiming responsibility or power – all with the aim of gathering information about their power and purposes, and to remind them that the Royal Navy was present, though how much attention they needed to pay to the ships was a problem. Given that British government policy was to oppose the Bolsheviks, almost any group other than the Bolsheviks could be given support. But the only group with both power and discipline were the German forces of occupation. Inevitably the British found themselves for a time relying on their erstwhile enemies to control the towns and cities in which they had forces.[4]

The French army occupied Odessa, but had no men to spare to take over at Nikolaiev or Sebastopol. Odessa was especially difficult, with several groups contending for control, while Sebastopol held what remained of the Russian Navy, but under German control, including a number of submarines, the weapon which the Royal Navy feared most; at Nicolaiev, the major shipbuilding base in the Black Sea, there were several incomplete submarines, which the navy was especially anxious should neither be completed nor should fall into Bolshevik hands. There were at least a dozen submarines in Sebastopol, a very dangerous force if the Russian Bolsheviks could regain them and send them out to attack their numerous enemies. When the French asked for British help 500 marines were collected from the ships in the Black Sea and the area and sent into Sebastopol. In that place it had been uncontrolled Russian sailors which had been the main security problem, all unpaid, unfed and undisciplined. They subsided and largely left the city when the British marines arrived. The British took over the Russian ships, voicing much disgust at the state they were in. By this time the Germans were keen to get home, and some had begun to refuse orders. The rail route through the Ukraine and Poland had turned dangerous, especially for the retreating German occupiers, whose trains tended to be stoned, if not worse, and the evacuation of the German troops by sea was planned, but it would take time to gather sufficient transport ships.

Shark returned to Constantinople on the last day of 1918 and went at once to Ismid, at the end of the Gulf of Ismid, where it received ammunition, 12-pounder shells, pistols, and black powder – useful weaponry for bombarding a shore, or for arming landing parties. It had been working continually by now for over four months, and had gone into the work directly from its commissioning without having had any really extensive trials to find any problems, and it was time for a refit; it went to Malta and was in dry dock for three weeks from 10 January. Meanwhile the crew was given generous leave, though when not on leave they had the tasks of scraping the ship's bottom or repainting. The ship returned to Mudros again on 21 February and next day was patrolling through the Dardanelles.[5]

No log exists for the next two months (March to May 1919), presumably because Lieutenant Bonham-Carter was replaced in command in April by Commander Eric Q Carter, who took the ship back to Britain. By the end of May the ship was at Chatham, where it was recommissioned, no doubt after a thorough inspection, and perhaps having undergone some of the delayed trials which had been skipped when it was originally commissioned.

The British presence in the Black Sea had been reduced at the end of 1918, perhaps too optimistically; then in April 1919 parts of the French fleet in the sea mutinied, demanding to be returned home. This mutiny was among the forces at Odessa and led to an immediate French withdrawal from the city; more trouble at Sebastopol persuaded the British to resume responsibility for that place. The Bolshevik attacks were persistent, if uncoordinated, but often they were locally successful, at least for a time. The Volunteer Army, an anti-Bolshevik force with some discipline, was concentrated in the Kerch peninsula and came under attack from a Bolshevik force in April; the battleship *Agamemnon* used its big guns to bombard the Bolshevik positions, who scattered. The unstable independent Ukraine had collapsed under the dual pressures of dissension within and Bolshevik moves without – the promise of a federal structure for Soviet Russia, and so much local autonomy, defused much of the Ukrainian opposition.

Shark returned to the eastern Mediterranean at the end of June, and went on a series of short voyages from Constantinople to Principo, to Samsun, to Batum, to Novorossisk, in part to deliver mail – it had collected 100 bags of mail for the region at Malta. By this time the Turkish Nationalist reaction to the severe peace terms dictated at Paris (the Treaty of Sevres) had begun to gather strength. The Allies had occupied Constantinople in a series of gradual developments and moves, which included the establishment of such institutions as the British Seaman's Hospital, an officers' club, and the YMCA. These were all the sort of British items one might find in a colony, and it made it seem that the British presence was becoming permanent, and not just a merely temporary GHQ as had been promised originally. In the latter part of 1919 the surrender of arms by forces in the interior of Anatolia and the demobilization of the Turkish armed forces slowed markedly, and in August the political reaction in the interior began with the beginnings of the organization of the revolutionary forces led by Mustafa Kemal, the later Ataturk.[6]

So the Allied problem with Russia had become a problem also with the Turks. In July *Shark* was patrolling in the Sea of Marmara, inspecting Turkish ships in search of arms being smuggled into European Turkey. A ferry was stopped and searched and sent in for further examination. *Shark* went into Gemlik to inspect the Turkish ships there, which included a torpedo-boat. This patrol was repeated in early August, but without the need to inspect so many ships. Back at Constantinople it took a Turkish ambassador and his staff across to the Asiatic side of the Bosporos, then took the captain of the cruiser *Ceres* out to his ship. Another patrol along the south Marmara coast followed. This time the interception of a Turkish caique proved fruitful: it was found to be carrying rifles, bayonets, and ammunition; it was made prize, the crew were arrested, and the ship was confiscated. (*Shark's* crew received prize money later; this must have been one of the last cases of prize money awards in the Navy.)

All this patrolling activity was designed to prevent the infiltration of Turkish arms and fighters into European Turkey, which was now wholly under Allied occupation. The Nationalists were pressing on towards the Marmara coast from central Anatolia, swimming easily through a sea of supporters. On its next patrol *Shark* went into the Gulf of Ismid once more, spending several days there and at Constantinople, largely spending the time on torpedo and firing practice.

The Russian Black Sea coast continued to be a problem. From Constantinople *Shark* sailed to Odessa, where it collected a Russian general and his staff and his guard and took them to Sebastopol. Attention now shifted to the Sea of Azov, where the coastal cities were coming under strong Bolshevik and other pressures. On 7 October *Shark* was off the Crimea, first at Sebastopol then at

Yalta, then a week later off Mariupol, deep inside the Sea of Azov. The shallow waters of the sea prevented the larger ships from operating, and only destroyers and some cruisers could get close to the shore. The initial investigation there showed the situation to be serious enough for ammunition to be served out to the guns, and on the 15th the ship cleared for action. Next day it was off the town of Ursov (Urzuf) about twenty miles west of Mariupol; there it opened fire on Bolshevik forces four times on that day and the next, and once more at other forces at the small town of Petrovski later. Clearly the Bolsheviks in the region were becoming more assertive. The ship cruised menacingly in the area for two more days, firing again at the Bolsheviks in Ursov. On the 20th it was in collision with a Russian tug, whether deliberately or not is not recorded, and was holed in the stern, though the damage was quickly repaired. On the 22nd it was relieved by its fellow destroyer *Seraph*, and left next day.

Shark was sent out of the Black Sea soon after this, reaching Malta on 27 October. It was replenished with oil, ammunition and stores, but then remained at Malta until January, being involved in manoeuvres and exercises, and firing and torpedo practices. No doubt the damage inflicted by the Russian tug was also investigated and a more permanent repair made. When the ship left Malta on 26 January it was mainly being used as a delivery and postal service. First it went to Constantinople, for the first time using the Corinth Canal rather than the much more dangerous passage between Greece and Crete. It returned the same way, but first went to call at Taranto. From there it returned to Malta, and then went to Smyrna, where the Greeks were in occupation and were fighting the Turkish Nationalists in the interior. It took some soldiers to Mudros, then went back to Smyrna, and then to Constantinople. For a change it then went to Salonika, back to Constantinople and then to Smyrna once more, conveying a general and his aide-de-camp. All this voyaging took less than two months, and one probable reason for using *Shark* was because the ship was in good condition after its Malta docking.

By this time tens of thousands of Russian refugees had escaped from the Bolsheviks on whatever ships they could reach, commandeer, or steal, and were spreading throughout the Mediterranean. On 20 March *Shark* was at Famagusta in Cyprus and helped in the disembarkation of one of these refugee ships, the SS *Kherson*; another ship, *Saratov*, arrived soon after and again the sailors were employed as porters and stevedores, moving people and baggage to the shore. Once that work was concluded the ship was again employed to sail from port to port, carrying people and mails and being generally present and available – Alexandria to Port Said, to Famagusta again, to Haifa and Jaffa in Palestine, back to Alexandria, and then along the Egyptian coast to Sollum and Mersa Matruh, and back to Alexandria. Finally it returned to Malta where it stayed for a fortnight.

Shark had therefore spent seven months either at Malta or shuffling about the eastern Mediterranean, with one short visit back to Britain. In June it was returned to the Turkish area, first to Smyrna then to Constantinople and Ismid, delivering mail and a general, and patrolling in its old territory in the eastern end of the Sea of Marmara. On 25 June it was at Mudanya, where landing parties from the battleship *Marlborough* were resisting advances and attacks by Nationalist Turks. *Shark* provided close cover to the armed parties, then did the same at Gemlik, where it prepared to fire, but in the end did not need to. Back at Constantinople it had some torpedo practice within the Bosporos. Then on 5 July it took mails to Sebastopol, still under Allied occupation, though the French had evacuated Odessa. As a gesture to an increasingly fragile Allied solidarity, the ship, back at Constantinople once more, was dressed overall on 14 July, Bastille Day.

Next day, it embarked three army officers and twenty-five soldiers and landed them at several places in succession along the Marmara coast wherever Nationalist power was present. It was not apparently intended that they should fight, but was another way of showing the flag, and of giving warning. *Shark* had to fire once, but successfully re-embarked all the soldiers and returned them and the information they had collected to Constantinople. *Shark* once more returned to Malta, arriving on 19 July, but then turned about and went back to the Black Sea.

Again the ship was being used mainly to deliver mails and to move people from one point to another – a Russian officer from Sebastopol to Yalta on 9 October, an American officer to Constantinople, Baroness Wrangel (the wife of the White Russian commander) and a collection of accompanying staff officers to Sebastopol. The ship then returned to Malta for the winter. It was docked and refitted, being recommissioned in March 1921, by which time it had a new captain, Commander Frederick Russell.[7]

V

There is another gap in the sequence of logs between late 1920 and 1922. At least some of the time *Shark* was undergoing maintenance at Malta, and it may be that the ship was becoming regarded as ineffective. There are comments in the Admiralty record that 'scouts' were not suitable ships for the Black Sea because of their limited endurance, and the lack of supplies of fuel oil available – *Scout* was one of the earliest of the 'S' class destroyers. However, *Shark* came back into the region in 1922, as the final crisis – the 'Chanak Crisis' – developed. It sailed back and forth between Constantinople and Chanak and Smyrna, the three main epicentres of the several elements of the crisis, in August and September, at the time when the Turks drove the Greeks out of Smyrna amid a great massacre and the burning of the city, and the British came to terms with the Turkish Nationalist successes. The British commander in Constantinople, General Sir Tim Harington, did not deliver a blunt ultimatum to the Turks as instructed by the Cabinet in London and so managed to secure an armistice, initiate new peace talks, and so avoided a war which would have been a disaster for both the British and the Turks. The British government had been abandoned by their (former) European allies, and had been refused help by their imperial dominion partners in an attempt to coerce the Turkish Nationalists. The prime victim of the crisis turned out to be the British prime minister, David Lloyd George.

Shark, however, was kept busy as usual, at least once in these months going to action stations in response to a local aspect of the several crises. It formed part of the regular patrol through the Dardanelles, calling repeatedly at Gallipoli and Kum Kale in the Dardanelles and at Mudros. Again it returned to Malta, going into dock there on 17 October 1922 and remained there until late November. The crisis between the Allies and Turkey was accompanied by constant exercises and manoeuvres by the British fleet in the Sea of Marmara. *Shark* took part in several of these during the winter of 1922/1923. A visit to Malta in late December (over Christmas) was to collect cordite and some sailors who were going to join the destroyer *Sparrowhawk*, so *Shark* was still being used as a messenger. The Dardanelles patrol was kept up, and *Shark*'s taxi-service continued in between these patrols.

A final crisis took place at Smyrna in January, bringing a major naval force together, including two battleships; *Shark* cleared for action but was not one of the ships which entered the harbour. The city had been under Turkish control since the fire the previous year, assisted by a massacre and the expulsion of the Greek population, and the armed ships entering the harbour clearly constituted a new crisis, originating essentially in Turkish assertiveness; all was smoothed over, however. At the end of February *Shark* sailed to Kios (or perhaps Chios) with the withdrawing forces, and then returned to Malta once more.

The new peace conference, held at Lausanne in Switzerland, after a break in February and March when the Turks walked out, finally produced an agreed text in July 1923. The reduction in tension brought *Shark* back to Britain after a final period of patrolling in the Dardanelles and the Sea of Marmara during the last stages of the negotiations. From Malta it returned once more to Chatham where it was again refitted and recommissioned in September – but, although assigned to the Atlantic fleet it was not employed, but was put on a care and maintenance basis, with an engineer lieutenant in command of a reduced crew.[8] This marked almost the end of the ship's active life.

For a ship built in the time of the greatest war so far on record, if only commissioned in the last four months of that war, *Shark* XI had had a very active and busy career. It had also seen more action, in the sense of firing its guns at enemies, than any of its predecessors or successors – even if most of this firing had actually taken place in what was theoretically peacetime. It had taken part in hostilities in the Adriatic, above all at Durazzo, and when shifted to the Aegean, it had bombarded Bolsheviks in Russia, and Turks in Asia Minor. Very few of its predecessors had ever fired their guns at any enemy, though its immediate predecessor and its two successors did so as they were sunk. Nevertheless, *Shark* XI had still, like its fellows, been used mainly in the auxiliary, but necessary, tasks which make it possible for a fleet to operate. And there was one more moment of activity to come, even more curious that anything it had done so far.

VI

From Chatham *Shark* was moved to Port Edgar on the Firth of Forth, still in a care and maintenance condition. It had an inspection by a commission of enquiry in February 1925; the ship was not moved on that occasion, and the Captain (D), commanding the flotilla of which it was a part, commented that the crew was 'cleaning ship every day', which is reminiscent of the final months of *Shark* IX at Portsmouth, when the ship was being cleaned right down to the moment when it was delivered to be sold. It must have been thoroughly disheartening to men who had joined the navy to do more than being used as cleaners. But *Shark* X had one more adventure to come.

In November 1925 the ship was brought from the Forth to Sheerness and then to Chatham, to be part of the Nore Reserve Flotilla. This was a time of much industrial unrest, centred particularly on the conditions and pay of the coal miners. Unions throughout the country were disturbed and agitated by the miners' plight, and there was talk of a general strike to provide support. This, by what seems to have been a series of accidents and mistakes by both the union leaders and politicians, eventuated in May 1926. This was the context of *Shark* XI's last 'campaign'.

At Chatham on 5 May the ship was oiled and provisioned, and ammunition was loaded. A General Strike had been called by the Trades Union Congress for midnight on May 3/4, and it actually began on the 4th as the word spread. At first few people know what to do in such an unprecedented situation, but the Admiralty evidently felt that preparation should be made for possible conflict. Certainly during the strike tempers became steadily more heated, and opinions voiced were increasingly extreme on both sides, and in government circles it was apprehended that a continuation of the strike would certainly threaten the position of Parliament and the government – the government was not slow in airing those fears and turning them into an accusation directed at the hapless Trades Union Congress, which was supposedly overseeing the strike, and now found itself presiding ineffectively over an apparent attempted revolution; certainly the whole affair was less a strike than a constitutional crisis.

The government's anti-strike measures increasingly involved the use of both the army and the navy. Convoys of lorries driven by volunteers were given military escorts, the Territorial Army was embodied as a supplementary police force, there were numerous soldiers with rifles and fixed bayonets on the London streets. The Admiralty used barges manned by Royal Navy sailors to protect and deliver raw materials to mills grinding flour, and to deliver newsprint for the use of the government's emergency newspaper, the *British Gazette*.

Parties of sailors were dispatched to take over the running of industrial plant which was considered crucial at many ports from Glasgow to Devonport to London; some of these interventions were very difficult and faced active resistance from the strikers, as at Cardiff, Hull and Newcastle, and above all at Glasgow. In the London area this meant intervening at the docks. At the Nore, the nearest naval command to the London area, the commander-in-chief, Admiral Sir William Goodenough, was warned as early as 1 May to conserve coal, gas, and electricity supplies. When the strike began, it was several days before it seemed necessary for naval parties to intervene, and when they did Goodenough (and the Admiralty) moved very delicately into the difficult situation. One party of sailors took over the operation of the Tilbury ferry; submarines went into several docks to provide power to maintain refrigeration in cold stores, which contained a large quantity of frozen meat which would have spoiled otherwise; stokers were used to keep the power stations going. Then several petrol depots were clearly seen to be vulnerable, and naval parties intervened to ensure that supplies continued to be sent out. At Thameshaven, the strikers dug up the road from the depot and cut the telephone wires; a naval party was sent ashore to repair the road, and when the men went to search for the cut wires they were harassed by, as the officer in charge reported, guerrillas.[9]

Besides the naval parties and the submarines, several other ships were moved into the docks for the emergency; 'U.C', 'Unrest, Civil', was the Admiralty's classification of the situation – commanders-in-chief had a file in their safes for such a contingency. The drillship *President*, formerly the sloop *Saxifrage*, was placed in the Albert Dock as an accommodation vessel for the various naval parties in the area; the destroyer *Sportive* was also there, and the destroyer *Tenedus* was in the Surrey Dock; the destroyer *Newark* was at Tilbury. Held in reserve at the Nore was *Ark Royal*, a seaplane carrier, and *Shakespeare*, a destroyer leader, both of which had substantial crews, and several more destroyers; at Thameshaven the monitor *Marshal Soult* and the destroyer *Shamrock* were stationed. This was a considerable contribution of naval power, though how far the strikers felt intimidated is not really known.

It is probable that it had more effect on the leaders of the strike, the union leaders in the TUC. This certainly had in some cases an effect on several of the TUC members who were by no means convinced that the strike was a sensible move. It is likely that the proposition that they were heading for revolution had a chilling effect on many of them, for they were generally of a socially and even politically conservative disposition, aiming to exploit the capitalist system, not overthrow it, but they knew that more extreme ideas were gaining ground among the strikers the longer the strike lasted. The increasing evidence that the government was quite willing to use its armed resources, and the steady if quiet increase in the military presence in London, must also have been a clear indication of the consequences they faced.

In this situation *Shark*'s activities during the strike are of interest. It was, as noted, oiled and armed on 5 May, the second day of the strike, in what was obviously a direct reaction to it. It was also fully crewed but it waited at Chatham for the next five days. On 10 May Vice Admiral Sir William Goodenough, the commander-in-chief at the Nore, came on board, with a river pilot. The ship sailed up the Thames flying the flag of the commander-in-chief as far as the Surrey Docks, where it anchored at 8.35 am.

The commander-in-chief disembarked at the docks, being on shore for an hour and a half. When he returned the ship moved a little way down the river to the Victoria Docks, where he went ashore again. The docks were one of the areas in London which were most solid in the strike, and where volunteers were busy at work as strike-breakers, though in London itself the strike was not well supported generally. The docks were clearly one of the most dangerous areas, if a conflict broke out, from the government's point of view. The commander-in-chief returned to the ship at 1.00 pm and *Shark* went further downstream to Purfleet and then to Gravesend, where the commander-in-chief landed again; he did so again at Thameshaven, and finally left the ship at Gravesend at 5.45 pm; the ship continued on to Chatham.

What this was all about is never stated, but it would seem to be in the nature of a reconnaissance by the commander-in-chief in case he had to take some sort of action. It could, of course, be merely a tour of inspection. He had parties of sailors at all the places he visited, but they had been there for several days already, and it is noticeable that he only made the journey the day after the serious trouble broke out at Thameshaven. There, not only had the strikers dug up the road and cut the telephone wires, they had stoned the drivers of some of the delivery lorries, while the petrol company executives had been extremely awkward about collecting supplies, each wanting to be first in the queue and each requiring to collect his own petrol, rather than, as Goodenough wanted, or simply taking a share of the whole mixture.

Goodenough does not mention this tour of inspection – or reconnaissance – in his reports, nor in his summary of the events, and the lessons to be learned, after it was all over.[10] It may thus be seen as something done on his own initiative. It was clearly the sort of move to be expected of a commander-in-chief who had sent his sailors into a difficult situation. It is not clear if the ships in the docks were actually fully armed, though it seems unlikely, but *Shark* certainly was, and while that may have been the obvious thing to do with a naval vessel, in other respects the naval situation in the docks was often as light-footed as it could be. It seems safe to conclude that Goodenough was prepared for any emergency, as was *Shark*.

In London it would clearly be the docks which would be the main focus of trouble if an insurrection broke out, and Admiral Goodenough apparently wished to become familiar with the potential field of conflict. (It was in a curious way reminiscent of the English government's use of the men of *Shark* I in London in 1696 to patrol and seek out possible subversives at a time when Parliament was due to meet, though the dockers of London were not to be confused with Jacobites; yet both subversive groups were unsuccessful.)

But this was not the only aspect which is evident in this short cruise. The situation in the country was becoming steadily more tense during 10 and 11 May, and it would seem that Goodenough was doing what admirals tend to do in moments of tension, sending an armed ship into the situation as a warning in the hope of cooling tempers, the sort of action taken by many of *Shark* X's predecessors, above all in the West Indies – *Shark* III and IV in the waters about South Carolina, Florida, and the Bahamas seems particularly apposite. The docks being one of the centres of the strike, by sailing as far as the Surrey Docks – the furthest inland of the several great London docks – *Shark* will have been noted by the strikers at all the docks which it passed on the way, and the commander-in-chief's ostentatious landings at several places were no doubt noted, as it was also that they were intended to be, and the whole performance was undoubtedly reported to the TUC's men who were in constant discussion about what to do during these days.

Next day, 11 May, a different performance was put on. At Chatham the Captain (D), commanding the local destroyer force, the Nore Reserve Flotilla, came on board *Shark* at 10.00 am. During the morning other destroyers of the flotilla – *Swallow*, *Turbulent*, *Shamrock* and *Steadfast*, all 'S' class destroyers contemporaneous with *Shark* – were gathered into a group at Chatham. Undoubtedly this, after the commander-in-chief's public display the day before, was also reported to the TUC. It was a clear and manifest threat that in the event of an attempt to overthrow the government and the governmental system, there was a substantial naval force available to act in defence of that system, just as there were numerous soldiers in London.

The general strike folded on the 12th, when the TUC determined that they would no longer support the miners in their separate strike; it was called off next day, but it only ended slowly in some areas, and the miners continued their own strike for several more months. The fact that elements among the other strikers, who had struck in sympathy with the miners, and not primarily with grievances of their own in mind, continued their action for some time is a clear sign that even in the few days of the general strike opinion among the strikers had shifted in a clearly revolutionary direction. Goodenough's daily reports on the situation in the London docks continued for another week, as the several striking groups reluctantly returned to work. The government's precautions were evidently fully justified; the fears of the TUC leaders were real. Only on the 18th, a week after the strike had been called off, was he able to report that all the strikes in the docks were over.

Shark was still at Chatham, but on 20 May the whole crew, except the coxswain, was dismissed from the ship.[11] Again, one wonders if the sailors had formed some common ground with the strikers – the men in the Admiralty dockyards and other establishments had in many cases been on strike – and so were removed before they could take some sort of action. The sailors were all given an extra week's leave. In the background of all this, for all those taking part and in the minds of every naval officer, was the collective memory of the events in Russia, where the sailors had been at the heart of the revolution. For revolutionaries, to persuade effective and disciplined groups like ships' crews to support them was always a priority. In the Black Sea and in the Baltic mutinous sailors with control of ships had often been decisive forces – and the French fleet in the Black Sea had mutinied in 1919, decisively reducing the effectiveness of Allied support for the anti-Bolshevik forces. It was to be only five years before elements of the Royal Navy at Invergordon staged their own strike. Any reasonably competent naval officer would understand the possibility of unrest in the navy.

Shark XI was used no more. It was in the Reserve at the Nore for the rest of 1925, then moved to the base at Rosyth on the Forth. In August 1927 it was formally recommissioned at Chatham, but it remained at Rosyth for the next four years, when it was sold off (in 1931). Its last adventure, into the heart of London, like its constant activity during its career in the Mediterranean and the Aegean and the Black Sea, had been less a vessel of war than as an anti-revolutionary instrument. It was not what the ship had been designed for, but it was a reflection of the unsettled time in which it existed. It was also a revival of the work done by most of its predecessors.

Chapter 13

Shark XII: a Submarine, 1934–1940

O ne of the lessons of the Great War was that at sea the submarine armed with torpedoes was an extremely effective weapon. They were, however, difficult to build, awkward to manoeuvre, just as inaccurate in firing their weapons as were other ships, and dangerous to be in. They were also not really submarines in the sense that, like a fish, they could exist permanently under the surface of the sea; the technical term for them is 'submersible', a vessel which can submerge for a limited time, usually several hours, but which must then surface for a variety of reasons, of which the replenishment of their batteries is one, and the need to vent the foul air accumulated by the crew breathing underwater is another. (On the other hand, 'submarine' is the popular term, and it will be used here.)

In the 1930s, as the 'S' class of destroyers were being phased out and sold, a new 'S' class, this time of submarines, was designed and constructed. The first of these were few, of 640 tons, and were soon succeeded by a slightly larger and improved version from 1934 onwards. This in time was also succeeded by another version, larger again, which began to be built in 1937, and which continued to be built until 1944 (the last of the class to be ordered were cancelled in 1945). The size of the earliest boats, and the way they grew larger, is very similar to the history of the earliest destroyers, it may be noted.

These new boats were frequently named from the decommissioned 'S' class destroyers, and the new *Shark* (*Shark* XII) was one of the second phase, built at Chatham and launched in May 1934. There were three more boats of the class launched in that year, but only four more in the next three years, and then the larger, third phase, version was designed. The second phase boats were armed with one 3-inch gun, and they had six torpedo tubes. In common with all submarines of that vintage, they were uncomfortable, dangerous, packed with equipment almost to the point where the crew had little room to move and live, and were of only a limited range and a limited period of submergence.

Shark the submarine was commissioned at Chatham in October 1934, five months after its launch, when the first captain, Lieutenant Commander

JG Roper, took command.[1] The early entries in the logs (each of which now covered only a month at a time) are oddly reminiscent of those for the first *Shark* in 1691 (and every newly built ship since) listing a series of tests and trials, loading of stores and ammunition, but instead of guns and sails and rigging and pease and beer, the entries mention a vacuum test, term trials, testing hydrophones, loading torpedoes, and submerging in the dock to test water tightness – but the process is much the same. It also took much longer: where the first *Shark* got through this process in a month or so, *Shark* XII did not go to sea until late November 1934, five months after its launching.

Exercises took place near Portsmouth in January and February 1935, and then the boat sailed to Gibraltar. Even in this first voyage it encountered one of the hazards of submarines at sea, when it had to change course suddenly off Cape Finisterre in order to avoid being run down by a merchantman – the submarines were so low in the water that they were barely visible, especially to lackadaisical watchmen in merchant ships. More exercises took place off Gibraltar, and then *Shark* accompanied the destroyer leader *Douglas* to Malta; *Douglas* was an extra large destroyer intended to lead a flotilla of other destroyers into battle. This one had become a sort of mother ship for the British submarines in the Mediterranean. On the voyage to Malta, *Shark* had to avoid being run down by other ships on three more occasions – the presence of *Douglas* does not seem to have afforded any protection.

Two months were spent at Malta undergoing repeated exercises. Each of these would typically consist of fake attacks on another Royal Navy ship – usually *Douglas* – using unarmed torpedoes, which had then to be recovered. But each exercise was very noticeably usually ended in the early evening, after which that part of the crew not on watch would be given leave. Submergence of the boat usually took place, but only for a short time. If other vessels were available, particularly a fleet of them, they would become the targets for the attacks, though they were usually warned in advance. It is tempting to believe that submarine tactics were scarcely developed in any substantive way by these exercises. Each exercise seems to have been effectively the same as the last.

The boat returned to Britain in mid-June 1935, taking ten days on the voyage from Malta to Portsmouth – submarines were not speedy craft. After exercises and participation in the Silver Jubilee review at Spithead, *Shark* returned to Malta. Wireless transmission trials took place, and then more exercises. These constituted the life of the craft and its crew for the next four months. Each exercise lasted a day, and was followed by anything from a day to a week in harbour.

On 25 November a new captain, Lieutenant Commander GH Bolus, took command, and the boat at once sailed to Alexandria in Egypt, but once there the routine was just the same as at Malta or Portsmouth: short exercises, including firing torpedoes at British ships, were mixed with short periods of submergence.[2]

1936 was, of course, the year in which Europe definitively turned towards war: the Nazi regime in Germany remilitarized the Rhineland, the civil war began in Spain. Already the year before the Fascist regime in Italy had begun its war of conquest in Ethiopia (Abyssinia) which continued through 1936. The quiet time in the Mediterranean was clearly over. The Ethiopian War brought a crisis in Britain's relations with Italy, and the failure of the British as controllers of the Suez Canal to prevent the passage of Italian forces into the Red Sea was a clear indication of the British failure of nerve; the Mediterranean Fleet was substantially reinforced during the crisis from the Home Fleet and elsewhere, which helped to expose the basic problem, that the number of possible enemies had grown during the early 1930s, and that it was becoming very difficult to contemplate a successful war if they combined.[3]

Shark's exercises continued in January of 1937, until the end of the month when it went on a cruise to Greece. This was a country where politics had been constantly messy since the end of the Great War, and in 1935 a republican regime had been replaced by a constitutional monarchy, which had effectively given way to a military dictatorship under General John Metaxas. During all the confusion and the changes of government and of constitutions, there had remained in the country a British Naval Mission, and Metaxas, like his predecessors in power, was happy for it to remain, since it represented a certain element of diplomatic support. The visit of *Shark* and other ships, part of the usual annual cruise for the fleet, was another gesture in the same direction.[4] On the other hand Metaxas was determined to play his own hand in the developing international situation, and was given little economic or financial support by his friend.

Shark returned to Malta after a week in Greek waters. By this time the boat and the crew were familiar with the waters near Valetta harbour in Malta and with those around Alexandria, but not elsewhere in the Mediterranean except the route back to Gibraltar. Perhaps with this deficiency in mind in April 1937 the boat's exercises developed into cooperation with a group of submarines, the large boat *Thames* (at 1,800 tons it was three times the size of *Shark*), and *Salmon* and *Sealion* (*Shark's* contemporaries) along with *Douglas*. A variety of bays and harbours around Malta were used for a change, and so experience in close inshore waters was gained. At the end of these manoeuvres the ship went into dock at Malta for examination, refit, and cleaning.[5]

The Spanish Civil War was rather more dangerous, since it did not remain confined to Spaniards: Germany and Italy intervened on the Nationalist side (or 'insurgent' as the navy called their ships) and Russia on the Republican side. There were hostilities in Gibraltar Bay (during which the British consulate in Algeciras was hit by a shell from an insurgent ship), and on the mainland close by, but not for long. Volunteers arrived to fight for the Republic, mainly; but it was Spaniards who mostly did the fighting and dying. The British government did its best to keep out of the matter, only occasionally metaphorically stamping its foot so that interference from outside lessened for a while. *Shark* was not involved, though the run to Gibraltar had become rather more dangerous than merely dodging uncaring merchantmen. In July 1937 it was at Gibraltar and found two 'insurgent' ships on patrol there, and a French destroyer in the harbour.

Shark was on its way to Plymouth for exercises, and on its return it stayed at Gibraltar for more exercises for three months. At one point it saw both the Italian hospital ship *Grandisca* passing, and the German *panzerschiff Deutschland* nearby. Later there was a United States ship in the area. And all the time, by now almost daily, *Shark* was exercising and manoeuvring both to gain expertise, and to make it clear that Gibraltar was on its guard. By late December it was back at Malta, and by late February 1938 its exercises had extended to patrols lasting several days each.

The naval affairs of the Mediterranean were now dominated by the expansion of the Spanish conflict, for Fascist Italy was using its submarines to sink 'enemy' ships without warning. The destroyer *Havock* was damaged, and a British tanker was sunk. These attacks were, if not entirely stopped, at least drastically curtailed for a time by the decisions of a conference at Nyon in France in February, in which Britain and France agreed to retaliate, but it soon started up again. At last, HMS *Endymion* sank an unidentified submarine – probably Italian – and the navy announced that other submarines which failed to identify themselves would also be sunk; the attacks stopped.

By 1938 it was obvious to the most insensitive that a wider European war would come in a fairly short time. *Shark*'s larger and longer patrols were probably a response to this. There were also more lengthy voyages designed to assist in the development and establishing of politically united fronts against the aggressor states. In March 1938, at the time when Hitler in Germany was annexing Austria, and the British and French had begun staff talks in anticipation of a joint campaign in the fairly near future *Shark* was one of a flotilla which paid a visit to the south of France.[6]

The flotilla consisted of *Aberdeen*, a sloop, and three submarines, *Shark*, *Salmon*, and *Sealion*. They sailed as a group from Malta on 16 March, went through the Bonifacio Strait between Sardinia and Corsica, and called for a week at Ajaccio in Corsica. Then they all sailed on the 21st and visited Villefranche next to Nice, also for a week. *Aberdeen* was there replaced by the much more formidable cruiser *Penelope*. It is very noticeable that this was all very deliberately close to Italy, both in geographical and in political terms, even very obviously provocative.

The ships had gone quite deliberately close to the Italian island of Sardinia on their voyage from Malta to Ajaccio; Villefranche was not only next door to Nice, but was very close to the Italian border, and was a part of the lands which the Italians were in the habit of claiming had been 'stolen' from them by France. Corsica where the ships had called was another. (Later in 1938 in the Italian Chamber of Deputies the assembled Fascist members stood and shouted 'Nice, Corsica, Tunisia', at the French ambassador, in an orchestrated display of typically Fascist bad manners.) Villefranche was also an old naval base employed by the Royal Navy in the eighteenth century. It is beyond belief that this cruise had not been planned to visit such places in ignorance of their significance to both France and Italy – the cruise was an obvious demonstration of political support for France. And perhaps a gesture to assist in the negotiations and staff talks which led eventually to the Franco-British alliance.

The Mediterranean fleet spent every summer in cruises to visit a variety of ports in the countries along the northern part of the sea. Greece was popular, as was Turkey; Italy was visited until the hostility of the Fascist regime became too obvious, when visits were scaled back; France being reckoned a friend was not much visited, and from 1936 Spain was wholly out of bounds as the civil war ground on. In 1938, after some negotiations, the fleet sent the battleship *Warspite* and a variety of squadrons to visit both Yugoslavia and Italy – but it was the former which received the greatest attention, while the Italian visitation was limited to Venice.

From France the ships returned to Malta, but later in 1938 *Shark* was part of another of these quasi-diplomatic 'good-will' excursions as part of the programme of the summer cruise – though it was actually rather more blatantly threatening in this case. This time the flotilla included the depot ship *Maidstone*, only recently completed, and in effect almost a cruiser in its armament (eight 4-inch guns), two of the largest submarines, *Thames* and *Clyde*, and *Shark*'s old companions and contemporaries *Salmon* and *Sealion*. *Warspite* and other groups of ships visited several places, but this group of depot-ship-plus-submarines went north along the whole of the Yugoslav coast almost to the Italian border.

Whereas the previous flotilla of the year had sailed along the west side of Italy, this one used the Adriatic side. The first destination was Cattaro (Kotor) in Montenegro, part of Yugoslavia, just to the north of the Italian satellite Albania (which Mussolini would annex not long after). Cattaro had been an important Austrian naval base in the Great War, and, being close to Italy, it might well become a new base for Italian ships in another war. The ships of the flotilla remained in that intricate and twisting channel for ten days. This would be a superb naval base, protected on all sides by steep hills, and with a helpfully deep channel and a well-defended entrance. These visits were, of course, intelligence missions as much as displays of force, and the commanders of every group of ships produced a detailed report on the places they visited and the contacts they made.[7]

In Kotor Bay it was noted that the best anchorage was Tivat, where the Yugoslav ships were based, but the most pleasant place was Kotor itself. Parties of men and officers went ashore either as tourists or as guests of the Yugoslav military. 'The naval and military officers were most hospitable and friendly, and did everything possible to make us feel at home. One wild party with the military in their summer camp in the mountains, presided over by a Serbian general, will be remembered in the Flotilla for many years.' It is unlikely that the captain of the *Maidstone,* who made this comment in his report, overlooked the fact that the Yugoslavs had long been at odds with Italy, and were always in search of international friends; a friendly relationship with the Mediterranean Fleet would obviously be helpful.

The ships then made their ways north along the Adriatic coast of Yugoslavia, threading between the islands and the mainland, including passing between the Italian island of Lagosta and the Yugoslav mainland, through the Korkula channel and past the Italian port of Zara (now Zadar). The lesson was surely quite obvious: that the Royal Navy was capable of sending silent ships underwater into Italian waters, and in the event of a war might well be able to use the base and inlet of Kotor as a naval base. Along the way the cutter of *Maidstone* sailed deep into the Gulf of Quarnaro (Kvarnaer) in the far north, taking three days for the voyage, and penetrating sixty miles inland; these were waters separating Yugoslav and Italian territories, close to the Italian bases at Trieste and Fiume; under no circumstances could this be considered a mere yachting cruise.

The cruise went as far north as Crikenica, a Yugoslav port only a little way south of the city of Fiume (Rijeka) (which had been (illegally) annexed by Italy in 1924 after being set up as a 'free city' in the peace treaties). It was now an Italian naval base, as were Trieste and Venice, only a short distance further north, which were being visited at the same time by other British ships. Again the lesson could not be clearer: the Italian navy in these northern Adriatic ports would be vulnerable in a war with Britain. (The fact that the Royal Navy did not venture to penetrate into the Adriatic during Hitler's War is immaterial, it was the threat which mattered.)

Shark and the rest returned to Malta by the end of August 1938 (the time of the Munich conference), but in the next year it sailed on more of these intimidatory cruises, to Mudros, now a fortified Greek naval base, to Alexandria, to Gibraltar, and a visit to Nice took place in March 1939, at the time when Hitler so spectacularly broke his word over Czechoslovakia and Neville Chamberlain resolved to abandon diplomacy and appeasement as hopeless.[8] The message again was obvious, that Britain and France opposed German expansion. Malta and Alexandria were the boat's bases in the course of 1939, where it was docked and its defects rectified.[9] Then in October it was summoned back to Britain; the war there had begun, but not (yet) in the Mediterranean. It is difficult to be sure, but it may well be that the threatening cruises made by *Shark* and its fellows to the south of France and Corsica, and along the Yugoslav coast, could have had some effect on the curious and impulsive and amoral mind of Mussolini, keeping him at home when the ally to whom he was attached by a 'Pact of Steel' went to war.

Shark had had as its captain in these cruises and demonstrations Lieutenant Commander GM Standen (from July 1937 to December 1938). Just as notable was his lieutenant, who had been in the boat since December 1936, Lieutenant MD Wanklyn, who became the most notable and successful submariner of the Mediterranean war. At the end of December 1938 a new captain, Lieutenant PM Buckley, was appointed to command, and it was under his command that *Shark* went to war.

Shark arrived at Portsmouth on 22 October and moved on to Rosyth almost at once. It became part of the 3rd Submarine Flotilla, along with four other submarines, though they did not move or operate as a group but as individual boats, each with a separate section of sea to patrol. By 1 November *Shark* was out on patrol off the Dutch coast. This patrol lasted a week, a longer period of time than the boat had ever spent on a cruise except those to the south of France and the Adriatic. After only a few patrols it was sent to Chatham for docking and a thorough check (though this had been done in Malta less than a year earlier).[10]

After undocking the ship, and the flotilla, was sent to Harwich which became its base for the next five months, based there in order to have easy access to the target area off Holland, but its time at Harwich was interrupted by a two-month refit at Sheerness in February and March 1940. From Harwich it was first sent on a series of short trials in the nearby waters, rather as it had done in the Mediterranean for so many years. Then its full patrol activity revived from late April.

For these early months the war in the North Sea was of a particular sort, very reminiscent of the situation in the Great War, inevitably. Both sides sent out patrols either of submarines or of surface ships, which usually failed to make any sort of contact. The main activity they relied on was minelaying. Each side sent out minelayers, surface ships and sometimes submarines, to plant minefields close to the enemy shores, and at the same time they each established major defensive minefields, which were hardly secret but which closed off large areas of the sea, so that their existence necessarily channelled ships along particular routes. These routes soon became known to the enemy and clandestine minelaying was conducted to ambush ships using those channels. And so on, a sort of deadly chess game whose successes were the sinking of ships and the deaths of seamen.

The North Sea was therefore a dangerous place and submarines survived only by taking great care. The submarines were also largely unsuccessful. It was only late in November that the first British submarine attack on an enemy ship took place, and December before the next; neither involved *Shark*. The only occasion when *Shark* was close to going into action was on 14 December when it sighted a squadron of German cruisers and destroyers, at least eight ships in all. *Shark* took refuge by diving deep, for there was no point in tackling such a force. The boat itself had probably been sighted, and as it was submerged the crew heard several underwater explosions, though these were not necessarily directed at it.[11]

The refit at Sheerness ended just before the German invasions of Denmark and Norway had begun. The whole of the British submarine force was sent out to attempt to interfere with the German transport arrangements. There is no log of these new patrols, but an Admiralty file preserves a series of tracings of the boats' courses and positions.[12] Each tracing shows the course of a submarine in the form of a straight-line course to the patrol area, and then an irregular series of movements, showing the area being covered, more or less comprehensively. *Shark* was again off the Dutch coast in April, and had no success in finding, let alone sinking, any enemy ships. Other submarines, whose patrol areas were closer to Norway, had some considerable successes; *Shark's* lack of success was due to the absence of targets in its patrol area, not to its inactivity.

The patrol beginning on 7 April was in the Skagerak off Christiansand in Norway, at first. This was the day after the German invasion of Norway began, and *Shark's* purpose, along with other submarines, was to harass the German maritime supply lines. The next day *Shark* sighted the depot ship *Saar* (though it was identified as *Brummer*) which was escorting two transports, the three ships sailing in line ahead. *Shark* found it difficult to get close enough to fire, and in the end it fired its torpedoes from a considerable distance. Either the boat itself was seen or the track of the torpedoes was spotted, but all three ships turned away, letting the torpedoes pass between them.[13]

This patrol was a difficult one. As *Shark* went out it was realized that the German anti-submarine measures were becoming steadily more effective. They used anti-submarine trawlers and aircraft, and both were armed with deadly weapons, depth charges and bombs. Their activities forced the submarines to stay submerged for long periods, a procedure very wearing for the crews. This was all in addition to the use of as many destroyers as was available, and the many mines which both sides had laid. Two enemy trawlers located *Shark* on 18 April and dropped six depth charges which exploded 'fairly close'.

The conquest of the Low Countries and France in late May and early June meant that the Dutch coastal patrol was reinstated, now with a better hope of locating enemy shipping. *Shark's* next patrol had begun on 7 May and on the 10th the crew realized that something was happening on the land, because they could see much air activity, and were close enough to the coast to hear gunfire. Otherwise the only notable incident was the appearance of a German aircraft, identified as a Heinkel, which made an attack, though with no success.

The boat returned to Rosyth on 24 May, and went out on patrol again on 11 June. The time from 7 June had been spent preparing for sea, loading provisions and so on. It cast off next day, seen off by Gracie Fields singing 'Wish Me Luck as You Wave me Goodbye', which one sailor commented should have been the other way about, and cruised in the Firth of Forth before returning to its base for two days. It finally set off on patrol on the 11th.[14] It patrolled in the North Sea for several days, during which nothing was sighted. It was ordered into a new area, but still sighted nothing. It returned from a fruitless patrol on 20 June. Then it went on an exercise, and sailed on a new patrol on 1 July.[15]

This was part of a new British submarine offensive aimed at intercepting German traffic along the Norwegian coast. This was now uniformly hostile territory so that, unlike when Norway was neutral, any shipping anywhere along the coast could be attacked. At first the patrol had a number of successes: *Snapper* sank a ship from a convoy on 3 July, *Thames* sank a torpedo-boat, and *Sealion* a transport. But in the end five British submarines were sunk in this operation.[16] *Shark* was one of them.

The boat was first posted as overdue on 7 July, which means it had failed to report in by radio at least once, perhaps twice, though Lieutenant Commander Buckley claimed he had certainly sent off one message that the ship was returning to port having suffered damage. Next day it was considered to be lost. But what had actually happened to it took several months to be understood. (In this it was very like the slow accumulation of information about the loss of *Shark* X at Jutland, but it was a much more lengthy process this time.)

The message that the ship had probably sunk and the crew were 'presumed dead', or at least missing, went out to the relatives soon after 8 July. The news that the survivors had actually been captured, not killed, arrived on 11 October, and a full list of their names came through the Geneva Red Cross, which functioned as an exchange system for such information. This list arrived on 20 October.

Then further information came from the interrogation of a German Air Force airman who had been captured. He was able to provide some details of what had happened. He admitted he had been in an aircraft on 6 July which had attacked a submarine. It had been on the surface, and was damaged by the aircraft's bombs, but not sunk. This attack took place near Skundesnes in southern Norway, and it was this positioning which enabled the Admiralty to decide that it was probably a record of the attack on *Shark*.

It emerged after the war, when the survivors could be interviewed, that the boat had been forced to stay submerged for all the previous day, and had surfaced at night because of the need to recharge its batteries – but this was

July and in the Northern Sea, when the nights are short, and it was probably not really full dark. The attack came from the air, and was evidently so sudden and so relatively accurate, that Captain Buckley was unable to take evasive measures. (It has to be said that a night attack by a bomber over water was highly unlikely to hit anything it aimed at; the accuracy of the bombing was surely mainly luck.)

The boat was damaged at the stern, evidently by a near miss. The rudder and the propeller were both damaged. The boat submerged to escape further attention, going down to 400ft, according to telegraphist Eaton, but it then emerged that several leaks had been started in the stern areas. The boat surfaced again, but it was clearly immobilized, at least for the moment. At about midnight it was located by a flock of bombers, fighters and seaplanes, evidently summoned by the original assailant. A Messerschmidt 109 strafed the 'bridge' – the conning tower presumably – and this caused a number of casualties. Eaton manned the Lewis gun and fired back and at least one aircraft was shot down. The airmen were rescued and made prisoner, a fate they must not have relished, since it put them in a damaged submarine under attack by their fellows.

The air attacks had caused further damage to the boat, and a fire had been started in the interior, which was being tackled by a party under Lieutenant Denis Bennett, the second in command. But with this fire, the casualties, and the fact that the fight with the aircraft had exhausted the boat's ammunition, it was clear that the fight was over. Three German minesweepers – *M 1803*, *M 1806*, and *M 1807* – arrived about dawn. Buckley, who was one of the wounded (he had a broken leg), surrendered. He saw to the destruction of any codes and maps – and presumably his log. A flying boat landed on the sea and took Buckley and Bennett prisoner, and rescued the German prisoners. The crew were left on board, while the minesweepers attempted to tow the boat into the nearest harbour. However, it soon sank, encouraged in this by the crew. All the survivors were taken off.[17]

None of this was known in Britain until October, and then only in an unverifiable outline. Then on 5 November it was learned that Buckley had been imprisoned at Stalag Luft XXA since September, by which time his broken leg had healed.[18] He was able to write to his father, who sent the letter on to the Admiralty. He also apologized that details had been published in the press. He explained that he had been beset by persistent *Daily Mail* reporters, and he complained at their intrusiveness, claiming that he had not told them much – they had apparently deduced a good deal more from what he had said and not said, and probably invented still more. The Admiralty, more familiar with the tactics of reporters, metaphorically shrugged its shoulders.

Further items of information trickled in. From Stockholm, whence in November had already come some plausible information, there came in December a report that gossip in Oslo – the British Naval Attaché in Stockholm had very good sources both there and in Norway – had mentioned a submarine being brought in to Tonsberg, on Oslo fjord; the boat then sank; two survivors were in hospital at Tonsberg. This item is included in the Admiralty file on *Shark*, so it must be assumed that the Admiralty made the connection, but it is not very convincing. *Shark* was certainly off Skudesnes when it was attacked, and was being towed into Stavanger when it sank; Tonsberg was a long way off, though the hospital may have been used. That the Admiralty connected this report with *Shark* is an indication of the paucity of accurate information they had. In January Buckley's father sent further word that his son was now in Oflag IXA camp.

There is also a curious handwritten note in the file, listing five names with ranks from lieutenant to gunner. The note comments that these five were United States sailors, and the United States, through the embassy in London, was attempting to have them all classified as officers, despite the stated rank of non-officer for three of them. There is no other indication to connect them with *Shark* than the inclusion of this note in *Shark's* file, but it would seem probable that *Shark* had these men on board when it was sunk – though it has to be said that neither of the men who recorded their memories of this cruise, Eaton and Buckley, mentioned them. Their names are not listed as members of the crew in any of the lists sent from the Red Cross in Geneva, so it seems that the Nazi authorities had separated them out from the rest, no doubt because of their American nationality and the international complications their presence in a British submarine acting with hostile intent could cause. Their status was clearly unusual; probably they were along as observers. The note is at the top of the file, and so it was the last item (dated January 1941) which had been added to it. There is no indication whether the American request was successful.

Once the investigations in 1945 into the submarine's fate had been concluded, awards were distributed. Buckley and six other ranks were each awarded the Distinguished Service Medal, Bennett and the warrant engineer the Distinguished Service Cross. The distinction was perhaps due to the fact that the latter were working in the interior during the fight, a much more dangerous place even than the conning tower.

Chapter 14

Shark XIII: a Destroyer, 1943–1944

A new *Shark* was built in 1943, another destroyer, twice the size, at 1,700 tons and 380ft in length, of *Shark* X or XI, well-armed with four 4.7-inch and two 40mm guns, and no less than eight torpedo tubes. This was a new class of destroyer – 'C' class – whose greater size was part of the general increase in destroyer sizes which had been going on ever since the type was first developed. (The French had a class of superdestroyers, up to 3,000 tons, which were more or less equivalent to a British light cruiser.) About thirty of the 'C' class ships were built in 1943 and 1944. The new *Shark* did not in fact last as such for very long. Even as it was being constructed its destiny was being discussed and changed.

One of the more notable contributions to the war at sea by a small country was that of the sailors of Norway, who had manned a considerable number of ships since the conquest of their country by Germany in a much-resented surprise invasion in 1940. They had come partly from the merchant ships which had been outside Norway when the country was invaded, and others were from those who had escaped from Norway since then – the most notable method was by boat and ship to Shetland by way of the 'Shetland bus'.[1] Many of those in the merchant ships had continued to sail in those ships, whose number made a considerable contribution to Allied transport capacity. Others manned a Norwegian navy in exile, but they had to be provided with ships by Britain. They had been assigned, among other ships, to some of the old Great War destroyers handed over to Britain in 1940 by the United States, which gained a string of valuable bases from Newfoundland to Trinidad in exchange – a far more valuable acquisition to the USA than the fifty ships were to Britain, but it was the deed which counted, not the balance of advantage. By 1943, however, these old ships, never very effective, were even more out of date than they had been at the time they were handed over; even then they could best be termed antiquated, and were now being kept well away from active warfare.

In 1943 two of these ships, manned by Norwegian sailors, were effectively without employment, and were held in Nova Scotia, where the crews were becoming distinctly restive at their lack of employment. Their morale was low, and men were deserting to find more productive employment ashore – there were plenty of jobs in Canadian factories. During that year a bureaucratic discussion in London took place over requests from the Norwegians, funnelled through their London embassy, for the men to be transferred to more active ships – which in effect meant handing over British ships to the Norwegian navy.

It was at first suggested that the Hunt class destroyer *La Combattante* be handed over to the Norwegians. This was a much better vessel than the ex-American destroyers they already had, being the former HMS *Haldon*, built in 1942. But it was pointed out that the Norwegians would hardly be pleased at being palmed off with a Free French discard. Rethinking took place.

It was then suggested that one of the new large destroyers of the 'C' class, *Success*, be loaned to the Norwegians. Objections were raised that as many destroyers as possible would be needed for the war with Japan which the navy was looking forward to fighting after Germany was beaten. The Norwegians countered this effortlessly and most effectively – it was after all a particularly weak argument – by stating that they would be happy to have their ships employed anywhere; Norway was not, of course, at war with Japan, at least not yet, and that could easily be rectified by King Olaf, who was one of the Norwegians in exile. The result of this bout of Admiralty infighting was that *Success* went on loan to the Royal Norwegian Navy in September 1943, and was renamed *Stord*.[2]

The crews of the two ex-American destroyers in Nova Scotia were not involved in the crewing of *Success/Stord*. Once one destroyer had been handed over, with the assurances given by the Norwegian command, however, it became easier to assign them a second, particularly as the lack of morale of the crews was due to lack of action – these were, of course, first class sailors, skilled and motivated, and the hesitation in the Admiralty in making use of them is well-nigh incomprehensible. Between them the crews of the two old ships were numerous enough to form a single 'C' class crew, with a little pruning. In November 1943, after another Norwegian request, the Admiralty nominated the new *Shark*, not yet fully operational, as the next to be transferred.

Shark (XIII) had been launched in June 1943. Engineer Lieutenant AJN Harling had taken command as early as April, and was responsible for the trials and the working up which took place. The crew was assigned in the next months, and was probably complete by October. Harling was replaced as lieutenant in command in February 1944, by Acting Lieutenant DCF Lloyd. His temporary rank indicates clearly that the ship's establishment was being changed, and the original British crew was soon transferred elsewhere. The offer of the ship to the Norwegians had been made at last in December 1943, and was accepted within ten days, early in January – in effect, considering the season and the effects on the speed of the diplomatic processes, this was virtually instantaneous. The ship was then crewed by the Norwegian sailors from Nova Scotia, whose transfer to Britain took some time to arrange.

Stord, meanwhile, was being employed on the hardest work of the war, the Arctic convoys ferrying war materials to northern Russian ports, which meant its crew sailed repeatedly past the coast of the country from which they were exiled. Apart from one episode it was kept at this work until almost the end of the fighting. But in the last phase of the war someone with diplomatic antennae in the Admiralty – or perhaps it was Norwegian pressure again, but the Admiralty was usually good at this sort of assignment – assigned the ship to take part in the liberation of Norway in May 1945. It went into Trondheim harbour to receive the surrender of German ships there, having earlier had the satisfaction of escorting some of the surrendering U-boats into British harbours.[3]

This satisfaction was not to be the fate of *Shark*. It was renamed *Svenner*, and the transferred crew had perhaps three months to become familiar with it. No doubt there are Norwegian records of the ship, but they are both inaccessible and unnecessary, for the ship's one moment of employment is known. It was assigned to the left guard for the invasion of Europe on 6 June 1944 – D-Day – as part of the escort for the landing forces on Sword Beach, the leftward invasion. *Stord* was also involved, but not in such an exposed position – this was the one duty it performed apart from the Russian convoys.

Shark/Svenner sailed across the English Channel during the night of 5/6 June. Off the coast of France it was attacked by three German torpedo-boats out of Le Havre on the morning of the invasion, torpedoed, and sunk. The three boats then escaped under the cover of the dense smoke screen which had been laid down by the Allied ships in order to hide their own activities. It was clearly an effective screen, even if on this occasion it was the enemy which benefited. On the other hand *Svenner* was in the way of an attack by the patrol boats on a much more valuable target, the command ship HMS *Largs*, which was able to manoeuvre to avoid their torpedoes. *Svenner* could therefore be said to have been doing its job. HMS *Swift* came to chase the German boats away, but stopped to rescue *Svenner's* crew; sixty-seven men were saved, thirty-three died. *Swift* was a sister ship of *Skark/Svenner*. *Svenner* was the only Allied ship to be sunk on that day.[4] *Swift* was sunk by a mine a fortnight later.

The last *Shark* had therefore been sunk, under a different name and with a foreign crew – but this was not by any means the only such change to a *Shark*: *Shark* VI had been made into *Salamander*, a fireship; *Shark* VII had faded away into ignominy as a convalescent hospital ship; *Shark* VIII had been delivered by its mutinous crew to foreigners. *Shark* XIII had at least taken the blows intended by the German torpedo-boats for something larger and more important – and this was the task of a destroyer.

Conclusion

For two and a half centuries – 1691–1944 – *Shark* was a name used by the Royal Navy for a succession of its smaller warships. *Sharks* therefore existed during the period when the British Navy was the pre-eminent naval power in the world. All of these ships were small, sloops and later destroyers, but such small ships were frequently the most useful naval units, able to go where line-of-battle ships or cruisers and battleships could not go, able to figure as a naval presence more economically than using the larger ships.

They rarely fought. Indeed some *Sharks* – III, IV, VI, VIII – clearly never fired their guns except in gunnery practice, but then actual fighting was not really the main purpose of a navy. It was most useful when the mere existence of its power was sufficient to prevent fighting. And it was this factor which particularly signified these *Sharks* as being useful vessels. It is typified perhaps best by the repeated visits of *Shark* III, IV and VII to the Bahamas, which clearly deterred most Spanish plots to seize the islands when the colony was at its most vulnerable. In this, Captain Woodes Rogers' repeated pleas for a naval presence at Nassau in the early years of the colony were sensible.

The *Sharks* rarely if ever distinguished themselves in any way. This is probably the basic reason why there are frequent gaps in the sequence of ships with that name – 1703–1710 after the ignominious capture of *Shark* II, 1755–1776 after the fading away of *Shark* IV, and the long gap between *Sharks* VII and IX, 1818–1893. The long slow stationary descent of *Shark* VII and its death by sinking into the Port Royal mud was scarcely an inspiration to the Admiralty to use the name again. Later gaps – 1911–1912, 1931–1934, 1940–1943 – were brief enough to be no more than the time needed to reassign the name to a new ship. At the same time, of course, the sheer number of ships being built in the twentieth century ensured that the name would inevitably be used when it became available. And it is the drastic shrinkage of the navy since 1945 which is presumably the reason the name has not been used again. The Admiralty – sorry, Ministry of Defence – could concentrate on more illustrious names for its few vessels; and besides, the last *Shark* had been given away and was sunk under a different name and a different nationality.

The history of *Sharks* in the British Navy was therefore unassuming, workmanlike, and of little or no account outside the fleet. They were a sequence of ships which did the minor chores of any navy. They turned up here and there to help struggling colonies (the Bahamas, the Turks and Caicos Islands), they carried messages and mails and important passengers, they escorted convoys and latterly the Grand Fleet, they went into shallow waters where the big ships could not go. This was all useful and even essential work, oiling the ponderous machinery of the fleet, diplomatically nudging unfriendly (or friendly) powers and peoples towards peace.

And they died variously. Five were sold off at the end of their useful lives, any usable parts no doubt being recycled, though the navy kept them going so long that there can have been little left of them, as for instance of IV after the hurricane, or of VII after two hurricanes and then rotting in harbour for over a decade. One *Shark* was so unsatisfactory that it was converted into a fireship, a type of vessel intended as a sacrifice, but not even permitted to be burnt. One *Shark* was captured by the enemy and another delivered to the enemy by its mutinous crew, sources of naval shame only just papered over by the more violent deaths of the later *Sharks*. One, the short-lived VI, was sunk in a storm, but this was the only one of the eight wooden ships to be so lost; but then these ships only rarely fought. Being attacked, they normally turned and ran, like *Shark* VII facing *Serapis* in the South Atlantic. It is perhaps an indication of the greater fragility of steel ships over wooden that three of the five made of that metal were sunk in fighting.

The metal versions, of course, were designed to fight, unlike their wooden predecessors. The sloops and gunboats made of wood were not expected to battle anyone, unless, like the xebecs and so on chased by *Shark* IV out of Gibraltar, they were smaller than it was. But the metal destroyers and submarines of the twentieth century were expected to go into battle against greatly superior forces, and, of course, they paid the penalty with their deaths.

Notes

Introduction
1. Richard Hakluyt, *The Principal Voyages of the English Nation*, Everyman ed. vol. 7, pp. 53–62.
2. *Oxford English Dictionary*, 'shark'; the modern German term for sturgeon is *stor*.

Chapter 1
1. The size and rigging of brigantines provoked several articles in *Mariner's Mirror* in 1922.
2. Noted as captain on 24 June 1692 in Syrett-DiNardo, with a reference to the House of Commons Journal of 22 April 1691, no doubt on his appointment to *Shark*, just launched.
3. ADM 36/3433, muster book of *Shark*, 1691–1693.
4. Philip Aubrey, *The Defeat of James II's Armada, 1692* (Leicester, 1979) ch. 3.
5. Clowes, *Royal Navy* 2.348–356; *Shark* is not mentioned.
6. Dated to 18 June in Colledge-Warlow, but it must have been earlier if Barker was appointed its captain on the 6th.
7. ADM 51/390, captain's journal of *Shark*, 1692; Stepney is noted as captain by Syrett-DiNardo on 10 January 1693, six months after his posting, as lieutenant, to *Shark*.
8. Aubrey, *Defeat* pp. 139–140.
9. Colin Harris, *Sir Cloudesley Shovell, Stuart Admiral* (Staplehurst, Kent, 2001) pp. 158–159.
10. Syrett-DiNardo.
11. ADM 36/3433, muster book of *Shark*, 1693.
12. Clowes, *Royal Navy* 2.357–360.
13. CSP Dom. 1693 p. 314.
14. Sam Willis, *The Admiral Benbow* (London, 2010) gives a useful description of events; he does not mention *Shark*.
15. Winston S Churchill, *Marlborough, his Life and Times*, 4 vols (London 1933–1938), vol. 1, ch. 25, argues strongly against his ancestor's guilt, though he was scarcely a disinterested witness; see also David Chandler, *Marlborough as Military Commander*, 2nd ed. (London, 1979) p. 47, who is judicious.
16. Like Durley, Cole arrived as a lieutenant; Syrett-DiNardo notes he was a captain by January 1697.
17. ADM 52/3970, Captain's log of *Shark*, 1695–1696.
18. CSP Dom. 1695 p. 97; ADM 106/486/150.
19. ADM 106/486/241, 242.
20. ADM 106/494/220.
21. ADM 106/483/86.
22. ADM 106/486/62, 90, 111.
23. ADM 106/483/149.
24. *Dispatch* was the second of the batch of brigantines built in 1691, of which *Shark* was the first; it was larger, but carried only two guns.
25. ADM 106/487/185.
26. ADM 106/494/392.
27. ADM 106/483/197.
28. ADM 106/483/190; 106/483/196, signed by both Cole and the boatswain.
29. ADM 106/485/178.
30. ADM 106/485/180.

31. ADM 106/486/100.
32. ADM 106/488/203.
33. This is probably William Jones (2), lieutenant from 30 January 1694, commander (a new rank just coming into use) from 23 May 1701, and captain on 15 February 1705; he was drowned on 24 August 1708 (Syrett-DiNardo).
34. ADM 51/3970, captain's log of *Shark*, 1697.
35. ADM 106/485/178.
36. CSP Dom. 1697, 341; ADM 106/3120; ADM 180/20/710.

Chapter 2

1. In Syrett-DiNardo the only John Carleton is noted as a lieutenant in 1679 and to have died on 12 February 1698; clearly either he did not die then, or another man of the same name captained *Shark*.
2. ADM 37/2391, muster book of *Shark*, 1699; ADM 106/525/310, 313, 315.
3. ADM 51/892, captain's log of *Shark*, 1699–1702.
4. ADM 106/525/346.
5. SP Dom. 1700–1702, 260.
6. Patrick Fitzgerald and Brian Lambkin, *Migration in Irish History, 1607–2007* (Basingstoke, 2008) pp. 122–127.
7. ADM 33/208, pay list of *Shark*, 1702.
8. Syrett-DiNardo; Fisher was promoted to captain in January 1705, but died in August.
9. ADM 1/5262/28, court martial of Captain Dampier.
10. CSP Dom. 1702–1703, 138, Josiah Burchett to Earl of Nottingham, 26 June 1703.
11. Stephen Martin-Leake, *The Life of Sir John Leake* revised by Geoffrey Callendar, vol. 1, (NRS, 1920) pp. 87–107.
12. A brief report is in Clowes, *Royal Navy* 2.301.
13. CSP Dom. 1702–1703, 177; Nottingham to Captain John Leake, 11 November 1702.
14. The fighting continued for several years; see DW Prowse, *A History of Newfoundland from the English, Colonial and Foreign Records* (London, 1896) ch. 6.
15. ADM 1/5264, courts martial of Captain George Fisher, 14 and 19 June 1703; no one seems to have noticed the second court.
16. Details from Colledge-Warlow, under the ships' names.

Chapter 3

1. The name is 'Legh' in the log, and so presumably this is the correct spelling, but 'Leigh' in the Admiralty documents – no doubt a clerk who knew better; I cannot locate him in Syrett-diNardo or anywhere else.
2. The name is unclear in the captain's log; the only *Rose* in service in 1711 was a sixth-rate, which was sold in 1712.
3. ADM 51/4339, captain's log of *Shark*, 1711–1713 and 1713–1714; ADM 180/19.
4. ADM 39/2392 and 2393, muster books of *Shark*, 1711 and 1714; ADM 33/284, pay list of *Shark*, 1711.
5. For example, Syrett-DiNardo lists none of them; a Francis Legh appears in a TNA document recording a lawsuit, but there is no necessary connection with *Shark's* captain.
6. ADM 51/4339, captain's log of *Shark*, 1715–1716; he does not seem to have ever been promoted beyond lieutenant; ADM 180/19.
7. The best modern account of the rebellion of 1715 is by Christopher Sinclair-Stevenson, *Inglorious Rebellion, the Jacobite Rebellions of 1708, 1715 and 1719* (London, 1971).
8. Brian Tunstall (ed.) *The Byng Papers* vol. III (NRS, 1932) p. 119.
9. *Byng Papers* III, pp. 130–131, 172.
10. *Byng Papers* III, pp. 180–184, 189.
11. *Byng Papers* III, pp. 199–200.
12. ADM 39/2394, muster book of *Shark*, 1715; ADM 33/302, pay list of *Shark*, 1716.

13. This seems to be the name in the captain's log; no Edward Mansfield is listed in Syrett-DiNardo, though he is named in a list of commissions by Josiah Burchett in the *Byng Papers* III, p. 107. Edward Mansell is a possible alternative reading of the name.

14. Syrett-DiNardo.

15. ADM 51/892, captain's log of *Shark*, 1717/8–1722.

16. ADM 1282; these letters are in a neat chronological group; they will not be annotated further.

17. David Cordingley, *Pirate Hunter of the Caribbean, the Adventurous Life of Captain Woodes Rogers* (New York, 2012) pp. 132–171.

18. A sailor, Rowland Hildesley, mate of the *Flamborough* (and probably the captain's son) wrote a letter describing the place, enclosed in ADM 1/2646/6.

19. ADM 51/357, captain's log of *Flamborough*, 1720.

20. For details of these men see Syrett-DiNardo; Brown and Wiseman are missing; Martin eventually rose to captain in 1740, and to rear admiral (superannuated) in 1756; the only *Shark* officer, so far, who rose so high; he died in 1779.

21. ADM 39/2396 and 2397, muster books of *Shark*, 1718 and 1718–1722.

22. Syrett-DiNardo; Sclater rose to captain in 1734; he died in 1750.

23. ADM 36/3414, muster book of *Shark*, April 1725.

24. ADM 51/892, captain's log of *Shark*, 1723–1725.

25. ADM 36/3413, muster book of *Shark*, April–May 1724.

26. Vernor W Crane, *The Southern Frontier 1670–1732* paperback ed. (New York, 1981, originally published in 1928).

27. ADM 36/3414 and 3415, muster books of *Shark*, 1725–1728.

28. Only Thomas is in Syrett-DiNardo, appointed as a lieutenant on 9 December 1729; neither Pike nor Pocock are listed.

29. ADM 36/3416, muster books of *Shark*, October 1728 to July 1729.

30. ADM 1/231, Admiral Charles Stewart to Admiralty Secretary, 16 March 1729/30, which is the source for much of the detail in the next pages, together with ADM 51/4339, captain's log of *Shark*, 1729–1730.

31. Cordingly, *Pirate Hunter* p. 229; the visits of *Aldborough* and *Shark* are not mentioned.

32. Richard Pares, *War and Trade in the West Indies 1739–1765* (Oxford, 1935) pp. 15–16.

33. He had been made commander on 30 June 1729, and became captain on 14 June 1731 (Syrett-DiNardo).

34. ADM 51/892, captain's log of *Shark*, 1730–1731.

35. However, Alexander did not reach commander until 1742, a slow ascent if he had a useful contact; perhaps their relationship was not so close, after all (Syrett-DiNardo).

36. The dates of his appointments as lieutenant and commander are not known, but he was promoted to captain in September (Syrett-DiNardo); as a fellow Scot, Admiral Stewart may well have interested himself in the rise of the son of a Scottish nobleman.

37. See the documents collected in ADM 1/231, which include Craufurd's report and his orders.

38. Promoted to lieutenant on 24 September (Syrett-DiNardo).

39. ADM 51/892, captain's log of *Shark*, June–October 1731.

40. ADM 51/4339, captain's log of *Shark*, 1731–1732.

41. Pares, *War and Trade* p. 16, quoting figures from the *Gentlemen's Magazine* (March, 1738).

42. ADM 51/4339, captain's log of *Shark*, May–June 1732.

43. Colledge-Warlow, 368.

Chapter 4

1. He had been a lieutenant since 1706, and a commander since 1729; he died within a year of ending his command of *Shark*, in 1740 (Syrett-DiNardo).

2. ADM 106/842/85, 86; 106/838/235, 240; ADM 180/3/529, Admiralty Progress Book.

3. ADM 51/893, captain's log of *Shark*, part 1.

4. ADM 106/838/266.

5. ADM 180/3/529–the cost of this refitting was £97.

6. ADM 106/842/91, 97, 101.

7. ADM 106/837/286, 287, 278.

8. Ibid, 294, 295.

9. ADM 106/851/78.

10. ADM 106/837/4, 5, 9, 13.

11. ADM 33/358, pay list of *Shark*, 1733–1739.

12. ADM 106/848/109; 106/851/34; increased complement: ADM 33/358.

13. ADM 106/851/94, 114.

14. ADM 106/851/102.

15. SP Col. *America and West Indies*, 1730.

16. Ibid, 1735–1736.

17. Ibid, 1731, report by Woodes Rogers.

18. A useful list is in Jan Rogozinski, *A Brief History of the Caribbean* (New York, 1999) pp. 161–162.

19. W Stitt Robinson, *The Southern Colonial Frontier, 1607–1763* (Albuquerque, 1979) pp. 186–187.

20. Ibid, 187–189.

21. SP Col. *American and West Indies*, 1737.

22. Richard Pares, *War and Trade in the West Indies, 1739–1763* (Cambridge, 1936).

23. CSP Col. *America and West Indies*, 1735–1736, 454.

24. ADM 106/915/470.

25. Sir Herbert Richmond, *The Navy in the War of 1739–1748*, vol 1 (Cambridge, 1920) p. 10.

26. ADM 106/893/47 and 913/47.

27. Syrett-DiNardo.

28. ADM 180/3/529.

29. ADM 354/110/49.

30. ADM 254/111/8, 157.

31. Swaysland himself was promoted to captain in January 1741 (Syrett-DiNardo); ADM 106/904/124; ADM 51/893, captain's log of *Shark*, July 1740–January 1741.

32. ADM 106/930/23 and 926/230.

33. ADM 33/363, pay list of *Shark*, 1740–June 1741.

34. Promoted to commander on 22 January (Syrett-DiNardo).

35. ADM 51/893, no 1, captain's log of *Shark* 1741.

36. ADM 106/926/230, 150, 154.

37. ADM 106/935/151.

38. ADM 106/938/314, 315, 317, 318, 324.

39. ADM 106/939/204/ 217, 225.

40. ADM 354/117/8, 116/169, 170.

41. He had been lieutenant since 1732 and was promoted to commander on 1 February (Syrett-DiNardo).

42. ADM 51/893, captain's log of *Shark*, 1743–1744.

43. Settee, a two-masted, lateen-rigged Mediterranean vessel, small and handy.

44. Another Mediterranean vessel, like a settee.

45. A three-masted ship, speedy, and much favoured by Algerine corsairs.

46. A single-masted coaster.

47. For the Worms negotiations see Sir Richard Lodge, *Studies in Eighteenth Century Diplomacy 1740–1748* (London, 1930) ch. 2.

48. ADM 51/893, captain's log of *Shark*, February–September 1744.

49. ADM 1/1602, Crookshank to Admiralty Secretary, 30 June 1744.

50. This is Robert Hughes (3) in Syrett-DiNardo, lieutenant in 1738, commander on 14 July 1744, and captain on 2 July 1745.

51. ADM 51/893, captain's log of *Shark*, September 1744–April 1745.

52. ADM 51/893, captain's log of *Shark*, April–May 1745.

53. ADM 106/1010/84.

54. Syrett-DiNardo.

55. Not listed in Syrett-DiNardo.
56. DNB, Christopher Middleton; WE May, 'The Shark and the '45', *Mariner's Mirror*, 53 (1967) pp. 281–285.
57. ADM 106/1010/95A, 96, 101, 104.
58. ADM 180/3/529.
59. ADM 180/3/529.
60. ADM 106/1010/232, 233, 237; 1013/120.
61. ADM 106/1010/238, 248, 262.
62. ADM 106/1010/268.
63. ADM 51/893, captain's log of *Shark*, November 1745–March 1746.
64. Frank McLynn, 'Sea Power and the Jacobite Rising of 1945', *Mariner's Mirror*, 67 (1981) pp. 163–172; a more detailed account is by John S Gibson, *Ships of the '45* (London, 1967).
65. This was the admiral later executed on the quarterdeck of his ship for apparently not trying hard enough.
66. Gibson, *Ships of the '45* pp. 56–57.
67. ADM 51/893, captain's log of *Shark*, March–July 1746.
68. ADM 106/1031/209.
69. ADM 106/1025/69, 83.
70. ADM 106/1031/246, 238.
71. The name is clearly 'Michell' in his correspondence, though too often (as in Syrett-DiNardo) taken to be 'Mitchell'.
72. ADM 1/2104, 15 February 1747.
73. ADM 106/1039/75, 77, 35.
74. ADM 1/2104 is the relevant one for *Shark*.
75. ADM 51/893, captain's log of *Shark*, 1746–1748.
76. Richard Harding, *The Emergence of Britain's Global Naval Supremacy, the War of 1739–1748* (Woodbridge, 2010) ch. 10.
77. ADM 106/1054/162, 165, 167; 1064/274.
78. ADM 33/412, pay list of *Shark*, 1743–1748.
79. Syrett-DiNardo; he became captain in 1758.
80. ADM 51/894, captain's log of *Shark* 1749–1752; ADM 180/3/529.
81. ADM 106/1068/71, 75; 354/140/242.
82. ADM 106/1068/101; 1070/252, 253; 1074/65.
83. ADM 106/1076/68; 1068/104, 256; 1070/80, 250.
84. ADM 1070/262, 268, 276.
85. ADM 1/306, correspondence of Commodore Holburne; Pares, *War and Trade* pp. 208–209; the matter of Tobago in the next paragraphs is not mentioned in Pares' book. The wider issue of French settlers on other 'neutral islands' continued to be a dispute throughout Holburne's command; the settlers simply refused to evacuate.
86. Lieutenant from 1748, he reached captain in 1765 (Syrett-Dinardo).
87. Lieutenant from 1744, captain in 1762 (Syrett-Dinardo).
88. Falkingham's letters describing his visit are in Holburne's volume of letters, ADM 1/306.
89. There are three specifically naval accounts of the hurricane and its aftermath, two by William Arthur, the Storekeeper, which are much the same (ADM 106/1088/27, 28) one by Commodore Holburne (ADM 106/1091/78) and *Shark's* log.
90. ADM 106/1100/69.
91. ADM 32/59, pay list of *Shark*, 1749–1752.
92. Lieutenant in 1747, (Syrett-DiNardo); neither O'Hara nor Drummond are mentioned again.
93. ADM 180/3/529.

Chapter 5
1. ADM 106/1236/181, 188.
2. He had been a lieutenant since 1755 and commander since 1768 (Syrett-DiNardo).

3. ADM 106/1233/291, 295, 321.

4. ADM 106/1233/118; 1236/62.

5. ADM 51/895, captain's log of *Shark*, March 1776–June 1777.

6. This correspondence is collected in SP 72/300/6; Chapman's version of the encounter is also in *Shark's* log for 28 July.

7. This is the starting point of Barbara Tuchman's version of the American Revolution, *The First Salute* (London 1989) though her beginning, at St Eustatius in November 1776, was five months after the protection – and implicit recognition of the rebels – which was given *Reprisal* by the French at Martinique.

8. It is not clear which Lieutenant Christian this was: a Brabazon Christian was promoted on 22 November, and (the later Sir) Hugh Cloberry Christian at an indeterminate date in 1778; Syrett-DiNardo does not record a man of that name being promoted in February 1777.

9. James Gambier (2), lieutenant on 12 February 1777, commander on 9 March 1778, captain on 9 October 1778 (Syrett-DiNardo) – such was the advantage of having an admiral as a father.

10. Made lieutenant on 15 March (Syrett-DiNardo).

11. ADM 52/679, pay list of *Shark* 1776.

12. ADM 106/1240/18, 19.

13. ADM 106/1239/226.

14. ADM 51/895, part 2, captain's log of *Shark* July 1777–August 1778.

15. ADM 52/679, pay list of *Shark* 1777.

16. No other account of the court martial than that in *Shark's* captain's journal has been found; there is nothing in Admiral Young's correspondence, nor is there any official record in the collection of Admiralty court martial papers.

17. Syrett-DiNardo; he died later in the year, perhaps yet another casualty of the West Indies 'climate'.

18. ADM 106/1244/216.

19. ADM 354/196/365.

20. Not listed in Colledge-Warlow.

21. ADM 354/196/383.

22. ADM 106/1244/293, 314; 51/840, captain's log of *Salamander*, November 1778 to September 1779.

23. ADM 51/841, captain's log of *Salamander*, September 2779–February 1781; Kinnall is not listed in Syrett-DiNardo; Finch, a cadet member of the family of the earls of Nottingham, was made lieutenant as he took command of *Salamander*, then commander in 1779, and captain in 1781.

24. It was recorded at the Admiralty in May 1780 (ADM 8/56) as in the Leeward Islands, anticipating its voyage.

25. Kenneth Breen, 'Sir George Rodney and St Eustatius in the American War: a Command and Naval Distraction, 1775–1781', *Mariner's Mirror*, 84 (1998) pp. 193–203.

26. Lieutenant from February 1776, commander in February 1781, and captain in 1783 (Syrett-DiNardo).

27. ADM 51/840, captain's log of *Salamander*, February 1781–June 1783.

28. John D Grainger, *The Battle of Yorktown, a Reassessment* (Woodbridge, 2005); David Syrett, *The Royal Navy in American Waters* (Aldershot, 1989), ch. 6; Piers Mackesy, *The War for America, 1775–1783* (Oxford, 1964) pp. 420–424.

29. Syrett-DiNardo; he went from lieutenant to captain within a month.

30. For these campaigns see AT Mahan, *The Influence of Sea Power on History, 1660–1783* (edition of London, 1965), ch. 13; Clowes, Royal Navy, 3, ch. 31, (by Mahan), and Mackesy, *War for America, 1775–1783* ch. 26.

31. Syrett-DiNardo; he eventually reached captain in 1809.

32. Colledge-Warlow, p. 368.

Chapter 6

1. A *Shark* is recorded as having been commissioned on 1 October 1779 and is listed among 'Convoys and Escorts', cruising on the East Coast of England (ADM 8/56); this is presumably *Shark* VI, though no other details are available.
2. Syrett-DiNardo have him dying on 15 September 1779, but also promoted to captain on 15 May 1780.
3. David Syrett, (ed.) *The Rodney Papers*, vol. 2 (NRS, 2007) pp. 647–648.
4. David Syrett, *The Royal Navy in American Waters, 1775–1783* (Aldershot, 1989) p. 159.
5. *Letter-Book and Order Book of George, Lord Rodney, Admiral of the White Squadron*, (New York Historical Society, New York, 1938) vol. 1, p. 90.
6. 'North America' is the place of the disaster in most modern lists; 'West Indies' in one; neither is specific; 'outside New York' would be more accurate.

Chapter 7

1. ADM 106/1248/309.
2. ADM 354/200/18, 50.
3. ADM 354/200/171.
4. Samuel Eliot Morrison, *John Paul Jones* (New York, 1959) ch. 13.
5. Syrett-Dinardo.
6. ADM 51/895, captain's log of *Shark*, February to November 1780.
7. ADM 106/1262/169, 171, 177, 196.
8. ADM 106/1248/148, 153, 163.
9. ADM 106/1262/184.
10. ADM 106/1248/176.
11. ADM 106/1262/219.
12. The name is McDouall in all the documents; Syrett-DiNardo alter this to 'McDougall', unjustifiably.
13. ADM 34/725, pay list of *Shark*, 1779–1780.
14. ADM 106/1258/480, 489, 1265/440, 1266/526.
15. ADM 34/725, pay list of *Shark*, May 1780–April 1781.
16. ADM 51/875, captain's log of *Shark*, November 1781 to November 1782.
17. The most detailed account of this expedition is, despite the self-deprecatory title, G Rutherford, 'Sidelights on Commodore Johnstone's Expedition to the Cape,' *Mariner's Mirror*, 28 (1942) pp. 189–212 and 290–307; for *Shark's* exploits see 207 and 306.
18. A quarter of a century later, Rear Admiral Charles Stirling called in at Rio, and was able to record a large quantity of military and naval information – people, fortifications, harbour installations, and so on: ADM 50/50, Stirling's Journal.
19. Morrison, *Jones*, p. 267.
20. Promoted to commander on 24 July 1781, and to captain on 22 January 1783 (Syrett-DiNardo).
21. ADM 106/1264/246 (McDouall), 295 (Maitland); at Sheerness the officers of the dockyard sent up yet another list: ADM 106/1268/575.
22. ADM 106/1264/300.
23. ADM 34/724, pay list of *Shark*, May 1781–January 1782.
24. ADM 51/895, captain's log of *Shark*, November 1781 to November 1782.
25. ADM 34/739, pay list of *Shark*, February 1782 to May 1783.
26. Became commander in October 1781, and captain in 1787 (Syrett-DiNardo).
27. ADM 51/895, captain's log of *Shark*, May 1783 to May 1784, and June 1784 to June 1785; 51/896, logs for June 1785 to March 1787 and April to November 1787.
28. See John Ehrman, *The Younger Pitt*, vol. 1, *The Years of Acclaim* (London, 1969) pp. 169–271; there is a brief summary in Roger Knight, *Britain against Napoleon, the Organisation of Victory, 1793–1815* (London, 2013) p. 25.
29. ADM 36/10624 and 10625, pay lists of *Shark*, 1783–1787.
30. Syrett-Dinardo: he rose to rear-admiral by 1808.

31. Syrett-Dinardo: he had been made commander on 21 September.
32. ADM 51/896, captains' logs of *Shark*, July to September 1793 (Dilkes), October 1793 to March 1794 (Brisac).
33. He rose to rear admiral in 1819; like Dilkes, this was effortless, the result of men above him on the captain's list dying.
34. Syrett-DiNardo: he had been commander since 1787 and became captain in 1793.
35. ADM 51/896, captain's log of *Shark*, March to September 1791; 51/863, log September 1791 to January 1793 (Legge), and January to September 1793 (Barker).
36. DW Prowse, *A History of Newfoundland, from English, Colonial, and Foreign Records* (London, 1896) p. 367.
37. ADM 7/575, abstract of log of *Shark*.
38. ADM 35/1652, pay list of *Shark*, July 1790 to September 1791.
39. ADM 35/1653, pay list of *Shark*, September 1791 to March 1793.
40. Syrett-Dinardo: he was made commander in 1780 and captain in 1787.
41. ADM 51/1104, captain's log of *Shark*, October 1794 to October 1795.
42. See Paul Butel, *The Atlantic*, trans. Iain Hamilton Grant (London, 1999) pp. 1–2.

Chapter 8

1. A single pay list of the ship exists: ADM 35/832, with this basic information; it will be considered in more detail later; ADM 180/23 and 180/4 have details of purchase and armament.
2. Syrett-DiNardo: neither of these men progressed beyond lieutenant, for reasons which will become clear.
3. Rif Winfield, *British Warships of the Age of Sail, 1793–1817* (London, 2005) p. 325.
4. Sir John Barrow, *The Life of Sir Sidney Smith*, vol. 1 (London, 1848) pp. 162–178.
5. Syrett-DiNardo.
6. James Gomm, *Narrative founded in a Series of events which took place in the Island of St Marcou* (London, 1801); Gomm was another old lieutenant, commissioned in that rank in 1782; he rose no further.
7. Tom Pocock, *A Thirst for Glory* (London, 1996).
8. John Watson (3) in Syrett-DiNardo; he reached commander rank in 1814.
9. ADM 180/4/102.
10. Robert O'Byrne, *Naval Biographical Dictionary*, 1849–cited in Syrett-Dinardo.

Chapter 9

1. ADM 51/1133, captain's log of *Shark*, November 1795 to October 1796; 51/1193, log of November 1796 to August 1797.
2. An account of the French attack by the Rev P Toque is printed in DW Prowse, *A History of Newfoundland from the English, Colonial, and Foreign Records* (London, 1896) pp. 368–371; *Shark* is, as usual, not mentioned. There is no evidence that the British ever used St Pierre. When investigated fifteen years later the island was deserted, its ruined buildings overgrown.
3. Syrett-DiNardo: lieutenant in 1794, commander in 1797, and captain in 1801, rising to rear admiral in 1830.
4. ADM 51/1234, captain's log of *Shark*, August 1797 to August 1798 and September 1798 to January 1799.
5. Prowse, *History of Newfoundland* pp. 372–373.
6. ADM 35/1653 and 1654, pay lists for *Shark*, 1793–1799.
7. Syrett-DiNardo.
8. Andrew Lambert, *The Challenge, Britain against America in the Naval War of 1812* (London, 2012) pp. 147–195; Clowes, *Royal Navy*, 6.75–86.
9. ADM 51/1400, captain's log of *Shark*, August 1799 to August 1800.
10. This convoy is noted in the *Naval Chronicle*, IV, pp. 157–158.
11. ADM 52/3473, master's log of *Shark*, 1799–1801.
12. Classed as a 'gunvessel' of fourteen guns in Colledge-Warlow.

13. Made commander in 1798 and captain in 1803 (Syrett-DiNardo); he rose to rear admiral in 1830.
14. ADM 51/1350, captain's log of *Shark*, February to October 1801.
15. Son of George III, duke of Cambridge, representing his father in the electorate.
16. ADM 1/1630, 29.
17. Syrett-DiNardo.
18. ADM 41/1431, captain's log of *Shark*, December 1801 to September 1802.
19. Printed as Appendix A in Philip Knight, (ed.) *Lady Nugent's Journal of her Residence in Jamaica from 1801 to 1805* (Kingston, Jamaica, 1966) p. 279.
20. Ibid, 61.
21. Made commander in 1802 (Syrett-DiNardo).
22. ADM 51/4499, captain's log of *Shark*, September 1802 to October 1803.
23. Michael Crater, *A History of the Bahamas* (London, 1968) p. 166; a summary is in Maya Jasanoff, *Liberty's Exiles, the Loss of America and the Renewing of the British Empire* (London, 2011) pp. 220–227.
24. Gordon S Wood, *Empire of Liberty, A History of the Early Republic, 1789–1815* (Oxford, 2009) pp. 367–372; George C. Herring, *From Colony to Superpower, U.S. Foreign Relations since 1776* (Oxford, 2008) pp. 202–109.
25. Wright, (ed.) *Lady Nugent's Journal* p. 72, 74–75.
26. CLR James, *The Black Jacobins* (London, 1938) ch. 12, 'The War of Independence'; there were risings in several islands after 1793: Jan Rogozinski, *A Brief History of the Caribbean* (New York, 1999) table 17, pp. 161–163.
27. The full name of 'T M' has not been discoverable; the muster lists do not contain a lieutenant with those initials, and the list in Syrett-DiNardo contains no less than fifteen possible names; he may, indeed, be a warrant officer, not a lieutenant.
28. ADM 35/1656, pay list of *Shark*, September 1800 to August 1803.
29. Lieutenant since 1793, commander in 1797 (Syrett-DiNardo); he rose to rear admiral in 1841.
30. ADM 51/1456, captain's log of *Shark*, February to May 1804.
31. Knight, (ed.) *Lady Nugent's Journal* p. 164.
32. The captains' logs for this period are at ADM 51/1456 (Ayscough), 1508, 1474, 1503, 1556, 2808, 1588, 1914, 2005, 1878, 1937 – this is the chronological sequence.
33. Edward a'Court, Charles White; all the men are in this and the next notes are listed in Syrett-DiNardo.
34. Edward Denman, Charles Newman Hunter.
35. John Ayscough, Hayes O'Grady, Joshua Rowley, Houston Stewart.
36. John Balderstone.
37. William Manners.
38. ADM 35/3868 and 4287, pay lists of *Shark*, 1813, and 1816–1818.
39. ADM 359/358/117.
40. David J Hepper, *British Warship Losses in the Age of Sail, 1650–1859* (Rotherfield, Essex, 1994) p. 156; there is no progress record in ADM 180 for the end of the ship.

Chapter 10

1. Robert C Stern, *Destroyer Battles* (Barnsley, 2008) gives a useful early history of the type.
2. See the history in John Tetsuro Sumida, *In Defence of Naval Supremacy, Finance, Technology and British Naval Policy, 1888–1914* (London, 1989).
3. David Lyon, *The First Destroyers* (London, 1996) discusses the development of these boats in detail.
4. Lyon, *First Destroyers* p. 97.
5. Details of sizes, armament, and so on, are in Colledge-Warlow under the ships' names; some are also in Lyon, *First Destroyers*.
6. Lyon, *First Destroyers*.
7. ADM 53/15704, log of *Shark*, 1896.

8. ADM 53/26206, 26210–26212, logs of *Shark* 1899. (Logs at this time covered only two months, and were laid out in a distinct and invariable pattern; there was little or no scope for comment or discussion; they are at times inexpressibly tedious.)
9. ADM 53/26214–26218, log of *Shark* 1903.
10. ADM 53/25219–25258, logs of *Shark*, 1904–1911.

Chapter 11

1. A neat summary of the work of destroyers in the Great War is in Taffrail, *Endless Story* (London, 1931) pp. 13–14.
2. ADM 53/26258–26261, logs of *Shark*, 1912–1913; *Navy List* 1912–1913.
3. I cannot resist a personal remark here: The ship visited Rothesay on the Isle of Bute on 24 April; my mother, who was a girl of nine at the time, and whose father, my grandfather, was the chief engineer on a Clan Line merchant ship, probably saw *Shark* in Rothesay harbour.
4. ADM 53/26261; 59968–59973, logs of *Shark* 1913–1914.
5. ADM 53/59978, log of *Shark* December 1914 and January 1915; Robert K Massie, *Castles of Steel* (London, 2004) pp. 337–360, for the Scarborough raid, with an account of *Shark's* doings on pp. 337–343; A J Marder, *From the Dreadnought to Scapa Flow*, London 1961–1970, 2.134–137.
6. Taffrail, *Endless Story*, makes this precise point (ch. 1), though to be sure he spoke from the captain's viewpoint, not that of the ordinary seamen.
7. ADM 53/59975–59981, logs of *Shark*, February 1915 to March 1916.
8. *V-48* was later sunk; it may have been the ship which torpedoed the battleship *Marlborough* without sinking it.
9. Marder, *Dreadnought*, 3.222 (very briefly); Taffrail, *Endless Story* pp. 174–180, and Massie, *Castles of Steel* pp. 607–609, for *Shark* at Jutland.
10. ADM 137/301 and 302, and 119/1643; Admiralty files on *Shark* and the Jutland enquiries.
11. Marder, *Dreadnought*, 3.221–223, comments that the Germans used their destroyers more aggressively than the British at Jutland – but the German aim in the North Sea was to whittle away at the British naval supremacy, and an aggressive use of destroyers, if a battleship, say, was sunk by them, would be worth losing several destroyers; the British had only to survive to win.

Chapter 12

1. ADM 53/59982, log of *Shark*, June to August 1918.
2. ADM 53/59983, log of *Shark*, September to October 1918; Kelly's report is in Paul G Halpern, *The Royal Navy in the Mediterranean, 1915–1918* (NRS, 1987) no. 256; for a clear account of the action see Paul G Halpern, *A Naval History of World War I* (London, 1994) pp. 175–177.
3. ADM 53/59984, log of *Shark*, November to December 1918.
4. For the events in South Russia see Peter Kenez, *Civil War in South Russia, 1919–1920* (California, 1977), and George A Brinkley, *The Volunteer Army and Allied Intervention in South Russia* (Notre Dame IN, 1966); also Richard H Ullman, *Anglo-Soviet Relations 1917–1921*, three vols, (Princeton NJ, 1961–1973), though only Brinkley has much to say on the naval activities in the Black Sea.
5. ADM 53/59984–59985, logs of *Shark*, November 1918 to February 1919; ADM 137/1733, Admiralty file on the Black Sea, 1918–1919.
6. Sir James E Edmonds, *The Occupation of Constantinople 1918–1923, Official History of the Great War* (transcribed by Neil Wells), (Uckfield, 2010); Bernard Lewis, *The Emergence of Modern Turkey*, 3rd ed. (Oxford, 2002) pp. 247–251.
7. ADM 53/59986–59994, logs of *Shark*, May 1919 to November 1920.
8. ADM 53/84829–84834, logs of *Shark*, July 1922 to August 1923.
9. ADM 1/8697/79 General Strike, Daily Reports; ADM 116/2432, use of submarines.
10. ADM 1/8705/184/26.
11. ADM 53/84839, log of *Shark*, May 1926.

Chapter 13

1. ADM 173/12973–12975, logs of *Shark*, 1934.
2. ADM 173/14324–14336, logs of *Shark*, 1935–1936.
3. Lawrence K Pratt, *East of Malta, West of Suez, Britain's Mediterranean Crisis, 1936–1939* (Cambridge, 1775), is a useful study of the issues involved in British Mediterranean naval strategy in this period. More generally see Stephen Roskill, *Naval Policy Between the Wars*, vol. 2, (London, 1976) ch. 9.
4. ADM 173/14948–14949, logs of *Shark*, January–February 1937.
5. ADM 173/14951, log of *Shark*, April 1937.
6. ADM 173/15513, log of *Shark*, March 1938.
7. The reports are collected in ADM 116/3903; see also ADM 173/15517–15518, logs of *Shark*, July–August 1938.
8. ADM 173/16085, log of *Shark*, March 1939.
9. ADM 199/2570, movements of *Shark*, 1939.
10. ADM 173/16092–16093, logs of *Shark*, October to November 1939.
11. ADM 173/16094, log of *Shark*, December 1937.
12. ADM 199/1840.
13. Ibid; Geir H Haarr, *The German Invasion of Norway, April 1940* (Barnsley, 2011) p. 390.
14. Telegraphist Eric Eaton, in an Imperial War Museum recording of his reminiscences, IWM 14140.
15. ADM 358/190, a file of material relevant to the sinking.
16. Jurgen Rohwer, *Chronology of the War at Sea, 1939–1945* (London, 2006) p. 30.
17. ADM 1/30435, recommendation for awards.
18. Buckley recorded his memories, along with much detail on his POW existence, for the Imperial War Museum, IWM 4759, where his contemporary account of the sinking and a POW notebook are also held (reference 4524); he continued in the navy on his release and rose to rear admiral.

Chapter 14

1. David Howarth, *The Shetland Bus*, new ed. (Lerwick, Shetland, 1998).
2. The discussion, the written part at least, is recorded in ADM 1/13353, destroyers loaned to the Royal Norwegian Navy.
3. See the entries for *Stord* in Jurgen Rohwer, *Chronology of the War at Sea, 1939–1945*, 3rd ed. (London, 2006).
4. Stephen Roskill, *The War at Sea*, vol. III, part II (London, 1961).

Index